THE
KINGDOM
IN
MARK

THE
KINGDOM
IN
MARK

A New Place and a New Time

WERNER H. KELBER

FORTRESS PRESS   Philadelphia

Library of Congress Catalog Card Number 73–88353

ISBN 0–8006–0268–4

4020H73   Printed in U.S.A.   1–268

To Norman Perrin

Table of Contents

Abbreviations

Bib	Biblica
BibLeb	Bibel und Leben
Bijdr	Bijdragen
BiR	Biblical Research
BJRL	Bulletin of the John Rylands Library
BZ	Biblische Zeitschrift
CBQ	Catholic Biblical Quarterly
EvTh	Evangelische Theologie
ExpT	Expository Times
HibJ	Hibbert Journal
HTR	Harvard Theological Review
Interpr	Interpretation
JBL	Journal of Biblical Literature
JRel	Journal of Religion
JTS	Journal of Theological Studies
NovTest	Novum Testamentum
NTS	New Testament Studies
RB	Revue Biblique
RHPhR	Revue d'Histoire et de Philosophie Religieuses
RSR	Recherches de Science Religieuse
ScJTh	Scottish Journal of Theology
SE	Studia Evangelica
ST	Studia Theologica

TDNT	Theological Dictionary of the New Testament
ThBl	Theologische Blätter
ThStKr	Theologische Studien und Kritiken
ThViat	Theologia Viatorum
TLZ	Theologische Literaturzeitung
TTZ	Trierer Theologische Zeitschrift
TZ	Theologische Zeitschrift
USQR	Union Seminary Quarterly Review
VD	Verbum Domini
ZNW	Zeitschrift für die neutestamentliche Wissenschaft
ZThK	Zeitschrift für Theologie und Kirche

Preface

This book is based upon my doctoral dissertation submitted to the faculty of the Divinity School of the University of Chicago in June 1970. Much work has gone into it since then. A rapid development in Markan studies made it necessary to reconsider individual sections, to integrate new material, and, in the end, to rewrite the whole. My basic thesis concerning the genesis and purpose of our oldest Christian gospel has, however, remained unaltered.

Among the scholars, past and present, who guided my thinking in fundamental ways, the following deserve special mention: Ernst Lohmeyer who discovered the significance of Galilee in Mark; Robert H. Lightfoot who insisted on the relevance of space and place in the gospels; Willi Marxsen who pioneered the redaction-critical exegesis of the oldest gospel; Theodore J. Weeden who brought the discipleship phenomenon in Mark into focus; Rudolf Pesch who contributed a magisterial work on chapter 13; Norman Perrin who during the last decade has prepared the ground for a theology of Mark.

The manuscript of this book was written while I was teaching at the University of Dayton, Dayton, Ohio. It is my pleasant obligation to sincerely thank Dr. Rocco M. Donatelli, Associate Dean of Arts and Sciences, Father Matthew Kohmescher, chairman of the Department of Theological Studies, and Dr. Richard A. Boulet, director of Graduate Studies in the Department. These gentlemen, each in his own way, encouraged my research and provided me with the most precious commodity of all: time. Many thanks also to my student assistant, Mark Taffera, who served as my life line to libraries during the months of writing, and who compiled the index of authors and of Scripture references.

As a member of the Markan Task Force I have profited from three years of seminar meetings and discussions. Of my colleagues who by their friendly criticism helped me toward finding my own concept of the Markan gospel I wish to mention: John D. Crossan, John R. Donahue,

Anitra Kolenkow, Robin Scroggs, Vernon K. Robins, and Theodore J. Weeden.

I have good memories of a night in Houston, Texas, spent in discussion with Dr. Friedrich Lang, my predecessor at Rice University. His unconventional view on the *theios anēr* theology further encouraged me to discount a direct Markan polemic against such a Christianity.

I owe a special word of gratitude to Kim Dewey, my former research assistant at the University of Dayton, now PhD candidate at the University of Chicago. Many of his helpful suggestions found their way into this book.

Words, the medium biblical scholars credit with life and power, cannot adequately express my indebtedness to my wife, Mary Ann. Without her this book could not have been written.

I dedicate this book to Norman Perrin, *Doktorvater*, mentor, and friend. To him I owe the greatest debt of gratitude.

THE
KINGDOM
IN
MARK

What we call the beginning is often the end
And to make an end is to make a beginning.
The end is where we start from.

T. S. Eliot, *Little Gidding*

A response to a world out of joint

Chapter I

ARRIVAL AND CONFLICT
OF THE KINGDOM

1:1—3:6

Most scholars are of the opinion that the gospel of Mark was composed in the decade preceding the destruction of Jerusalem, sometime during the years A.D. 60-70. It is the contention of this study that the gospel came into existence sometime after A.D. 70 under the impact of the city's devastation. This thesis rests on the claim that there was a body of Christians directly involved in and deeply affected by the fall of Jerusalem. For them, as for their fellow Jews, the disaster caused dreadful physical suffering and hardship. Owing to the unique position Jerusalem held in Jewish and, we shall see, Jewish Christian faith, the religious implications of the fall were likewise profound. Apocalyptic expectations, hopes for messianic intervention, and a redemption of Davidic promises were singularly tied to the city and its temple. It was here that the temporal and spatial coordinates crossed to form the global fixed-point, the divine center of the universe. Without Jerusalem the people were bereft of orientation in space and time, at once displaced and without future. With the fall of the city their entire basis of existence had collapsed.

Was there any compelling reason for Christians to continue living in faith? What they needed was a new place and a new time. To meet the present crisis, a system was required which could account for the disaster, create a new configuration of time and space, and provide a sense of continuity and stability. This is precisely what was done. Just as the crucifixion did not put an end to the Christian movement, but merely marked the beginning of theological reflection on the significance of Jesus, so did this second major catastrophe in early Christianity—the fall of Jerusalem—by no means signal the end of Christian history, but rather

1

the beginning of a reorientation of history. The composition of the Markan gospel arose out of the need for a new comprehensive field of vision subsequent to the collapse of a particular Christian worldview.

Against this historical backdrop the very first words of the Markan composition, "the beginning of the gospel," are of notable significance. That Mark opens his work by announcing that this is its beginning, is indeed curious. Ought it not to be taken for granted that he does not commence with the tail end of the story? Obviously he wishes to make an issue of this "beginning." There are three ways in which this all-important *archē* functions in Mark's gospel.

First, *archē* is a response to the experience of a terminal point in history. The destruction of the center of life spelled the end of all hope. All known paradigms of hope were consumed in the flames of the conflagration, and the survivors had to come to terms with the city of promise reduced to ashes and a faith refuted by the enemy's victory. The Christian traditions which had reached Mark from earlier times had been rendered obsolete. Because they did not answer to the challenge of the hour, let alone account for the loss of meaning and life, they appeared to be irrelevant. Mark responds to the unparalleled crisis by reshaping and transforming his traditions into the (for Christians) radically new form of gospel which allows him to make a new beginning. This beginning is the answer to the end of Jerusalem and the implied end of history. In the face of the end Mark posits a beginning.

Second, *archē* indicates *merely* the beginning of something the final consummation of which is yet to come. One of the more startling aspects of the gospel is that it does not commence with the critical experience which precipitated its composition. Mark regresses into the past of Jesus' life. Deprived of hope in his own present, but intent on building a new future, he returns to the very beginnings of Christian hope. He retraces the life of Jesus in search for clues to his own experience. If the Christians follow his guide along the way of Jesus, they will learn how they got caught in the crisis and, knowing its genesis, discover an opening toward a new future. They have to reconsider the life of Jesus from beginning to end, in order to be released into a new beginning at the point of the gospel's ending. There is thus a correlation between beginning and ending.[1] Only if they start from the right beginning, i.e., from the very

---

1. One of the very few scholars who noticed this is Robert P. Meye, *Jesus and the Twelve* (Grand Rapids, Mich.: Eerdmans, 1968), pp. 211–13, and *idem*, "Mark 16:8 —The Ending of Mark's Gospel," *BiR*, 14 (1969), pp. 33–43.

beginning, will they perceive how the end of their hope came about and know what the true end is. This suggests that the *archē* reduces the whole gospel to a prologue of a new future for the Markan Christians. The entire work stands at the beginning of something new.

Third, *archē* serves an important structural purpose in the text of the gospel. Implying that more is to come, *archē* invites the reader to discriminate between introduction and gospel in full measure. This is confirmed by a recurrence of the term gospel in 1:14, at which point it presents Jesus' own proclamation. The "beginning of the gospel" is thus 1:1–13, i.e., John's preparation of the way, and the baptism and temptation of Jesus. The gospel in full, 1:14–15, concurs with Jesus' first public utterance;[2] 1:14–15 is clearly thrust into pivotal position. This all the more so since Jesus' inaugural message constitutes the only instance in Mark, and indeed in the synoptic tradition, where the gospel's content is *expressis verbis* spelled out. The full gospel message of 1:14–15 is thus endowed with programmatic consequence. It furnishes the key to the Markan Jesus' life and death. All aspects of his ministry will have to be read in the light of this gospel program.[3]

THE GOSPEL PROGRAM

We begin our consideration of 1:14–15 by recalling that it was Mark who imported the term gospel into the synoptic stream of tradition.[4] Hence, the careful spacing of gospel in the first fifteen verses, which serves to distinguish the prolegomena from the gospel's program, can be attributed to Mark; 1:14 itself is largely a redactional product,[5] and the principal message in 1:15 is flanked on both sides by a redactional refer-

2. Among studies on 1:14–15 see Benjamin W. Bacon, "The Prologue of Mark: A Study of Sources and Structure," *JBL*, 26 (1907), pp. 84–106; N. F. Freese, "Der Anfang des Markusevangeliums," *ThStKr*, 104 (1932), pp. 429–38; Allen Wikgren, "Archē Tou Euangeliou," *JBL*, 61 (1942), pp. 11–20; Oscar J. F. Seitz, "Praeparatio Evangelica in the Markan Prologue," *JBL*, 82 (1963), pp. 201–06. The most significant studies in recent times are Leander E. Keck, "The Introduction to Mark's Gospel," *NTS*, 12 (1966), pp. 352–70; Rudolf Pesch, "Anfang des Evangeliums Jesu Christi," *Die Zeit Jesu* (H. Schlier Festschrift), Günther Bornkamm and Karl Rahner, eds. (Freiburg: Herder, 1970), pp. 108–44; Aloysius M. Ambrozic, *The Hidden Kingdom*, The Catholic Biblical Quarterly—Monograph Series, No. 2 (Washington, D.C.: The Catholic Biblical Association of America, 1972), pp. 4–31.
3. Karl-Georg Reploh, *Markus—Lehrer der Gemeinde*, Stuttgarter Biblische Monographien, No. 9 (Stuttgart: Katholisches Bibelwerk, 1969), p. 15 calls 1:14–15 a "Schlüsselstelle zum Verständnis des Evangeliums."
4. The argument is convincingly presented by Willi Marxsen, *Mark the Evangelist*, trans. Roy A. Harrisville *et al.* (Nashville, Tenn.: Abingdon Press, 1969), pp. 117–50.
5. Ambrozic, *Kingdom*, p. 4.

ence to gospel.[6] Mark will likewise have assembled and shaped the material with which to give content to gospel, the term of his choice.[7] In principle, our earlier observation remains valid; 1:14–15 manifests the controlling idea of the whole. But in view of the redactional structuring of 1:1–15 we must qualify that position. Mark 1:14–15 provides the hermeneutical key not primarily to the ministry of Jesus, but first and foremost to Markan theology. Underlining the prominence of 1:14–15 by the conspicuous position he designed for it at the outset of his work, Mark put on the lips of Jesus the program and leading motif of his own theology. Jesus has become the medium of the Markan message, and this message is directed to and, in all probability, dictated by the Markan condition.[8]

Since Mark chose gospel as a heading for Jesus' message, the redactional function and concept of this term must be clarified. On this matter W. Marxsen's insights deserve to be reviewed.[9] With the exception of 1:1 and 1:14–15, the evangelist introduces gospel in such a manner that it follows on the heels of a preceding reference to Jesus. Thus in 8:35 Jesus calls upon his followers to lose their lives "for my sake and for the gospel's." In 10:29 Jesus commends those who abandon everything and everybody "for my sake and for the sake of the gospel." In 13:9 Jesus foretells persecution and death which in turn will precipitate his followers' public testimony "for my sake," and in 13:10 he emphasizes the need to preach the "gospel." As for 14:9, Marxsen could have made an even more convincing argument, had he considered the verse in a slightly broader context, because the mentioning of the woman's anointment, which will be remembered "wherever the gospel is preached" (14:9), follows in the wake of Jesus' dire prognosis that "you will not always have me" (14:7c). In this latter case, the absent Jesus is replaced by the preached gospel.

If, as we have argued, the gospel has to be strictly understood from the viewpoint of the Markan present, it seems sound to advance one step for-

6. Reploh, *Lehrer,* p. 15.
7. Mark derived the material of 1:15 largely from early Christian missionary tradition. See Rudolf Bultmann, *History of the Synoptic Tradition,* trans. John Marsh, 3rd ed. (New York: Harper & Row, 1963). p. 341; Ernst Lohmeyer, *Das Evangelium des Markus,* 17th ed. (Göttingen: Vandenhoeck & Ruprecht, 1967), pp. 29–30; Norman Perrin, *The Kingdom of God in the Teaching of Jesus* (Philadelphia: Westminster Press, 1963), pp. 200–01.
8. Pesch, "Anfang," at once oversimplifies redactional contributions by acknowledging only 1:1 and 1:15c as Markan, and unduly complicates exegesis by assigning 1:2–15b to a pre-Markan redactor.
9. Marxsen, *Mark,* pp. 117–38, 146–50.

ward and posit as a preliminary rule that the gospel functions in such a manner as to extend Jesus into the Markan present. What lies at the root of the Markan gospel is therefore the desire to remain in living attachment to Jesus and to preserve continuity between Jesus and the Markan community of followers. This motif of *repraesentatio* will have to be firmly kept in mind when dealing with the program of 1:14–15. In part, Jesus' first proclamation in public, this gospel in the full sense, is likely to have been formulated in such a way as to answer the Markan community's need for the representation of Jesus.

From there one must not immediately jump to the conclusion that the person of Jesus has become the content of the gospel. At this point we register our disagreement with Marxsen when he sees the role of *repraesentatio* most adequately played out by the resurrected Christ: "In and by his gospel, the Risen Lord re-presents his own life on this earth."[10] In so far as Christ initiates and proclaims the gospel, he is its author. But since the gospel's proclamation renders Christ contemporary with the Markan community, he is sum and substance of the gospel. In Marxsen's view, Jesus Christ is both author and content, subject and object of his gospel. Mark supposedly achieves this omnivalent function of Jesus by fusing the historical Jesus with the resurrected Christ to the point that the former is totally absorbed by the latter. As a corollary to this, Marxsen can postulate a close correspondence between the gospel of Mark and that of Paul. He cites with approval G. Friedrich's definition of the Pauline gospel because it is one which Marxsen believes applies with equal precision to Mark: "If we were to sum up the content of the gospel in a single word, it would be Jesus the Christ."[11] In the last analysis the gospel is therefore Jesus' self-proclamation as the Christ. It is with this concept of gospel that Marxsen approaches 1:14–15. Taking for granted that the crucial verses furnish a model case for Jesus' self-proclamation, and adopting the majority reading of *ēngiken* as a statement of nearness, he arrives at the conclusion that in 1:14–15 Jesus announces his own imminent coming, i.e., his parousia: "Briefly put the gospel declares: I am coming soon."[12]

Marxsen's gospel theory set a tone and gave directives which from the outset pulled the redaction-critical exposition of the Markan gospel into a theological orbit that bears odd resemblance to, generally speaking,

10. *Ibid.*, p. 131.
11. *Ibid.*, p. 130.
12. *Ibid.*, p. 134.

Pauline, Lutheran, existentialist maxims. Specifically, his gospel theory must be challenged on four points.

/   First, although Marxsen acknowledges the summarizing significance of 1:14–15,[13] he spends little time on its exegesis, but is anxious to bring it in line with his own concept of gospel.

2   Second, Marxsen shortcuts the theological distance which separates a Mark from a Paul. Christ, the crucified and resurrected One, undoubtedly comprises the substance of the Pauline gospel. But this concept is not, we shall see, fundamental to the Markan gospel. Furthermore, Paul's gospel never even approximates a narrative form, because it is not motivated by the need to retrace the past life of Jesus. Unless proven otherwise, Pauline influence on Mark remains an illegitimate assumption,[14] and the identification of the two gospels' concepts obstructs the path to the authentic Markan theology. There ought to be a deeper appreciation of the Markan gospel on its own terms before outside help is sought.[15]

3 ,   Third, if it is assumed that the gospel is the functional equivalent of Christ, it seems only logical to conclude that "Christ himself is the gospel."[16] This formula, Christ equals gospel, appears to be so solidly established Christian knowledge as to be above questioning. And yet, to define the Markan project as "the gospel which Christ, the Risen Lord, proclaims *and* which proclaims Christ, the Risen Lord,"[17] is to define it according to the canon of the school of existentialist exegesis.[18] By christologically maximizing the content of gospel, Marxsen has exaggerated the *repraesentatio* motif into a hermeneutical principle of modern persuasion. If gospel is indeed indistinguishable from Jesus Christ, then passages such as 8:35, 10:29, 13:9–10, and 14:7–9 amount to christological tautologism, the very thing Mark would likely have avoided by his novel insert of gospel.

4   Fourth, that our gospels perform the synchronization of the earthly Jesus with the resurrected Lord is a standard principle of modern gospel interpretation. Only as risen Christ is Jesus said to have authored the

---

13. *Ibid.*, p. 66.

14. Martin Werner, *Der Einfluss Paulinischer Theologie im Markusevangelium* (Giessen: Töpelmann, 1923). The author discounts Pauline influence on Mark, a thesis which has not been overturned.

15. Refreshingly to the point, Ambrozic, *Kingdom*, p. 8: "The primary source for discovering the meaning of Mark's 'gospel' should be the Gospel of Mark."

16. Marxsen, *Mark*, p. 148.

17. *Ibid.*, p. 149.

18. See Keck, "Introduction," p. 358: ". . . Marxsen has simply modernized Mark's theology into Marxsen's."

gospel and preached to the Markan Christians. But does this reflect the religious logic of Mark? As indicated above, we will operate on the assumption that the gospel marks a religious *regressus ad originem* (not, of course, to be confused with the historically inspired, questing return *ad fontes*), a retelling of the sacred past of Jesus in a manner most meaningful to the Markan contemporaries.[19]

Sooner or later a study of 1:14–15 stumbles against the controversial *ēngiken*. Imminent nearness or present arrival, that is the question which has haunted exegesis to this day.

EXCURSUS

The controversy surrounding the term *ēngiken* was born with C. H. Dodd's thesis of Jesus' realized eschatology. As for 1:14–15, this exegete built his case in great measure upon a linguistic analysis of *engizein* (1:15) and the Q verb *phthanein* (Matt. 12:28b/Luke 11:20b) in the LXX and Hellenistic literature.[20] It is discovered that the two verbs translate either the Hebrew *naga'* or the Aramaic *m'ta*, and furthermore that both originals carry the meaning "to arrive." Due to their common Semitic background the *ephthasen* in Q and the Markan *ēngiken* are declared interchangeable, as a result of which both Q and Mark are said to assert the arrival of the Kingdom as a present reality. Being of the conviction that Q and Mark approximate "the original tradition of the words and works of Jesus,"[21] Dodd is now prompted to infer that the manifest arrival of the Kingdom constitutes "the fixed point from which our interpretation of the teaching regarding the Kingdom of God must start."[22] Henceforth, Dodd proceeds to reconcile potential or real future Kingdom sayings to Jesus' fundamental message of the realized Kingdom.[23] It may be said that the methodological basis for Dodd's realized eschatology lies in an examination of single words.

W. G. Kümmel[24] commences his work on the eschatological message of Jesus with an examination of *engys* and *engizein* in the New Testament. In its usage of *engys* the New Testament is said to be "completely uniform."[25] Consistently the term denotes the nearness of an event, but never its actual arrival. Likewise, the verb *engizein* occurs in the New Testament and especially in the

---

19. For similar observations see Ambrozic, *Kingdom*, pp. 9–13.

20. The gist of Charles H. Dodd's analysis is contained in *The Parables of the Kingdom*, rev. ed. (New York: Charles Scribner's Sons, 1961), pp. 28–40, as well as in "The Kingdom of God Has Come," *ExpT*, 48 (1936–37), pp. 138–42. For a review of Dodd's thesis, see Perrin, *Kingdom*, pp. 64–68.

21. Dodd, *Parables*, p. 26.

22. *Ibid.*, p. 35.

23. See especially Dodd's forced interpretation of 9:1, *Ibid.*, pp. 37–38.

24. Werner Georg Kümmel, *Promise and Fulfilment*, trans. Dorothea M. Barton, Studies in Biblical Theology, No. 23 (London: SCM Press, 1966).

25. *Ibid.*, p. 20.

gospels "without exception"[26] in the sense of "coming near." In light of this understanding of nearness, Mark 1:15 will have to be rendered with "The Kingdom of God is coming near," or else the evangelist "must have been guilty either of an extremely grave misunderstanding of Jesus' fundamental message concerning the coming of the Kingdom of God or of an incomprehensible inconsistency in . . . [his] use of words."[27] The comparatively imminent arrival of the Kingdom is therefore the understanding most germane to the teaching of Jesus. Kümmel's reading of 1:15 is in the main deduced from an analysis of *engys* and *engizein*.

R. H. Fuller[28] makes Mark 1:15 the basis of his discussion of the Kingdom of God in the proclamation of Jesus, and promptly conducts yet another inquiry into the meaning of *engizein* in the New Testament. Similar to Kümmel, this author determines that throughout the New Testament *engizein* refers to events which have not yet occurred, but are forthcoming in the very near future. With this, the future propensity of the Markan *engiken* seemed assured once and for all. However, Fuller expresses a certain uneasiness about his futuristic interpretation, presumably because he is impressed by the overall powerful wording of 1:15 which might well incline toward a reading in terms of present realization. For a moment he ponders the possibility of considering *engiken* within the total context of 1:15, but quickly dismisses the idea because "the context does not demand the exceptional meaning here."[29] From then on Fuller steers a compromise course between a fully realized eschatology and a futuristically oriented one. Resorting to evidence from outside the New Testament, he turns to three occurrences of *engizein* in Deutero-Isaiah. In each case he finds *engizein* being used to render the "dynamic, present meaning" of the Hebrew participle of *qrb* and feels for this reason justified in modifying his strictly future understanding of the Greek verb.[30] Aside from its future direction the *engiken* is now said to indicate a happening in the present as well. The Kingdom of God is in the person and through the ministry of Jesus "operative in advance."[31] Fuller arrives at this proleptic notion of 1:15 by way of a series of detailed word studies.

The three examples shed light upon the methodological guidelines which have swayed an understanding of 1:14–15. Aside from the fact that all three studies appear somewhat forced to serve preconceptions which may, or may not, correctly assess Jesus' Kingdom proclamation, these interpretations arrive at far-reaching theological conclusions by narrowly focusing upon the single words *engizein* and the cognate *phthanein*. The meaning of *engiken* is dictated by a consensus which was achieved through a lexicographical polling of the

26. *Ibid.*, p. 24.

27. *Ibid.*

28. Reginald H. Fuller, *The Mission and Achievement of Jesus*, Studies in Biblical Theology, No. 12 (Chicago: Alec R. Allenson, Inc., 1954), pp. 20–35.

29. *Ibid.*, p. 24.

30. *Ibid.*

31. *Ibid.*

verb *engizein* and its cognate in the New Testament, the LXX, Hellenistic texts, and the Old Testament. It has been said that the whole controversy demonstrated nothing but "the ambiguity surrounding the meaning of both Greek words under discussion, as well as around the possible underlying Semitic verbs."[32] Clearly the issue is not resolved by one more scholar holding up a newly discovered scrap of evidence indicating "nearness," merely to be countered by another one who has come across a hitherto overlooked passage supporting "arrival." The basic deficiency of this approach lies in the failure to come to grips with the semantic significance of words in their contextual settings. It is the context which molds the meaning of words, while single words are pliable and accommodating to their semantic environment. The aggregate and not the monad mediates the meaning. A single word set aside in isolation does not operate as the carrier of the message, but rather the total configuration of words in their status of interlocking.[33]

As regards 1:14–15, the exclusive reliance upon a single word led to remarkably inconclusive results. When taken by itself, the *ēngiken* is a subtle and ambiguous phrase, devoid of any self-explanatory power. The verb's intended delivery will have to be inferred from the contextual unit made up by the two verses. Yet, what will emerge as the plausible contextual meaning cannot be fully determined until it is viewed as an organic ingredient in an even larger unit, the entirety of Markan theology—eschatology.

Section 1:14 provides the general setting for the gospel of God, and the recitative *hoti*, the equivalent of quotation marks, stages the words of 1:15 in the form of a direct address. 1:15 is divided into *kerygma* (15a) and *parenesis* (15b), the proclamation proper and the ethical conclusions to be drawn from it.

By their advanced position the two verbs *peplērōtai* and *ēngiken* in 1:15a dominate the content of the message, and it is further to be noted that the curtain rises with the unambiguous and commanding *peplērōtai*. No other New Testament theologian saw fit to put on the lips of Jesus the bold assertion: fulfilled has been the time! Elsewhere the time has not arrived yet (1 Thess. 5:1), or it is close at hand (Rev. 1:3; 22:10), or it has grown very short (1 Cor. 7:29). Even the Johannine Christ announces frankly: "My time has not yet fully come" (John 7:8). Nor are Matthew and Luke ready to adopt Mark's powerful time saying. The eschatological time statement in 1:15a sets a precedent in New Testament literature.

32. Robert F. Berkey, "Engizein, Phthanein, and Realized Eschatology," *JBL*, 82 (1963), p. 181.

33. G. Kittel's *Theological Dictionary of the New Testament*, which operates in large part on the basis of isolated word studies, has been subjected to profound criticism by James Barr, *The Semantics of Biblical Language* (London: Oxford University Press, 1961).

Furthermore, 1:15a is the only instance in the New Testament where a time saying of such force is joined together with a Kingdom saying. Reading the controversial *ēngiken* in the wake of the unprecedented time phrase, the former assumes the meaning of arrival.[34] The time is fulfilled because the Kingdom has in fact made its arrival. Both the singular eschatological force of the initial time saying, and the conjunction of this time saying with a Kingdom saying suggests an interpretation of 1:15a in terms of present arrival and realized fulfillment: the eschatological time has been fulfilled and the Kingdom of God has arrived.[35]

While Luke deviates entirely from the Markan model, Matthew considerably weakens the purpose of 1:14–15 and transforms Mark's emphasis on present arrival into one of preparatory anticipation of the Kingdom. A brief review of the five major alterations which the Markan original underwent at the hand of Matthew will further clarify the Markan focus.

First, Matt. 4:17 does not constitute Jesus' inaugural address, for he has already conversed with the Baptist (3:15) and repudiated the demands of Satan (4:4, 7, 10). Second, Matthew does not introduce the term gospel until 4:23, so that Jesus' proclamation in 4:17 cannot qualify as the sum and substance of the gospel proper. Third, Jesus' message falls short of Markan originality, for this *same* message has been preached before by the Baptist (3:2; 4:17). Fourth, as indicated above, Matthew omits the time saying which in Mark serves to accentuate the presence of the Kingdom. Fifth, Matthew reverses the order of the Kingdom saying and the injunction to repentance, and, most importantly, he inserts the particle *gar* after *ēngiken*. As a result of these changes, Jesus' proclamation is deprived of its programmatic character, and what is announced in Matt. 4:17 is not the present arrival, but the imminent coming of the Kingdom. Repentance for Matthew is an act of preparation, because (*gar*) the Kingdom is at hand. It is in this manner that he responds to what in Mark is a firm insistence on arrival and present reality of the Kingdom.

Central to 1:14–15 is not the announcement of the Kingdom's imminent advent, but that of its establishment in the fullness of time and at a definite place. The Jesus "from Nazareth in Galilee" (1:9) left the wilderness

34. This same point was made by Matthew Black, "The Kingdom of God Has Come," *ExpT*, 63 (1951–52), p. 290, and by P. Joüon, "Notes Philologiques sur les Évangiles," *RSR*, 17 (1927), p. 538.
35. Two scholars have recently deviated from the majority reading of 1:15 in terms of imminence, and argued in favor of present arrival: Reploh, *Lehrer*, p. 20, *passim*, and Ambrozic, *Kingdom*, p. 21, *passim*.

and "came into Galilee" (1:14) to announce there his gospel program. The Kingdom has accomplished its realization, and it has done so in Galilee. This then is the gospel program of the Markan Jesus: There is full time in Galilee, for it is here that the Kingdom of God has attained its earthly destination. The principal identity of Jesus is that of proclaimer and bearer of the Kingdom; all aspects of his career must be viewed in light of his programmatic Kingdom deed.

Eschatology is of ultimate concern to Mark, and the realized eschatology of the Galilean Kingdom serves as premise for, and holds the hermeneutical key to Markan theology.[36] Not the risen Christ, but the presence of the Kingdom in Galilee constitutes the gist of the gospel program. Essentially it is this program which makes the new beginning in the aftermath of the catastrophe. It is in response to the crisis in history that Mark announces the presence of the Kingdom in Galilee. The beginning is localized in Galilee and actualized in the fullness of time.

Our exegetical efforts have as yet not exhausted the implications of 1:14–15. The grammatical nature of *peplērōtai* and *ēngiken*, both being perfect tenses, deserves special attention. Just as the bulk of the material in 1:14–15 gives the impression of having undergone a process of studied selection and composition, so does the use of the perfect tense also appear to be deliberate. As a rule, the perfect expresses both a punctiliar and a linear quality; it marks the point of departure which carries with it a resultative force. The temporal significance conventionally associated with the perfect tense is that of the "continuance of a completed action."[37] The two verbs may therefore be expected to refer to an event, which happened in the past but continues to be of relevance for the present. That this is the force of *peplērōtai* and *ēngiken* is all the more likely, because it seems to spring directly from the redactional vantage point. The evangelist looks back upon the Galilean past and sees the Kingdom as having arrived with the person of Jesus, but he is fully aware of the implications this advent is having for his own people who live decades after

---

36. See Franz Mussner, "Gottesherrschaft und Sendung Jesu nach Mk 1, 14 f.," *Praesentia Salutis* (Düsseldorf: Patmos, 1967), pp. 90–93. Keck, "Introduction," p. 368, holds that 1:14–15 has no "consequences in the narrative that follows . . ." With this we disagree because we believe that the Markan gospel is preeminently the gospel of the Kingdom. Keck considers 1:1–15 the prologue, and 1:16–20, the call of the first disciples, "as the paradigmatic inauguration of the whole" (p. 363). Our study, it will become obvious, is far from relegating discipleship to the periphery. Kingdom theology and discipleship are closely interwoven. The disciples are called to witness the Kingdom, because they are going to be in charge of the Kingdom.
37. Friedrich W. Blass and Albert Debrunner, *A Greek Grammar of the New Testament*, trans. Robert W. Funk (Chicago: University of Chicago Press, 1961), p. 175.

the fact. Indeed, the redaction critic will posit that Mark is eminently conscious of the Galilean Kingdom's currency in his own time, or else he would not have reported the happening at all. His perspective of the past of Jesus is informed by the dimension of his own present. He delves into the past and re-creates it, but only to the extent that it affects his condition and speaks to his concerns. In this manner, the Kingdom of Jesus' past is given priority in Mark's presentation, because it carries heavy weight with his own present.

With this we have arrived at a fundamental question. Why was it that approximately forty years after the death of Jesus the thoroughly eschatological message of the arrival of the Kingdom of God was recounted to a Christian people? In what sense can the Galilean advent of the Kingdom be relevant to a people who have experienced the fall of Jerusalem? This is one of the root problems of Markan theology-eschatology, and it will preoccupy this study to the end.

The above insights allow us to see the *repraesentatio* motif of the Markan gospel in clearer light. Obviously it is going too far to say, as does Marxsen, that Christ preaches himself in the gospel, for the sum and substance of the gospel proclamation is the Kingdom. To argue that Jesus is synonymous with the Kingdom, or present in the preached word of the Kingdom, is to miss the mark of *repraesentatio* which distinguishes the Markan gospel from the other gospels. Looking at 1:14–15 from the angle of *repraesentatio*, however, the Kingdom emerges as a meaningful concept, for in it resides the power to bridge the gulf that separates the past of Jesus from the present of Mark. The Kingdom may well continue after Jesus has died, and through it the people may link up with and share the Jesus of the past. This presupposes that in some form and fashion Jesus' Kingdom has become a present reality for the Markan people.[38] But it also presupposes that Mark does not ascribe primary significance to the resurrected Lord. The Christ who speaks and acts in the gospel is the Jesus of Nazareth in Galilee (1:9), the Son of God (1:1, 11), installed into office at baptism and not by resurrection! It is this Jesus who in his inaugural message extends the Kingdom to a people who are robbed of full time, and who in a moment of void and destruction may worry about Jesus' absence from their midst.

The second part of Jesus' address, the *parenesis* (15b) summons the

---

38. The precise nature of the Kingdom's presence in the community will be discussed in Chap. II.

people to "repent and believe on the basis of the gospel."[39] In a general sense, *metanoia* involves a total commitment to God, achieved not merely by renouncing all that is evil and sinful, but by a break with one's former mode of living altogether.[40] In view of this all-inclusive nature of *metanoia* it is worth contemplating whether the concept is necessarily confined to religious-spiritual conduct, denoting change of heart and humiliation in sackcloth and ashes. H. Braun[41] has pointed out that at Qumran repentance was something to be accomplished by a turning away from the world (of nonsectarians), the subsequent entry into the new community, and the handing over of all material possessions to the community's administrative body. At least we will have to keep in mind that *metanoia* implicates a practical, physical potential, indicating change of place and life direction. It is to be noted in this connection that already the precursor's baptism of repentance effected a break with place, an exodus of "all the country of Judea and all the people of Jerusalem" (1:5). As regards the counsel of faith, it is well to recall J. Robinson's[42] observation that "Mark has no single person or act as the object of faith, and no specific credal statement as the content of faith." This suggests that the Markan *pistis* took shape under religious conditions quite different from those which gave birth to the Pauline *pistis* in the crucified and resurrected Lord. Generally, the Markan *pistis* is not concerned with belief in somebody, i.e., the Christ of the cross, but *pistis* constitutes an attitude on the part of man, characterized by such attributes as confidence, fearlessness, courage, and perseverance in the face of experiences to the contrary.[43] To sum up the *parenesis*, the Markan people are called upon to undergo a drastic change of heart (and place?) and to summon up their courage in virtue of the presence of the Kingdom.

Admittedly this interpretation raises more questions than it can answer at this point. The vast majority of exegetes who settle for the nearness of

---

39. Notwithstanding Mark's well-known preference for *eis* in places where one normally expects *en* (Cuthbert H. Turner, "Marcan Usage: Notes, Critical and Exegetical, on the Second Gospel," *JTS*, 26 [1924–25], pp. 14–20), the singular phrase *pisteuein en* is likely to express a redactional purpose in a verse so carefully constructed by Mark. The *en* must be given its literal force. The gospel of the Kingdom is the ground which sustains a life in faith.

40. Johannes Behm, "metanoeō, metanoia," *TDNT*, 4, p. 1002.

41. Herbert Braun, "'Umkehr' in spätjüdisch-häretischer und frühchristlicher Sicht," *ZThK*, 50 (1953), pp. 243–58.

42. James M. Robinson, *The Problem of History in Mark*, Studies in Biblical Theology, No. 21 (London: SCM Press, 1957), p. 75.

43. In Mark, fear is the improper, and faith the proper attitude. Both postures are, however, surpassed by "seeing," the eschatological experience par excellence.

the Kingdom can readily perceive *metanoia* and *pistis* as initiatory acts destined to smooth the path for the coming of the Kingdom. In part it was this counsel of repentance and faith which persuaded scholars to opt in favor of the Kingdom's imminent forthcoming, for its full realization was considered incompatible with what seemed to be a note of preparation. In part it was also under the influence of such decidedly future-oriented sayings as 9:1, 13:30, and 13:33 that exegetes were tempted to bring 1:15 into harmony with the gospel's overriding future orientation. But our desire to reduce complex lines of thought and seeming contradictions to an intellectually satisfying picture may deprive us of comprehending the total vision. By striving for an unhealthy balance on this matter, exegesis has paid the high price of obstructing the gateway to the inner dynamics of the Kingdom in Mark.

Having committed ourselves to the Galilean realization of the Kingdom, we are required to set aside the traditional interpretation in terms of preparedness for the coming Kingdom. Repentance and faith, we suggest, do not constitute acts of preparation, but signal the direct consequences ensuing from the Kingdom's presence. A radical break with the former mode of living and confidence in view of the eschatological happening in Galilee—those are the claims imposed upon a people who live in the wake of the irruption of the Kingdom.

This interpretation has every appearance of distortion, because the *parenesis* seems to cancel out the *kerygma* of the Kingdom. What is the meaning of repentance in the fullness of the Kingdom, and why is one to believe if the Kingdom has in fact arrived? What is the nature of this realized Kingdom that it provokes the ethical call to change? Again, we must remember that this is a program designed to appeal to a people who live under conditions of virtual unfulfillment. Tension and conflict, so candidly engraved in this Kingdom message, reflect Markan experiences. The paradoxical juxtaposition of fulfillment and unfulfillment, and the seeming inconsistency between the advent of the Kingdom and its resultant ethical call are meant to speak into the situation of crisis. The Kingdom has come, an exit is opened, and the present impasse could well be overcome. The people can, as indeed they must, make a change, lift themselves out of their hopeless condition, and live up to the fullness of the Galilean Kingdom.

The enlistment of Simon, Andrew, James, and John into the service of discipleship (1:16–20) from the outset accords a communal dimension to the Kingdom. Moreover, this first public gesture on the part of Jesus reveals in what way the Kingdom affects people. It consists of people and it bids for people (1:17c), but in the curious sense of dislodging these first participants from their native environment. The nucleus of the Kingdom is called into being neither by a foundation ceremony, nor by a ritual laying on of hands, but by a forced departure of four men away from their professional and personal lives. The disciples are given new directions and they are about to strike a new course. As the Kingdom begins to involve people, it severs their ties to the past, puts them on the way, and transplants them into a totally new mode of existence.

COLLISION OF KINGDOMS

Beyond breakup and motion, the Kingdom breathes the spirit of conflict, and establishes itself over against adversaries on various fronts. It has been observed that 1:16–3:12 "stands under the theme of a power struggle"[44] which erupts at successive junctures between Jesus and Satan, the Son of God and the demons, and the Son of Man and his earthly opponents.[45] This conflict had been initiated by Jesus himself in the wilderness confrontation (1:12–13). The spirit-filled Son of God had searched out and challenged Satan on his own ground. As he emerged from the contest, the time was ripe for the announcement of the advent of the Kingdom. Born out of a demonic power struggle, the Kingdom will henceforth assert its presence wherever the initial conflict is continued.[46]

As Jesus enters Capernaum in the company of the four recruits he finds himself immediately engaged in a confrontation with hostile forces (1:21–28). Presumably in reaction to his teaching with authority, an unclean spirit screams aloud. The spirit recognizes, quite properly from his perspective, that Jesus' mission is bent on overthrowing the demonic power structure: "Have you come to destroy us" (1:24d)? We owe it to the perception of this demonic spirit that Jesus' universal purpose is disclosed. He came to crush not merely a single proponent of the powers of darkness, but the Kingdom of Evil proper. Jesus responds to the spirit's astute awareness of the situation by "rebuking" him. This rendering of *epitimaō* with "rebuke" or "reproach" is, however, inadequate, for more is involved

---

44. Leander E. Keck, "Mark 3, 7–12 and Mark's Christology," *JBL*, 84 (1965), p. 352.
45. Robinson, *History*, pp. 34–35.
46. As regards the significance of the temptation scene and the issue of eschatological tension in history, we generally adopt the position of Robinson, *History*, pp. 33–42, over against that of Ernest Best, *The Temptation and the Passion: The Markan Soteriology*, Society for New Testament Studies, Monograph Series, No. 2 (Cambridge: Cambridge University Press, 1965), pp. 3–60, *passim*.

than a gesture of disapproval or a word of correction. The term connotes an aggressive effort to wrest the power away from an opponent.[47] Jesus' commanding word "Be silent and come out of him" (1:25b), divests the spirit of his position of power and authority. The spirit's defeat is violently signalled by the man's lapsing into convulsions and a loud cry at the moment of exit (1:26). This exorcism, it is obvious, far exceeds the limits of a verbal confrontation. What we witness is a physical power struggle between two diametrically opposed antagonists. Jesus' exorcising ministry amounts to a clash between two Kingdoms. As he brings his newly gained authority into play, and by actualizing his new word of teaching (which concerns the Kingdom!), he makes a reality of God's rule on earth. To do battle on behalf of the Kingdom of God is the intrinsic purpose of the exorcism.[48]

It is beyond dispute that the story of the power struggle at Capernaum also makes a christological point. Jesus occupies the center, not only because he emerges victorious, but more so because his full identity as the Nazarene, the Holy One of God, comes to light. Still a word of warning must be expressed against viewing 1:21–28 solely as an epiphany story. There is first Mark's well-known attempt to have the demons' christological confessions suppressed (1:34; 3:11–12). The Son of God christology is not given free rein; rather it is subordinated to and its full manifestation impeded by another theological purpose, conventionally referred to as the Messianic Secret. Second, the response of the crowd to Jesus' act of domination is highly revealing. The onlookers' question is: "*What* is this?" (1:27c), and not "*Who* is this?," as one might expect them to ask out of pure christological curiosity.[49] Third, the Capernaum story provides a good example of a word of Jesus being turned into work and action. To put the same point differently, the christological verbalization is set into the context of an apocalyptic power struggle. It is in the process of the overthrow of evil and out of the mouth of the enemy that Jesus' authority is revealed. Fundamental to the story is the struggle of two Kingdoms.

47. Howard C. Kee, "The Terminology of Mark's Exorcism Stories," *NTS*, 14 (1968), pp. 232–46.
48. The relationship between exorcisms and Kingdom is clearly brought out by Kee, *ibid.* See also Karl Kertelge, *Die Wunder Jesu im Markusevangelium*, Studien zum Alten und Neuen Testament, No. 23 (Munich: Kösel, 1970), pp. 86–87. This function of the exorcisms is on a par with the theology of Q, see Matthew 12:28/Luke 11:20.
49. Rudolf Pesch, "Ein Tag vollmächtigen Wirkens Jesu in Kapharnaum," *BibLeb*, 9 (1968), p. 118, argues a redactional alteration from the original *tis* of the question to a *ti*.

The conflict at Capernaum carries significance beyond its own account and into the successive career of Jesus. Markan summaries bring the exorcisms into the limelight (1:34, 39; 3:11), stressing the continued importance of the hostile encounters. To all appearances, the struggle at Capernaum merely marks the overture to a conflict which pervades throughout the Galilean ministry. In imitation of the master's scheme and style the disciples are to carry on the battle (3:15; 6:7, 13), but at times their efforts are reported to have come to nought (9:18, 28–29). They seem not fully able to continue or maintain the struggle on behalf of the Kingdom of God.

There exists a close affinity between the exorcisms and the healing miracles.[50] This is why the Capernaum exorcism is immediately followed by the healing of Simon's mother-in-law (1:29–31). The Markan summaries, by singling out exorcisms and healings (1:34; 3:10–11), likewise recognize the functional similarity between these two types of activity.

The first miracle considered worthy of a theological reflection equal to that of the Capernaum exorcism is the healing of the leper (1:40–45). The condition of the sick man seems not unlike that of the demoniacs. He begs Jesus to make him clean (1:40: *katharisai*), and Jesus responds by performing a cleansing (1:41c: *katharisthēti*; 1:42b: *ekatharisthēti*). It is as though the leper was plagued by an unclean spirit. Because the disease brings him once again face to face with the powers of evil, Jesus is moved by a feeling of anger.[51] The cleansing itself is indicated by the exodus of the leprosy (1:42a: *apēlthen ap' autou hē lepra*). After the healing Jesus again harbors strong feelings toward the man (1:43: *embrimēsamenos autō*) and immediately orders his departure (1:43: *euthys exebalen auton*). The general state of agitation and the forced exodus strike a clear parallel between the nature of an exorcism and that of a healing.[52]

Exorcisms and healings are the two principal approaches used to translate the Kingdom program into action. In both cases, Jesus intrudes upon enemy territory, challenges and subdues the forces of evil which are in the way of the fulfillment of the Kingdom of God. This is the manner in which he mounts warfare so long as he moves about in the north.[53] To

---

50. Robinson, *History*, pp. 40–42; Kertelge, *Wunder*, pp. 86–87.

51. Against substantial manuscript evidence we read *orgistheis* and not *splangchnistheis*, because a change from anger to mercy seems more plausible than an alteration vice versa. See Vincent Taylor, *The Gospel According to St. Mark* (London: Macmillan and Co., 1963), p. 187; Gustav Stählin, *"orgē," TDNT*, 5, p. 428, n. 328.

52. Kertelge, *Wunder*, p. 73: "Die Heilung des Aussätzigen stellt somit eine Variation des Themas der Dämonenaustreibung dar."

53. The only exception to this is the healing of the blind Bartimaeus (10:46–52).

the Christians who suffered a crucial defeat this sounds a promising note. The disaster they experienced carries no ultimate significance, for the real battle is still in process. The Kingdom of God is not lost, but at present crucially involved in combat against the Kingdom of Satan.

KINGDOM IN DEFIANCE

The five controversy stories (2:1–12, 15–17, 18–22, 23–28; 3:1–6) carry the conflict onto an altogether different plane which permits tentative glimpses into communal conditions. Evidence must no longer be accumulated to press the point of the "post-Easter" perspective of the issues under discussion.[54] More recently, H.-W. Kuhn[55] resumed the form-critical analysis and demonstrated that the first four of the five controversy stories were joined together in a unified pre-Markan narrative cycle. But Kuhn made such minimal concessions to the redaction as to render the redaction-critical task virtually obsolete. Without inquiring into the provenance of each word of the conflict stories, it is possible to detect a good many more redactional traces. Furthermore, it seems Mark chose to deal with forgiveness of sins, association with outcasts, the practice of fasting, and Sabbath observance because these were issues of vital concern to him and his people. The controversy stories will therefore provide us with a structural outline of the Markan communal conditions as well as that of an opposing group.

2:1–12, the healing of the paralytic, is a composite literary product. Secondarily interjected into a miracle story (2:1–5, 11–12) is a conflict report (2:6–10) which now has a muffling effect on the miracle theology. The emphasis is not on Jesus the miracle worker, but on Jesus who performs a miracle through the problematic power of the forgiveness of sins. The intrusion of the controversial element and the accompanying shift from the miraculous toward forgiveness of sins is very likely of redactional making. There is first Mark's well-known device of intercalations.[56] Secondly, the interpolated section is at the beginning and

---

54. Bultmann, *Tradition*, pp. 12–19.

55. Heinz-Wolfgang Kuhn, *Ältere Sammlungen im Markusevangelium*, Studien zur Umwelt des Neuen Testaments, No. 8 (Göttingen: Vandenhoeck & Ruprecht, 1971), pp. 53–98.

56. Ernest v. Dobschütz, "Zur Erzählkunst des Markus," *ZNW*, 27 (1928), pp. 193–98; T. A. Burkill, "Anti-Semitism in St. Mark's Gospel," *NovTest*, 3 (1959), p. 37, n. 2; Robert H. Stein, "The Proper Methodology for Ascertaining a Markan Redaction History," *NovTest*, 31 (1971), pp. 192–94.

ending labeled by two "Markan insertions,"[57] a technique whereby near-identical frame-verses enclose items of redactional significance. The first case occurs in 2:6 (*dialogizomenoi en tais kardiais autōn*) and 2:8b (*dialogizesthe en tais kardiais hymōn*), focusing upon forgiveness of sins, and the second case concerns 2:9b (*egeire kai aron ton krabbaton sou*) and 2:11a (*egeire, aron ton krabbaton sou*), emphasizing the Son of Man's authority to forgive sins on earth. Third, the opening verse of the redactional interpolation (2:6) is a total Markan creation.[58] Fourth, the title Son of Man and its use in reference to earthly power in 2:10 is fundamental to Mark's christological purpose.[59] Last not least, it is a distinct tendency in Mark to put a strain on christological features which lend themselves to a *theios anēr* interpretation.[60] Thus it is Mark who casts Jesus in antithesis to an opposition viewpoint. The Son of Man acts as the spokesman of Markan interests, defending what in the eyes of the adversaries is outright blasphemy, i.e., the right to forgive sins on earth.

Table fellowship with outcasts (2:15-17) constitutes an apothegm culminating in Jesus' crucial word (2:17). This latter, originally an isolated logion,[61] deflects the preceding table fellowship theme toward a more general application. The application is extended to sinners, not tax collectors and sinners, the special occasion is fellowship in an unspecified sense, not merely feasting and eating, and Jesus himself, not Levi the tax collector, plays the host. While it cannot be proven that it was Mark who added 2:17, the interests reflected by this verse are those of Mark. The Markan Jesus defines his objective in terms of a mission to the very people who were traditionally excluded.[62] The inclusive nature of the new

---

57. The Markan insertion technique was discovered by John R. Donahue, "Temple and Trial in Mark 14," pp. 7-8, 29-31, an unpublished paper. The technique will be discussed in chapters two and three of Donahue's forthcoming book *Are You the Christ? The Trial Narrative in the Gospel of Mark*, to be published in the *SBL Dissertation Series*.

58. The use of *ēn* or *ēsan* in conjunction with a participle as an auxiliary is Markan, see Turner, "Marcan Usage," *JTS*. 28 (1926-27), p. 349; the insertion technique is Markan; the introduction of the scribes is Markan (1:22; 3:22).

59. Norman Perrin, "The Creative Use of the Son of Man Traditions by Mark," *USQR*, 23 (1968), pp. 357-65. This essay is included in Perrin, *A Modern Pilgrimage in New Testament Christology* (Philadelphia: Fortress Press, 1974).

60. Keck, "Christology," pp. 354, 357; Paul J. Achtemeier, "The Origin and Function of the Pre-Marcan Miracle Catenae," *JBL*, 91 (1972), pp. 218-21.

61. Bultmann, *Tradition*, p. 18; Martin Dibelius, *From Tradition to Gospel*, trans. B. L. Woolf (New York: Scribner, 1935), p. 64, n. 1.

62. Kuhn, *Sammlungen*, pp. 89-95, has strenuously advocated the synonymity of sinners and Gentiles in the tradition. In the redaction the Gentile theme will surface in 4:35-8:21, see Chap. III; it is not yet apparent in 2:15-17.

community of the Kingdom is in tension with a more traditional, exclusivist notion of community.

Complex religious developments have left their mark upon the fasting controversy (2:18–22).[63] The traditional theme underwent a metamorphosis to the point of a complete reversal of the original intention. For while the core of the tradition espoused the non-observance of fasting (2:18–19a), the latter adaptation assumes a situation in which fasting has become a fact of life (2:19b–20). An additional sayings collection concerning new patches and old garments, and new wine and old wineskins introduces the by now well-known element of tension and opposition. No compromise is allowed between the new arrangement and an older order of things.[64] Whether or not the qualifying "on that day" (2:20b) and the radical sayings collection are Markan additions,[65] it is in this latest version that the issue of fasting makes contact with the Markan situation. Complete freedom from fasting has lost its appeal for Mark, for Good Friday has been appointed as the day of weekly fasting.[66] The death of Jesus, not the day of his resurrection (!), provides the stimulus for a reordering of time. By implication, the present is experienced as a time of dominical absence. With Jesus' death the disciples are in a state of sorrowful waiting, and fasting on the day of crucifixion is the proper attitude to take between the times.[67] More directly, Jesus endorses the weekday of his death as a day of fasting, and in the process dissociates the Markan people from an older order of fasting.

Two Sabbath conflicts (2:23–28; 3:1–6) conclude the Markan controversy sequence. In the first case, a pre-Markan unit may well have reached its natural ending with the two questions posed in 2:25, 26, because at 2:27 Mark employs the redactional citation formula *kai elegen*

---

63. T. A. Burkill, *New Light on the Oldest Gospel* (Ithaca, N.Y.: Cornell University Press, 1972), pp. 39–47.

64. The fasting is not meant to be a concession to Jewish piety, but rather an irreconcilable break with the Jewish days of fasting, see Ernst Haenchen, *Der Weg Jesu*, 2nd ed. rev. (Berlin: Walter de Gruyter & Co., 1968), p. 118.

65. That "on that day" (2:20b) is a Markan addition has been claimed by Lohmeyer, *Markus*, pp. 60–61, and Walter Grundmann, *Das Evangelium nach Markus* (Berlin: Evangelische Verlagsanstalt, 1965), p. 66.

66. For an extensive argument in favor of Good Friday as the day of fasting, see Kuhn, *Sammlungen*, pp. 61–72.

67. Both the experience of Jesus' absence and that of the present as an interim period are recognized Markan features. On absence, see Theodore J. Weeden, *Mark —Traditions in Conflict* (Philadelphia: Fortress Press, 1971), pp. 101–17; Neill Q. Hamilton, "Resurrection Tradition and the Composition of Mark," *JBL*, 84 (1965), pp. 415–21. On the present interim, see Ambrozic, *Kingdom*, pp. 197–202.

autois[68] to offer his own comment on the tradition.[69] The traditional story settles the specific issue of plucking corn on Sabbath by reference to Scripture, without however passing a resolution on the Sabbath question per se. While the opponents have their legal basis undermined, the suspension of the holy day has as yet not been declared the rule of the day. The Markan redaction undertakes a formal ruling on the Sabbath question. There exists a new order of values and the Sabbath has to take second place. The day is not categorically invalidated, but as a matter of principle subordinated to man and his needs. 2:28 enunciates the christological point, the Son of Man's lordship over the Sabbath. Thus the Sabbath is set free, and the Christian freedom from Sabbatical claims is traced to the Son of Man's fundamental authority.

As in the first controversy (2:1–12) so are also in the last one (3:1–6) conflict and miracle combined in creative interaction, whereby the miracle serves as a vehicle for the conflict. Inserted into the miracle tradition is the conflict scene, with repetitious redactional comments indicating the transitional points (3:3a: *kai legei tō anthrōpō*; 3:5c: *legei tō anthrōpō*). It is also in the conflict material that redactional features are most conspicuous. *Periblepsesthai* (3:5a), to look around, is a uniquely Markan verb which has judgmental overtones when used in reference to the person of Jesus.[70] *Pōrōsis tēs kardias* (3:5b), hardness of heart, carries very special weight in Markan theology.[71] By virtual consensus, the climactic 3:6 is considered redactional.[72] The healing miracle lays bare the very depth of the conflict. The authority of the Son of Man exposes the opponents' hardness of heart, as well as their inauspicious deliberations. In the end, the whole conflict turns out to be one between the desire to save life and the plan to take life. It is a life-and-death struggle and Jesus is to become the victim.

There emerges from these controversies the basic features of the

---

68. Joachim Jeremias, *The Parables of Jesus*, trans. S. H. Hooke, 6th ed. (New York: Charles Scribner's Sons, 1963), p. 14.
69. Taylor, *St. Mark*, p. 218; Alfred Suhl, *Die Funktion der alttestamentlichen Zitate und Anspielungen im Markusevangelium* (Gütersloh: Gerd Mohn, 1965), p. 82. This is not to say that Mark is the sole creator of 2:27–28; but he purposefully inserted the saying here.
70. Six out of seven occurrences in the New Testament appear in Mark; Luke 6:10 is dependent on Mark.
71. Joachim Gnilka, *Die Verstockung Israels*, Studien zum Alten und Neuen Testament, No. 3 (Munich: Kösel, 1961), p. 32.
72. Taylor, *St. Mark*, p. 220; Eduard Schweizer, *The Good News According to Mark*, trans. Donald H. Madvig (Richmond, Va.: John Knox Press, 1970), p. 74; Bultmann, *Tradition*, p. 63.

Markan community. Humans exercise the supreme authority to forgive sins; a highly positive attitude is assumed toward Gentiles; Friday, the day of the crucifixion, is commemorated by fasting, while the Sabbath has become unhinged. In effect, what is advocated is a new communal identity of inclusiveness, a new order of priorities, and the beginnings of a calendrical reconsideration of time. All this is done in the name of the Son of Man and in full consciousness of the eschatological novelty of the undertaking. But it is also done in direct opposition to another order of life which appears to be stamped with a Jewish hallmark. In this other camp forgiveness of sins is considered the prerogative of God, sinners live in violation of the communal holiness, and the weekly fast days and Sabbath are observed in the spirit of Jewish piety.

The conclusion seems inescapable that we are confronted with a struggle between "church" and "synagogue." But to this we must object. The major flaw in this thesis is that the Markan argument is not set up in such a way that it could meet the Jewish position in any meaningful manner. Above all, it is the christological logic which must remain foreign to Jewish readers. That the Son of Man has power to forgive sins and authority to abrogate the Sabbath is at best puzzling, at worst nonsensical to someone uninitiated in the Christian identification and experience of this Son of Man. It is as though Mark presupposes christological knowledge. Since the controversy section is controlled by the Son of Man title, it would have to be a Son of Man christology. Instead of a Jewish-Christian struggle we might therefore better assume an internal Christian situation[73] in which Mark uses Son of Man to establish rapport with his opponents because it was under this title that Jesus was known to them.

It is true, Mark has cast the opposition in the role of the Jewish establishment figures. But he is not primarily motivated by historical interests. The past must speak to the present. Mark's opponents see their own argumentation and piety mirrored in that of the scribes and Pharisees. Their attitude toward Jesus resembles that of the scribes and Pharisees, as indeed these Jewish Christians are in large measure indistinguishable from their fellow Jews. But theirs is also the spirit which put Jesus to death.

---

73. This is also argued by Kuhn, *Sammlungen*, pp. 84–98, on behalf of the pre-Markan tradition. But as so often, what Kuhn claims for the tradition, we would claim for the redaction.

CONCLUSION

Mark creates a new beginning by announcing the arrival and present reality of the Kingdom in Galilee. This forms the premise for his gospel. Irrespective of what happened in and to Jerusalem, it is in Galilee where the mission of Jesus is continued. There the Kingdom of God is pitted against the Kingdom of Satan in a struggle which will decide the fate of history. History did therefore not come to an end, but it has on the contrary reached its critical stage with the arrival and apocalyptic engagement of the Kingdom in Galilee.

The beginning of the Kingdom spells the ending of an older order of things. Specifically, the Kingdom generates a radical alternative to a Jewish Christian way of life. New life in the Kingdom is gained only at the price of repentance, change, and a breaking loose from the traditional order. As the example of Jesus shows, the rejection of the tradition and the adoption of the new freedom of the Kingdom may be so provocative an undertaking as to bring on death.

The Kingdom comprises neither a state of perfection nor a time without tension. Born out of conflict, it releases struggle and provokes opposition. It is by virtue of its eschatological novelty that it exists in dialectical relationship with the demonic Kingdom and in antithesis to an older ordering of life. If rightly understood, therefore, rupture, conflict and suffering do not result from the end of the city of life, but from the beginning of the Kingdom in history. But because the Kingdom has arrived in a state of conflict, it is still a matter of belief.

Chapter II

THE MYSTERY
OF THE KINGDOM

4:1-34

The Markan Jesus delivers two major speeches, evenly divided into the northern and southern spheres, the Galilean and Jerusalem sections of the ministry, yet both appealing to the root experience of the Markan Christians' eschatology. At the Lake of Galilee the topic is the mystery of the Kingdom (4:1–34), and on the Mount of Olives it is the parousia of the Son of Man that receives special treatment (13:5–37). The Jerusalem speech has been provided with a redactionally construed introduction (13:1–4), which functions as a kind of rostrum for the speech proper.[1] At first glance redactional efforts do not seem to have gone to similar lengths in setting the stage for the Galilean speech. And yet, in 3:20–35, the section immediately preceding the speech, the familiar theme of opposition is resumed, carried to a new peak, and then redactionally tied to the layout of the speech. This dramatic interaction between the solidification of the opposition (3:20–35) and the external arrangement of the Kingdom speech deserves our first attention.[2]

In 3:20–35 two types of opposition forces arrive on the scene, the relatives of Jesus and the Jerusalem scribes. The family declares Jesus mentally deranged, while the delegation sent from Jerusalem suspects him of being possessed by Satan himself. Jesus responds to the Jerusalem charges by speaking for the first time "in parables" (3:23a: *en parabolais*). From now on, speaking "in parables" becomes Jesus' habitual mode of speech

1. See Chap. VI.
2. J. Coutts, "Those Outside (Mark 4, 10–12)," *SE*, 2 (1963), pp. 155–57.

reserved for the opposition. While Jesus stays inside a house with a crowd sitting "about him" (3:32a: *peri auton*), his own mother, brothers, and sisters are said to be "standing outside" (3:31b: *exō stēkontes*), asking for him "outside" (3:32c: *exō*). In a surprise move, Jesus rejects his own blood relatives and instead identifies "those about him" (3:34a: *tous peri auton*) as those truly related to Jesus. Thus immediately preceeding the speech, a distinction is drawn between insiders and outsiders. Subsequently, this carefully drafted division is sustained and brought to bear upon the speech setting. At the outset the parable of the sower is addressed to a "very large crowd" (4:1b), and this public address is qualified as a teaching "in parables" (4:2a: *en parabolais*). Afterward, Jesus enters into secret session together with "those about him with the Twelve" (4:10b: *oi peri auton syn tois dōdeka*) and initiates them into the hidden meaning of the parable. In the formulation "those about him" we recognize Mark's previous designation of the true community of believers (3:32a, 34a). And again, these insiders are marked off against "those outside" (4:11c: *ekeinois de tois exō*) to whom everything occurs "in parables" (4:11c: *en parabolais*). The purpose of this rigid division of people is obvious. Only the insiders, the disciples and those about Jesus, are granted full access to his message. Henceforth, they are privileged with full comprehension and they ought to be able to follow Jesus. The outsiders, on the other hand, will lack any deeper understanding of Jesus' message and mission because they will have been excluded from his esoteric instruction.

This solidification of both the opposition and the *familia dei* causes an unforeseen division, because the dividing line does not naturally fall between friend and enemy, but consigns those who would above all others be expected to be on the inside, the family of Jesus, to the outside. It was Mark himself who with the aid of his interpolation technique conjoined relatives and scribes into this unlikely fraternity of shared hostility. He intercalated the debate with the scribes (3:22–30) into the episode concerning Jesus' relatives (3:20–21, 31–35). As a result, the house mentioned at the outset (3:20a) furnishes the crucial locale for the total scene, setting apart insiders from outsiders, while scribes and relatives are fused together into one solid block of opposition. The two groups have become united in a common cause against Jesus and his disciples. Since the scribal opposition is for the first time brought into relation with Jerusalem (3:22a), one may wonder whether Jerusalem could not provide a clue to Mark's curious interest in affiliating the relatives with the scribes. At this point we cannot but recognize that this strange break precedes the mystery speech. It is not until the disciples have been dissociated from the relatives and scribes that they are being entrusted with the secret message.[3]

TRADITION AND REDACTION

The first two verses of Chapter 4 are fully explicable as a redactional construct. Both the *kai* parataxis[4] and the frequent use of *palin*[5] are noted Markan features. The link-phrase *kai palin* occurs twenty times in Mark, four times in Matthew, and only once in Luke. The use of *archesthai* (*ērxato—ērxanto*) in conjunction with a present infinitive is characteristic of all Synoptics, but the construction clearly predominates in Mark.[6] Both *didaskein* and *didachē* belong to the very core of the redactional vocabulary.[7] Markan appreciation for the Galilean lakeside scenery has been well observed by W. Marxsen.[8] In 4:1–2 *thalassa* occurs no less than three times. Jesus commences his teaching *para tēn thalassan*; as the people press upon him he enters the boat and takes his seat *en tē thalassē*;[9] the audience stays behind on land *pros tēn thalassan*. *Thalassa* in reference to the Lake of Galilee occurs seventeen times in Mark and only fourteen times in Matthew; Luke mentions the northern lake five times, but chooses to call it *limnē*. The specific phrasing *para tēn thalassan* turns up three more times in redactional verses (1:16; 2:13; 5:21). The term *ochlos* is part of the synoptic vocabulary, but Mark employs it thirty-seven times, Matthew forty-eight times, and Luke thirty-nine times. "Allowing for the relative lengths of the three Gospels, the preponderance is clearly with Mark."[10] The wording *pas ho ochlos* is found in three more redactional verses (2:13; 9:15; 11:18). *Ochlos pleistos* is a unique formu-

---

3. Perhaps S. G. F. Brandon, *Jesus and the Zealots* (New York: Charles Scribner's Sons, 1967), p. 275, hits upon a nerve when he states: "So categorical a repudiation of the blood relationship and its replacing by discipleship-relationship is truly amazing, when it is recalled what the prestige of the blood-relationship to Jesus meant in the Jerusalem Church."

4. John C. Hawkins, *Horae Synopticae* (Oxford: Clarendon, 1909), pp. 150–52.

5. Cuthbert H. Turner, "Marcan Usage: Notes, Critical and Exegetical, on the Second Gospel," *JTS*, 29 (1927–28), pp. 283–87.

6. Turner, "Marcan Usage," *JTS*, 28 (1926–27), pp. 352–53.

7. Eduard Schweizer, "Anmerkungen zur Theologie des Markus," *Neotestamentica* (Zurich: Zwingli Verlag, 1963), pp. 95–97.

8. Willi Marxsen, *Mark the Evangelist*, trans. Roy A. Harrisville *et al.* (Nashville, Tenn.: Abingdon Press, 1969), pp. 57–75.

9. Mark emphasizes not the sitting in the boat, but the sitting in the sea! This is reminiscent of a motif from royal ideology according to which the king is enthroned at the center of the primeval flood (Ps. 29:10; Ezek. 28:2).

10. Turner, "Marcan Usage," *JTS*, 29 (1927–28), p. 237.

lation in Mark, but it appears to be deliberately coined so as to strike a contrast between the largeness of the initial crowd and the intimate circle of true believers thereafter. The fact that Jesus delivers his major speeches in a sitting position (4:1c; 13:3a) may be a conscious attempt to correlate the two events. More recently redactional fondness for the expression *epi tēs gēs* has been noted.[11] Both the Markan citation formula *kai elegen autois* and the redactional *en parabolais* were already identified above. In sum, linguistic analysis reveals Mark as the author of the two introductory verses 4:1-2.

The parable of the sower (4:3-9) appears to be virtually untouched by the redaction; a few, though crucial, Markan characteristics will be discovered in the interpretation (4:14-20). It is, however, noteworthy that parable and interpretation are somewhat set apart by a Jesus saying (4:11-12) which appears to be out of touch with the parable theology. That this foreign element has intruded between parable and interpretation is confirmed by the fact that the intervening logion has been provided with the Markan citation formula. Verses 4:11-12 are thus marked as a redactional insert. The same citation formula is two more times employed in Chapter 4 (4:21, 24), and in each case it serves to present a set of formerly isolated sayings (4:21-23, 24-25). These cursory observations allow of a first appraisal of tradition and redaction in Chapter 4. Already in the tradition prior to Mark, parables were supplied with allegorical explanations.[12] If the parable of the sower was at an early stage connected with an interpretation, the natural linkage between the two units would seem to be a question concerning the meaning of the parable. D. Daube[13] has called attention to an established rabbinical parable pattern, dating back to the first century, which is composed of three parts: first, a pronouncement by the master directed to the general public, second, departure of the outsiders and question by the insiders, and third, a deeper explanation of the initial announcement. We assume the existence of a pre-Markan parable tradition which was made up of three constituent parts: parable, question, and interpretation of the parable. Mark carefully designed the lakeside setting and placed this parable

11. Aloysius M. Ambrozic, *The Hidden Kingdom*, The Catholic Biblical Quarterly—Monograph Series, No. 2 (Washington, D.C.: The Catholic Biblical Association of America, 1972), p. 124.

12. Joachim Jeremias, *The Parables of Jesus*, trans. S. H. Hooke, 6th ed. (New York: Charles Scribner's Sons, 1963), p. 79.

13. David Daube, "Public Pronouncement and Private Explanation in the Gospels," *ExpT*, 57 (1946), pp. 175-77.

tradition into the frame of a speech of Jesus (4:1–2, 33–34). For as yet unexplained reasons he disconnected the parable from its interpretation by the inclusion of a lengthy Jesus logion (4:11–12). To alleviate existing tension between the parable tradition and the intruding word of Jesus, this latter insertion was at both ends smoothed out by additional redactional cushions (4:10, 13). Furthermore, Mark expanded the speech complex by two additional sayings units (4:21–23, 24–25).

Regarding the parables of the seed growing secretly (4:26–29) and the mustard seed (4:30–32), H.-W. Kuhn[14] claimed that these two were united with the parable of the sower and its interpretation in a pre-Markan parable collection. The three parables are internally connected by the key words "sower," "seed," and "sowing," all three speak into a present situation of failure and eschatological void, and all bear the label of the pre-Markan citation formula *kai elegen*. But Kuhn's efforts to prove a thematic coherence between the three parables appear forced. Two parables are clearly marked as Kingdom parables, while the parable of the sower is unrelated to the Kingdom theme. Not until the Markan redaction makes its influence felt, are all three parables brought under the control of the leading Kingdom motif.

Why would in the state of the tradition a non-Kingdom parable be joined together with a set of Kingdom parables, if their common purpose was not to convey the message of the Kingdom, but to create confidence in a situation of rampant hopelessness? Why demand the service of Kingdom parables, if they cannot function in a Kingdom capacity? Of course, it is quite possible that neither the parable of the seed growing secretly nor the parable of the mustard seed were originally conceived as Kingdom parables at all. Considerable clumsiness in the formulation of the introductory formulae to the two parables (4:26, 30) indicates that introduction and parable did not always belong together; disconnected from their Kingdom identifications the two parables do not intrinsically pertain to the Kingdom. But what was their concern prior to the Markan redaction? Despite Kuhn's efforts, Bultmann's judgment on this matter remains valid: "The original meaning of many similitudes has become irrecoverable."[15]

On the other hand, if one looks at the problem from a redaction-critical

---

14. Heinz-Wolfgang Kuhn, *Ältere Sammlungen im Markusevangelium*, Studien zur Umwelt des Neuen Testaments, No. 8 (Göttingen: Vandenhoeck & Ruprecht, 1971), pp. 99–146.
15. Rudolf Bultmann, *History of the Synoptic Tradition*, trans. John Marsh, 3rd ed. (New York: Harper & Row, 1963), p. 199.

angle, one is immediately struck by the fact that two Kingdom parables
found their way into a speech unit which under the influence of the
redaction has become preoccupied with the Kingdom theme. Did Mark,
then, compose the introductory verses 4:26, 30? We cannot know for sure.
The citation formula *kai elegen*, in any case, is not so easily dismissed as
un-Markan. M. Zerwick[16] has demonstrated its possible Markan usage in
4:9, 26, 30, as well as in 12:35, 38. It is quite plausible that Mark adopted
the two parables and arranged their present position in the speech, because they fitted ideally his Kingdom theology. We will thus have to
assume an overall substantial redactional involvement in 4:1–34. The core
of the tradition (4:3–9, 14–20) was wedged apart by a redactional insertion (4:11–12), enlarged by redactional accretions (4:21–23, 24–25, 26–
29, 30–32), and its uneven edges smoothed by redactional transitions
(4:10, 13); the whole complex was placed into the format of a redactionally designed speech (4:1–2, 33–34).

The original parable tradition had a straightforwardly illustrative,
elucidative function, and the idea of hardening of heart or concealment
lay beyond its horizon. Neither the parable nor its interpretation confronted the audience in the form of a punitive riddle whose chief purpose
it is to remain unintelligible, and to blind and condemn the outsiders.
Nor was the parable tradition in any sense dominated by the Kingdom
theme.[17] But it is, on the other hand, important to note that the tradition
was already in need of an explication. Mark, we will see, radicalized this
element of special interpretation into a wholly new idea.

We commence our evaluation of the Markan redaction with 4:10. The
change of scenery indicated by the un-Markan *kata monas* and the question concerning the parabolic message may yet be the residual parts of
the tradition. But two redactional alterations indicate Mark's manner of
bending the conventional pattern toward a new viewpoint. First, there
are "those about him with the twelve" who direct the question to Jesus.
The phrase is wholly Markan. *Hoi dōdeka* receives preferential treatment
by the redaction (3:14, 16; 6:7; 9:35; 10:32; 11:11), *hoi peri auton* resumes the former designation of the true relatives of Jesus (3:32a, 34a),
and the conjunction of the two groups with the preposition *syn* is equally
Markan, as a comparison with the redactional 8:34a shows. It is possible

16. Maximilian Zerwick, *Untersuchungen zum Markus-Stil: Ein Beitrag zur stilistischen Durcharbeitung des Neuen Testaments* (Rome: Pontifical Biblical Institute,
1937), p. 38.
17. Also admitted by Kuhn, *Sammlungen*, p. 126, n. 15.

that, according to the tradition, only the disciples were privileged to be the recipients of the secret message.[18] Mark, however, expands the traditional circle of the twelve by including the formerly chosen group of true believers.[19] The twelve and "those about him" now form an esoteric alliance, the exclusive insiders to whom Jesus will entrust what to the outsiders remains obscure.

A second alteration concerns the plural *tas parabolas*. Although only one parable was narrated, the ensuing question takes an interest in "the parables." Mark, it stands to reason, has to speak of parables after he had expanded the tradition to the point at which more than one parable is presented. Apart from the parable of the seed growing secretly and the parable of the mustard seed, the two sayings units 4:21–23 and 4:24–25 deserve attention with respect to their possible parabolic quality. Is Mark likely to view these two collections of sayings as autonomous parables, and not merely as agglomerations of scattered logia? This theory has been advanced by J. Jeremias,[20] and it can be supported on structural grounds. The parable of the sower begins and ends with an injunction to "hearing" (4:3a: *akouete*; 4:9b: *akouetō*). Once again we encounter Mark's technique of encapsulating a crucial message with identical terms.[21] The final *akouetō*, moreover, is part of an apocalyptic code word which has been attached to the parable by what was tentatively identified as a Markan citation formula (*kai elegen*). This same code word was used to mark the formal conclusion of the first sayings unit (4:23), while the second sayings unit was provided with a formal introduction (4:24b: *blepete ti akouete*) which is not unlike that of the parable of the sower (4:3a: *akouete*). The same formal characteristics which distinguished the presentation of the parable of the sower are being employed to structure the two sayings units. Hence, Mark's speaking of parables in 4:10 has to be taken literally. What follows the interpolation 4:11–12 is a secret speech of Jesus which consists of altogether five parables (4:13–20, 21–23, 24–25, 26–29, 30–32).

18. Willi Marxsen, "Redaktionsgeschichtliche Erklärung der sogenannten Parabeltheorie des Markus," *ZThK*, 52 (1955), pp. 258–60.

19. Thus already Johannes Weiss, *Das Älteste Evangelium* (Göttingen: Vandenhoeck & Ruprecht, 1903), p. 61: "Mir scheint zweifellos, dass der Bearbeiter das Bestreben gehabt hat, den Kreis der Zwölfe zu erweitern, z.B. 4:10." For a different view, see Robert P. Meye, "Mark 4, 10: 'Those about Him with the Twelve,'" *SE*, 2 (1963), pp. 211–18; also *Jesus and the Twelve* (Grand Rapids, Mich.: Eerdmans, 1968), pp. 152–56, *passim*. The author translates "those of the twelve," and argues for a narrow circle of disciples within the wider circle of the twelve.

20. Jeremias, *Parables*, p. 14, n. 11; see also Jan Lambrecht, "Die fünf Parabeln in Mk 4," *Bijdr*, 29 (1968), pp. 25–53.

21. See Mark's gospel-frame in 1:14–15.

The first word addressed to the exclusive circle of insiders reveals that they are being entrusted with the mystery of the Kingdom of God. Following closely the Markan word order, we translate: "To you the mystery has been given which concerns the Kingdom of God" (4:11b). Redactionally inserted between the parable of the sower and its interpretation, this Kingdom saying now functions as the leading motif of the subsequent parable speech, governing the interpretation of each of the five parables.[22] Undoubtedly, the mystery has as its object the Kingdom, but the precise nature of this mystery remains as yet undisclosed. The singular *mystērion* is not likely to signal a variety of revelations, but rather one particular insight into the nature of the Kingdom. It is this disclosure of the nature of the Kingdom which will be granted in the secret parable speech.

The *mystērion* which is to become the privileged possession of the insiders is contrasted with the experience *en parabolais* on the part of the outsiders. There is general agreement that a literal rendering of *en parabolais* with "in parables" fails to give an adequate impression of the Markan Jesus' relation toward outsiders. Both the Greek *parabolē* and its Hebrew equivalent *māšāl* embrace a wide range of meaning, including such figures of speech as proverb, folk saying, taunt, wisdom saying, similitude, and riddle. Given the nature of Mark's polemical context—the division of audience into insiders and outsiders, and communication to the outsiders *en parabolais*—we follow the majority opinion in adopting "in riddles" as the appropriate rendering of the *en parabolais*.[23] The redactional "in riddles" therefore characterizes the effect Jesus has or creates toward the outside world. That this understanding transcends any specific concern for parables is confirmed by 4:11c. No matter whether we translate with Ambrozic[24] that "everything comes in parables," or with Gnilka[25] that "everything turns into riddles," or with Jeremias[26] that "all things are imparted in riddles," the crucial point is that Jesus is not said to *speak in parables* to outsiders, rather that everything is or *occurs in riddles* to the outsiders (*ta panta ginetai*). This is neither a statement on Jesus' specific use of parables, nor even on the purpose of his teaching in general, but

---

22. Karl-Georg Reploh, *Markus—Lehrer der Gemeinde*, Stuttgarter Biblische Monographien, No. 9 (Stuttgart: Katholisches Bibelwerk, 1969), pp. 63–71.
23. Matthew (13:35) derives scriptural justification for *en parabolais* from Ps. 78:2; in this psalm verse the *māšāl* is synonymous with *ḥîdāh*, riddle, dark saying.
24. Ambrozic, *Kingdom*, p. 79.
25. Joachim Gnilka, *Die Verstockung Israels*, Studien zum Alten und Neuen Testament, No. 3 (Munich: Kösel, 1961), p. 27.
26. Jeremias, *Parables*, p. 16.

on the nature of his ministry as a whole. The whole ministry is *en parabolais*, i.e., an enigma to outside recognition. This points beyond a specific theory on parables! Certainly, the Markan Jesus does not, as is so often claimed,[27] make it a matter of policy to use parables as instruments of punishment. Indeed, the parable of the sower (4:3–9) which is taught to outsiders is not even introduced as a "parable," but quite appropriately as a teaching "in riddles" (4:2a). To the outsiders Jesus relates in parabolic, riddling fashion, but the insiders will be given a chance to learn that he was actually lecturing on the present state of the Kingdom. Rather than punish, the parables will help to reveal what to the outside forms an inaccessible riddle, and to the inside takes on the appearance of a mystery. Basically, what the Galilean speech advances is a further elaboration of the Kingdom theme, but not a thesis on parables. Of central concern is the nature and mission of the Kingdom, and how it effects a division between insiders and outsiders, and a corollary distinction between mystery and riddle.

This point of view is essentially restated in 4:33–34, a Markan summation of the speech complex. Earlier we assigned the two verses to the redaction.[28] *Lalein ton logon* (4:33a, 34a) is in the synoptic tradition limited to Mark (2:2c; 8:32a). *Logos* is aptly rendered with "message," for it entails Jesus' fundamental program and is but a different term for the "gospel" of the Kingdom.[29] The term is therefore ideally suited for the purpose of summarizing Jesus' first speech. The crucial clause 4:33b will also be assigned to the redaction. Mark's extended use of *dynamai*, and its frequent application in a weakened sense, corresponding to our "can," "could," "may," or "might," has been demonstrated by C. H. Turner.[30] Jesus transmits his *logos* "as they could hear," or "in proportion to their capacity."[31] 4:33b, we conclude, features the Markan motif of the riddling nature of Jesus' message. There is finally the phrase *kat 'idian*, evidently of redactional making (6:31 32; 7:33; 9:2, 28; 13:3), which in 4:34b serves to point up the aspect of inside revelation. Of course, the three

27. Dennis E. Nineham, *The Gospel of St. Mark* (Baltimore, Md.: Penguin Books, Inc., 1963), p. 136; T. A. Burkill, *Mysterious Revelation* (Ithaca, N.Y.: Cornell University Press, 1963), p. 100; Vincent Taylor, *The Gospel According to St. Mark* (London: Macmillan and Co., 1963), p. 257; Ambrozic, *Kingdom*, p. 79.
28. Eduard Schweizer, *The Good News According to Mark*, trans. D. H. Madvig (Richmond, Va.: John Knox Press, 1970), pp. 105–07.
29. Burkill, *Revelation*, p. 172; Taylor, *St. Mark*, p. 271; Ulrich Luz, "Das Geheimnismotiv und die Markinische Christologie," *ZNW*, 56 (1965), p. 16.
30. Turner, "Marcan Usage," *JTS*, 28 (1926–27), pp. 354–55.
31. *Ibid.*

hapax legomena in 4:34 provide formidable ammunition against Markan authorship. But the *tois idiois mathētais* is explicable as a direct outgrowth of the preceding *kat 'idian*, stressing the notion of private instruction. *Epilyein* is a technical term called for in a summarizing statement on esoteric teaching. *Chōris* springs from Mark's desire to emphasize the exclusively parabolic nature of Jesus' message.[32] All three terms issue Markan motifs and they combine to recapitulate the anomalous effects Jesus' ministry is having upon people. There is not a single feature in 4:33–34 which could come into collision with the theological scheme of the speech. 4:1–2, the introduction, 4:11–12, the redactional insert, and 4:33–34, the summation, are linked up by a web of redactional interaction, providing the structural underpinning for the total speech. The two references to *autois* in 4:33a and 4:34a resume the *autois* of 4:2a, indicating the crowd of outsiders. The *toiautais parabolais pollais* in 4:33a, Jesus' stance toward the outside world, will have to be read in the established sense of *en parabolais* in 4:2a. Obviously, Jesus' communication will not from now on be limited to parables.[33] The *toiautais parabolais* in 4:33a is a generalized plural, referring to the parabolic impact Jesus' *logos* will have upon the outside world. The *chōris parabolēs* in 4:34a will likewise point to the *logos'* being darkened by a film of incomprehensibility, and not to a career given to teaching in parables. The injunction to "hearing" addressed to the outside crowd in 4:3a and 4:9b is echoed in 4:33b, displaying the outsiders' limited hearing capacity. Finally, the universalizing *panta* in 4:34b reiterates the *ta panta* of 4:11c. In substance, Jesus' message is communicated in parabolic form (4:33a), which provokes inadequate outside response (4:33b); Jesus takes the parabolic position as a matter of principle (4:34a), and provides only the insiders with the key to unlock the whole (4:34b).

4:11–12 has long been used as a *locus classicus* for the Christian concept according to which Jesus through the agency of unintelligible parables condemns Israel to a state of hardness of heart. "The passage accounts for the unbelief of the Jews," states B. Lindars[34] with a degree of overconfidence. We have already argued that 4:11c must be considered apart from any specific question of parables. Jesus' whole life is a "para-

---

32. Minette de Tillesse, *Le Secret Messianique dans L'Évangile de Marc* (Paris: Cerf, 1968), pp. 181–85.

33. This is an important logical consideration, well stated by Theodore J. Weeden, *Mark—Traditions in Conflict* (Philadelphia: Fortress Press, 1971), p. 143.

34. Barnabas Lindars, *New Testament Apologetic* (Philadelphia: Westminster Press, 1961), p. 159; Gnilka, *Verstockung*, p. 49.

ble," but it is with the aid of parables that, to some, access is granted to the mystery of his Kingdom. More importantly, the judgmental concept founders on two grounds. First, Mark does not at this point advocate a hardening of heart, and second, Israel does not match the identity of the outsiders.

As regards the hardening of heart theory, it is significant to note that Isaiah 6:9–10 has in its Markan version (4:12) undergone two important alterations. Against the Massora, Septuagint, Targum, Matthew 13:14, and Acts 28:26, the Markan text reverses the order of hearing followed by seeing. Mark's emphasis is on seeing. Against the Massora, Septuagint, Targum, Matthew 13:14–15 and Acts 28:26–27, the Markan text does not contain the reference to the fattening of the heart, the very basis for the hardening theory.[35] Accordingly, a word of caution is in order against prematurely reading a theory of the hardening of heart into Mark. Undoubtedly, this is the view into which Mark was developed by Matthew. The latter replaced the final *hina* by a causal *hoti*. As a result, Jesus speaks in parables *because* the people lack insight; and there exists deficient insight because "this people's heart has grown dull" (Matt. 13:15: *epachynthē gar he kardia tou laou toutou*). Hence, the Matthaean Jesus addresses the people with incomprehensible parables as unrelenting punishment for their failure to respond with an open heart to him, and the people fail to acknowledge him, because their natural condition precludes any revelatory perception. By contrast, Mark strikes out the hardening text, stresses the riddling nature of Jesus' whole ministry, and emphasizes the blindness of the outsiders. Rather than a hardening of heart, a theory of concealment might be closer to the Markan point. There is no desire to lock the people into a vicious circle of crime and punishment, but definitely the intent to insulate Jesus' mission against outside recognition. The correlatives of blindness and seeing, lack of hearing and full comprehension, an opaque life "in parables" and enlightenment in private session move us into the theological orbit of hiddenness and revelation, which is at the core of the Messianic Secret.

As regards the punishment of Israel, Matthew puts "this people" in the place of Mark's outsiders (Matt. 13:15), and upgrades the blessed disciples (Matt. 13:16). Now it is a confrontation between the disciples and the Jews, or the "church" versus the "synagogue." Mark, we noticed before, is uninformed by a Christian-Jewish clash, but seems to be respond-

35. Thomas W. Manson, *The Teaching of Jesus* (Cambridge: Cambridge University Press, 1931), p. 78.

ing to a Christian conflict *intra muros*. We further recall the strange division which had occurred prior to the Galilean speech. The scribal authorities together with the family of Jesus had come to encounter ostracism, while the twelve and "those about him" had been elevated to the rank of insiders. Only after the disciples and "those about him" were extricated from official Jewish influence and isolated from the authority of the family of Jesus, had they been given the inside information. But, it is proper to ask in the spirit of Mark, will these insiders take the secret information to heart? Will they let themselves be touched by the mystery of the Kingdom? As early as 4:13, even before the parable speech proper, Jesus seems to have doubts about the insiders' mental capacity, and in 8:18 the disciples will be charged with the same imperception which had formerly been the inalienable characteristic of the outside audience. At that point, we shall see, the insiders will have joined company with the outsiders. Was the Galilean mystery speech, then, to no effect at all?

We have anticipated strains and stresses which in the early Galilean period are virtually dormant, and we must now return to the redaction and summarize its consequences in 4:1–34. Mark appended a code word to the parable of the sower, partly to round it off, but in the main to alert the readers to its undecoded state of nature. A carefully staged break between an inside and an outside audience, redactional alterations in 4:10, and the insertion of the mystery motif in 4:11b serve to exaggerate the traditional motif of parabolic explanation into a situation of esoteric initiation versus outside unperceptiveness. The secret parable speech is the exclusive property of the insiders; the outsiders are left with the unexplained riddle of the parable of the sower. The Kingdom saying 4:11b is the most unusual feature in all of 4:1–34, and its interpolation imposes a wholly new idea upon the parable tradition, for neither was this Kingdom logion formerly associated with parables, nor had the pre-Markan parable source stood under the control of a Kingdom theme. In its present position, 4:11b exerts its Kingdom influence upon the five subsequent parables. Mark selected and shaped the material of the secret parable speech so as to make it serviceable to the leading Kingdom motif. One way or another each parable makes the same point.[36] Each of the five parables functions as the bearer of the mystery of the Kingdom which in Mark's judgment is at the heart of the parable of the sower. Vice versa, the meaning of the parable of the sower which had remained unperceived by the outsiders is through the vehicle of the five Kingdom parables revealed to the disciples and "those about him."

36. Reploh, *Lehrer*, p. 73.

HIDDENNESS AND REVELATION

The allegorical interpretation 4:14–20 is under the commanding influence of the Kingdom saying 4:11b transformed into a parable, whose own interpretation does not lie in an explanation of details, but in a single insight into the mystery of the Kingdom. Neither the person of the sower, nor the nature of the soil holds the center of interest. The main protagonist is *ho logos*, and its fate in the world makes up the plot of the parable. In just seven verses *ho logos* is reiterated eight times; four times in conjunction with *akouein*. The logos, we are informed, both suffers a multiple loss and gains a massive victory. A three-fold failure is set over against a three-fold success,[37] but it is the period of crisis to which special importance is attached. We detect in the absolute use of *ho logos* and in the emphasis on the hearing of *ho logos* (4:3a, 9b, 23, 33b) the voice of the redactor (4:33–34). Whatever the traditional thrust of 4:14–20, under redactional control the parable narrates the story of the logos of the Kingdom, and it is narrated out of the Markan experience of disillusionment. Satan has intruded into the community and is playing havoc among the people; the demonic conflict is extended into the Markan generation. There is general lack of fulfillment, and persecutions and suffering seem to defy the arrival of the Kingdom. But the suffering is accorded the eschatological designation of "tribulation" (4:17b: *thlipseōs*) and thereby integrated into a larger scheme of things. The crisis of the present is but an overture to the future parousia (13:19, 24). Contrasting the bad harvest with a vast yield, the parable brings hope and encouragement into a present situation of frustration. Defeat and disaster are undeniable, but so is the fact that the seed has been sown which is to bear fruit in abundance. Even though the crisis of the present appears to hold little for the future, it is, nevertheless, a crisis which by its very nature forecasts victory. Even if the present experience is contrary to the Kingdom, it still cannot challenge its reality, for this contradiction between its obvious impotence and its powerful outcome is built into the history of the Kingdom.

The two parables, 4:21–23 and 4:24–25, are made up of four sayings, each one of which already served in the Q tradition. Mark selected the logia,[38] because he discovered a common truth in them, and he cast them

---

37. Mark describes a true climax: thirty-fold—sixty-fold—hundred-fold. Matthew (13:25) reverses the climax into an anticlimax, which sounds a note of growing disappointment: not all seed yields hundred-fold, some only sixty-fold, and some as little as thirty-fold.

38. Reploh, *Lehrer*, pp. 61–62; Taylor, *St. Mark*, p. 262.

into the mold of parables which in the context of the mystery speech expose the true condition of the Kingdom.

In Mark the saying 4:21 refers to the "coming" of the lamp, whereas Matthew speaks of the "shining" (Matt. 5:15), and Luke of the "lighting" (Luke 11:33) of the lamp. In Mark the eschatological point breaks through the parabolic imagery. This lamp logion is concerned with the status of hiddenness and revelation, and the rhetorical form of the question implies that it is the latter which guarantees authentic existence. Verse 4:22 articulates the contrast between concealment and manifestation in terms fundamental to the whole speech:

> *krypton   —phanerousthai*
> *apokryphon—phaneron*

The clue to the understanding lies in the construction with the final *hina* (4:22b): what is hidden, is hidden in order to be revealed! Nothing remains under cover, because it is the very nature of a cryptic condition that it urges toward its apocalypse. The present hiddenness therefore finds its *raison d'être in the* imminent revelation. The concluding code word (4:23) calls attention to the secret meaning enclosed in the parable. This is the mystery of the Kingdom, that it is subject to the great eschatological reversal. It "comes," not to be invisible, but to be seen in the open; it will exchange its covert condition for the status of epiphany. In effect, the present hiddenness of the Kingdom testifies to its impending apocalypse.

The two parables 4:21–23 and 4:24–25 are arranged according to structural considerations quite similar to those detected in 1:15: *kerygma* is followed by *parenesis*. The second parable (4:24–25) regulates the conduct of people who live under the covert/overt auspices of the Kingdom. In Mark the measure logion (4:24c)[39] is lengthened by the addition of *kai prostethēsetai hymin* (4:24d); the clause reinforces the notion of reciprocal enhancement already expressed in the preceding *metrēthēsetai hymin* (4:24c): "By what measure you measure, you will be measured yourselves—and still more will be given to you." This same theory of enhancement is set forth in the following 4:25a: "For he who has, still more will be given to him." The parable concludes with the theory of progressive diminution, the precise antithesis to progressive enhancement: "From

---

39. In Matthew (7:2) the saying of the measure warns against passing judgment on a brother. In the Lukan context (6:38) this same saying postulates what might be called the theory of reciprocity: a measure for measure mode of procedure controls ethical conduct.

him, who has not, even what he has will be taken away." These rules of enhancement and diminution are to be differentiated from the theory of total reversal which was the point of the previous parable. The eschatological rule of reversal implies that hiddenness is turned into the opposite, as darkness is turned into light. The theories of enhancement and diminution imply that conditions will not be turned upside down, but intensified, for better and for worse. This *parenetic* correlation between "having" and "having more," and "not having" and "having even less" parallels the kerygmatic antithesis between the present and the future state, or the covert and the overt Kingdom. Void and in want of fulfillment as the present may well be, it still provides centers of meaning and consequence, for in it the future takes shape. Loyalty to the Kingdom now will reap compensations many times over. Those who acknowledge and live according to the conditions set by the invisible Kingdom, will be rewarded, and they will be rewarded beyond all expectations. This is what the people are summoned to grasp; whoever endorses the Kingdom in its hidden state and proceeds to measure the world with an eschatological yardstick, will enter into the fullness of the Kingdom; whoever fails to accept the reality of the Kingdom now, forfeits entry into the Kingdom then.

In contrast to the parable of the logos (4:14–20), the parable of the seed growing secretly (4:26–29) is not designed to dwell on the antipodes of the seed's humble beginnings on one end and the abundant produce of the harvest on the other. This time full attention is given to the period between sowing and final yield (4:27–28). After the farmer has sown the seed, he settles down to live the rhythm of an ordinary life (4:27a). In the meantime the seed ripens, grows, and develops into a cornstalk without the farmer's agency. Not only does the farmer not intervene on behalf of the corn, but the whole development is said to elude his comprehension (4:27b). He initiated a process which now runs "of its own accord" (4:28a: *automatē*). The insistence on the farmer's lack of cooperation is not meant to encourage human passivity, or to counter the doctrine of synergism, or to check Zealotic urges, but solely to bring out God's exclusive control over the time which elapses between seeding and reaping. If, therefore, the parable focuses upon the "meantime" of growth, it is not the developmental process as such which is stressed, but the inevitability and divinely ordained destiny of the Kingdom's maturation process. Once set into motion, the Kingdom pursues its foreordained course, and progresses with immanent necessity and unshakeable vitality toward its consummation. The point is the irresistibility with which the Kingdom runs its course toward fulfillment. To the Markan people who live between sowing and harvest, this conveys a strong note of encouragement. The seed has been sown, a beginning is made, the Kingdom's course is set into motion. Now nothing can stop it from reaching its goal. Living under the impact of the irruption of the Kingdom, the Christians can rest assured that its concealed present will inevitably make way to its revealed glory.[40]

That the parable of the mustard seed (4:30–32) pits the minuteness of the seed against the magnitude of the full-grown plant is commonly accepted. Less known is the fact that we are now in a position to demonstrate how Mark took pains to press the point of contrast. There exists a close verbal correspondence between 4:31b and 4:31c/32a:

> *hotan sparē epi tēs gēs*
> *epi tēs gēs, kai hotan sparē.*

Arranged according to the chiastic pattern of a-b-b-a, the two members bring the spotlight down upon the enclosed line: *mikroteron on pantōn tōn spermatōn* (4:31c).[41] The whole composition is a classic case of a Markan insertion. Additional confirmation comes from Matthew who straightens Mark's rugged syntax, and from Luke, widely considered to be close to the Q version, who shows complete ignorance of the insertion procedure. Mark reinforces an already existing motif of contrast by playing up the smallness of the seed. Seed and plant now provide a stunning elaboration of the extreme ends of the Kingdom's total expanse. The beginnings of the Kingdom are set in opposition to its ending, and no direct consideration is given to what happens in between. This parable forms the crowning finale of the mystery speech, because it articulates the speech's central point more cogently than any previous parable. The mystery of the Kingdom resides in the paradoxical polarity between its embryonic state of little importance and its developed state of universal majesty.

It is striking that none of the parables in 4:14–32 dwell on motifs which generally prevail in the synoptic parable tradition, be it the eschatological dimension of the imminence of judgment, the lateness of the hour, pre-

---

40. Rudolf Schnackenburg, *God's Rule and Kingdom*, trans. John Murray (New York: Herder and Herder, 1963), p. 154.

41. The insertion was noticed by Hawkins, *Horae*, p. 135; Charles H. Dodd, *The Parables of the Kingdom*, rev. ed. (New York: Charles Scribner's Sons, 1961), p. 153; Taylor, *St. Mark*, p. 270. For the most extensive discussion on the state of tradition and redaction in 4:30–32, see Ambrozic, *Kingdom*, pp. 122–34.

paredness in view of the parousia, the suddenness of the Kingdom's irruption, or the social dimension of the loving concern for the outcasts, the reintegration of the lost, the rejection of the self-righteous, and mercy toward repentant sinners.

Carefully selected and stripped of their original purpose, these five parables were compiled and reshaped in order to function as the bearers of the mystery of the Kingdom of God. In one form or another each parable accentuates the same point. For whether a massive loss is contrasted with a plentiful success, or whether a phase of hiddenness is set over against a phase of public disclosure, or whether man's present conduct is said to condition his authentic future, or whether an uncontrollable movement is posited which leads from the covert to the overt, or whether an infinitesimally tiny seed is measured against the cosmic tree of life—all five parables total up to one single insight: the Kingdom in miniature will phase into the Kingdom which covers the length and breadth of the land. This is the mystery of the Kingdom explained.

CONCLUSION

The mystery speech is born out of the Markan experience of a present not holding what the Kingdom promised to bring. Measured on the basis of the limited success its propagation knew, the truth of the gospel of the Kingdom seems in doubt. Essentially, the Kingdom has come under Satan's heavy attack, and it is about to be choked in demonic embrace. In this situation the speech aims at providing consolation and dispelling feelings of despair and rootlessness. Careful measure is taken to design a broad framework out of which hope can persuasively be delivered to a hopeless people. A seed has been sown, the inaugural program (1:14–15) stands confirmed, and the Kingdom has indeed become a reality. But as the seed will yet have to grow to become the tree it was intended to be, so will likewise the Kingdom arrive at its prime time only after having accomplished the passage through the middle time. At the present moment, therefore, the Kingdom is a blessing in disguise, invisible and hence a matter of faith (1:15b). Born out of conflict, God's rule on earth exists in, and suffers a state of conflict. Suffering and persecution at this time in history are the "normal" experience, and in no way indicative of the Kingdom's innate defects. That the Kingdom will move out of present darkness into light and liberation is as certain as is the movement from eclipse into the phase of full manifestation.

The Kingdom has a past, a present, and a future, and Mark develops and correlates the three dimensions into a meaningful synthesis. Jesus' past opens up to the Markan present, because the Kingdom of God constitutes Jesus' legacy to his followers. In a sense, the Kingdom continues the authority of Jesus into the Markan present (motif of *repraesentatio!*). What has become obvious now is that the Kingdom continues a Jesus *in all his hiddenness.* As his power and personality are extended into the present by means of the Kingdom, so is also his accompanying Secret lengthened to the point that it conditions the present status of the Kingdom.[42] The anonymity of the King corresponds to the hiddenness of the Kingdom, and past and present are joined together by a bond of the unrevealed. It is proper to say, then, that the Markan people live in the hiddenness of the Kingdom. And yet, they are not totally incarcerated in their present misery, for the present is open to the future. Their crisis is but the prenatal darkness which inevitably precedes the breakthrough toward life and light. Nor are they merely the cogs in a divinely supervised clockwork of history, for it is out of their very experience of crisis that they are called to shape their future destiny, for better and for worse.

The Kingdom of God which had made its appearance in Jesus' first public utterance in Galilee, is concealed at the present time, only to be made manifest at some future point. In effect, we see Mark writing a history of the Kingdom,[43] and he does so in order to assign to his own people a place of hope in the midst of it. He isolates their present experience and cushions it at both ends by the fundamentals of the Kingdom. The people have now come to live in an interregnum, in a zone of invisibility, suspended between Jesus' covert reign of the past and his overt reign in the future. Theirs is a transitory existence, rooted in the epochal event of the past and propelled by the promise of a great future. Crisis and conflict are not denied, but integrated and explained. If their current experience seems contrary to the promise of the Kingdom, it is because they were unaware of the complete history, and the full dimensions of the

---

42. Even though the observation was made in relation to the life of the historical Jesus, A. Schweitzer, *The Quest of the Historical Jesus*, trans. W. Montgomery in 1910 from first German edition (New York: Macmillan, 1968), p. 349, was basically correct when he remarked in response to W. Wrede's theory of the Messianic Secret: "He [Wrede] is unwilling to recognize that there is a second, wider circle of mystery which has to do, not with Jesus' messiahship, but with his preaching of the Kingdom, with the mystery of the Kingdom of God in the wider sense. . . ."

43. Nils A. Dahl, "The Parables of Growth," *StTh*, 5 (1951), p. 157: "We may say that the parables of growth teach that the Kingdom has a 'history,' a period of its secret presence preceding its final revelation."

Kingdom. By suffering trials and tribulation they do in fact participate in and act out the mysterious drama of the Kingdom.

For one last moment we must return to the dramatic setting of the mystery speech. For while this revelation of the history of the Kingdom was meant to provide orientation for Christians in Markan times, its full implication will only become intelligible if we observe carefully the manner in which the speech is staged as an event of the past. We are again referring to the fact that the mystery of the Kingdom had been disclosed as a piece of inside information to "those about him" and the twelve. At this stage, then, these insiders are to know the history of the Kingdom in outline. But now as before we must reiterate our doubts. Will the disciples accept this message? Can they tolerate the fact that the Kingdom in fullness is as yet to come in the future? Should the time ever arise for them, would they be able to endure the drought of the interregnum? Most importantly, will this collegiate of the Twelve and "those about him" ever remember that it had been in Galilee, in Jesus' only Galilean speech, that the master had spoken of the three phases of the Kingdom? Only the remainder of the gospel story can tell whether they grasped and lived this mystery of the Kingdom.

Chapter III

EXPANSION AND UNITY
OF THE KINGDOM

4:35—8:21

Mark's predilection for Galilee and his specific interest in closely tying Jesus' Kingdom activity to Galilee is too clearly pronounced a feature to be overlooked. Jesus' own Galilean identity is assured with the first mentioning of his earthly background (1:9). The subsequent gospel program (1:14–15) serves in part to anchor the Kingdom in its Galilean base of operations. The beginning was thus in Galilee. Jesus' first two miracles which take up the Kingdom's battle by means of exorcising (1:21–28) and healing (1:29–31), are located in the Galilean seaport of Capernaum. In the case of the exorcism, Mark specified the concluding geographical reference by the redactional additum *tēs Galilaias* (1:28).[1] This first miracle generates a movement that spreads Jesus' fame as a preacher of the Kingdom "throughout all the surrounding region of Galilee." The Kingdom is a dynamic force which extends itself into all of Galilee. But we also observe the incipient stirrings of a counterforce which is attempting to check the advance of the Kingdom. With A. Kuby[2] we detect in 1:35–38 a first indication of strained relations between Jesus and his disciples. Simon and those with him arrive at Jesus' retreat outside Capernaum, wondering why he would not stay and enjoy his fame for everyone is searching for him (1:37). They are inclined to hold back Jesus, thus di-

1. Rudolf Pesch, "Ein Tag vollmächtigen Wirkens Jesu in Kapharnaum," *BibLeb*, 9 (1968), p. 118.
2. Alfred Kuby, "Zur Konzeption des Markus-Evangeliums," *ZNW*, 49 (1958), p. 55; also Theodore J. Weeden, *Mark—Traditions in Conflict* (Philadelphia: Fortress Press, 1971), pp. 27–30; 149, n. 17.

verting him from a purpose which is to take him far beyond the city limits of Capernaum.[3] He is therefore defying the disciples' request to return, when he pronounces the missionary goal of his ministry: the gospel of the Kingdom must be preached elsewhere, for this is what his life is all about.[4] The summarizing verse 1:39 reiterates the point that in *all* of Galilee the Kingdom is being ushered in by word and deed.

For all the importance Mark attaches to Galilee, his full concept of Galilee, or "all of Galilee" still remains strangely obscure. Does he use it in an ethnic sense, or in a geographical sense, or in a combination of the two? If he understands Galilee ethnically, it will hardly refer to the Gentiles. He never explicates his notion of Galilee on the basis of Isaiah 9:1-2, the very passage which envisions a "Galilee of the nations." More importantly, Jesus has as yet not stepped on Gentile territory, nor have any Gentiles come into Galilee to him. On the contrary, Jesus has up to this point conducted his ministry in an exclusively Jewish environment. All his dealings have been with Jewish people, his activities in the synagogues were necessarily directed toward Jewish audiences, and the controversies have arisen out of a thoroughly Jewish milieu. This might lend support to the thesis that Mark uses Galilee to express his concern for the Jewish Christians of his time, that Galilee is wherever Jewish Christians live, and the Kingdom is expanded to cover all the Christians. But this is not altogether correct, because we have already observed Mark's efforts to overcome the limitations set by a distinctly Jewish point of view (controversy stories). It must also be added that in 3:7-12, a Markan summary report, a mixed Jewish-Gentile gathering is depicted. If Galilee has any geographical significance at all, it may be that its territory seems to be bounded on the east by the lake of Galilee. Crucial events, such as the founding of the Kingdom community (1:16-20; 3:13), the aforementioned ecumenical gathering (3:7-12), as well as the mystery speech (4:1-34) have been located nearer to the western shore of the lake, but no attempt has as yet been made to depict Jesus as crossing over to the other side.

In 4:35-8:21 the idea of the lake as the boundary line of Galilee is broken down. The principal drama of this section portrays Jesus undertaking a number of voyages on and across the Lake of Galilee. We will tentatively assume that these journeys serve to generate a further expan-

3. We shall have ample opportunity to observe the disciples' intransigence about the Kingdom's goal-oriented drive.

4. Against Pesch, "Kapharnaum," p. 266, we take 1:38d to be a Markan *gar* clause; see also C. H. Bird, "Some *gar* Clauses in St. Mark's Gospel," *JTS*, 4 (1953), pp. 171-87.

sion of the Kingdom. If Galilee is indeed geographically limited to an area west of the lake, the Kingdom and all it represents will then be extended to places outside of Galilee. Or should one assume that this reach beyond the sea merely completes the Kingdom's drive to cover "all of Galilee?"

As for the literary history of 4:35–8:21, P. Achtemeier has reconstructed a "pre-Markan cycle of miracle stories, circulating in the form of two catenae,"[5] out of which Mark composed this very section. Each catena consisted of five miracle stories, which were arranged in analogous order —a sea miracle, three healing miracles, and a feeding miracle.[6] Even though these miracles were in their pre-Markan condition not organized into a continuous story line, they appear to be molded on a homogeneous religious concept, the *theios anēr* theology. Whether it is the use of the title Son of God or of the theophany formula *egō eimi*, fear and awe in view of miraculous deeds or the spectacle of healing power directly emanating from the healer to the patient, intimations of the Moses figure or an uncanny authority over nature—these and other features contained in the body of the miracle tradition bring out its epiphanic character. Jesus, according to this tradition, is a miracle worker, human but endowed with superhuman powers.[7]

Achtemeier has laid the significant form-critical groundwork, and it is incumbent upon us to discern the pertinent redaction-critical implications. His studies stimulate many questions for redaction criticism. Does Mark uncritically reproduce this miracle tradition, or does he subject it to his editorial interpretation? Does he actively challenge the *theios anēr* theology, or is he primarily interested in making the material serviceable to his very own purpose, without directly taking issue with the tradition's central point? Why does he adopt two catenae, instead of dropping one of them? Is he insensitive to the charge of being repetitious? What purpose, if any, do plain doublets as the sea miracles or the wondrous feedings serve in the context of the gospel?

5. Paul J. Achtemeier, "Toward the Isolation of Pre-Markan Miracle Catenae," *JBL*, 89 (1970), p. 290.
6. Heinz-Wolfgang Kuhn (*Ältere Sammlungen im Markusevangelium*, Studien zur Umwelt des Neuen Testaments, No. 8 [Göttingen: Vandenhoeck & Ruprecht, 1971], pp. 191–213) recognizes a sequence of only six miracles in 4:35–5:53, 6:32–52. He overlooks the clearly identifiable parallel structures of the two catenae. Achtemeier's analysis is more persuasive.
7. More recently Paul J. Achtemeier, "The Origin and Function of the Pre-Marcan Miracle Catenae," *JBL*, 91 (1972), pp. 198–221, uncovered the eucharistic meal as the historical locus of this miracle tradition. Being part of the eucharistic liturgy, these texts served to reveal the risen Lord as present among the participants.

Obviously, our angle of vision is different from that of Achtemeier. He views the present Markan order of events as largely conditioned by the underlying source, whereas we will observe Mark's use of the source as being dictated by a definite theological concept of his own. Principally, we will demonstrate how Mark joins the miracle units together with the aid of the itinerary connective of six voyages, thus welding the many stories into the one story he wishes to tell.

THE JEWISH DESIGNATION

There is evidence that the miracle story of the Stilling of the Storm (4:35–41) has been furnished with a Markan introduction (4:35). Both the *kai* parataxis[8] and the use of *legein* in the present tense[9] reflect redactional touches. The doubling of the time reference points up the concern for temporal continuity with the antecedent event.[10] It was on the day of the mystery speech, and late on that day after the secret initiation had come to a conclusion, that Jesus embarked on the voyage. *Eis to peran* and/or *diaperan* introduce the all-important crossing motif. Judiciously spaced throughout 4:35–8:21, the terms signal an actual crossing of the lake, be it from the western bank to an area east of the lake, or vice versa.[11] This crossing motif is a major contributing element in the redactional formation of the voyage framework, and it serves to integrate the miracle units into a new whole. The *autois* in 4:35, following in the wake of Jesus' private session with the insiders, refers to the disciples. It is, however, striking that in the miracle the disciples are never singled out under this term. It is thus not implausible to assume that the traditional miracle story provided no active role for the disciples at all. In that case, Mark would have brought them into the story by closely connecting it to the preceding mystery speech.[12] While 4:35 both prepares for the voyage drama and links up with the mystery speech, the following verse 4:36

8. John C. Hawkins, *Horae Synopticae* (Oxford: Clarendon, 1909), pp. 150–52.

9. John C. Doudna, *The Greek of the Gospel of Mark* (Philadelphia: Society of Biblical Literature and Exegesis, 1961), p. 41.

10. For the redactional nature of the doubling of a time reference, see Pesch, "Kapharnaum," p. 188.

11. Commentators consistently argue that *eis to peran* indicates a movement to the eastern border of the lake. But not so in Mark. Out of five instances the phrase is used in the voyage section (4:35; 5:1, 21; 6:45; 8:13), 5:21 and 8:13 mark a crossing from east to west. Markan familiarity with *peran* is proven by the redactional 3:8.

12. Karl Kertelge, *Die Wunder Jesu im Markusevangelium*, Studien zum Alten und Neuen Testament, No. 23 (Munich: Kösel, 1970), p. 99.

appears to clash with the dramatic setting of the mystery speech. The dismissal of the crowd overlooks the fact that Jesus had some time earlier (4:10) withdrawn from the crowd, and the "other boats" have not been prepared for and are forgotten afterward. With 4:36 then we touch upon the bedrock of the tradition. As the beginning of the story, so is also part of its ending composed by Mark. Jesus' harsh rebuke of the disciples (4:40), coupled with their fearful reaction (4:41a) is an essential aspect of Mark's discipleship theology. The onlookers' confession, however, (4:41c, d) is again a standard feature of *theios anēr* miracle stories. What surfaces as the traditional core of the story is a sea miracle which manifests Jesus' superiority over a demonic nature.

Into this miracle story Mark has introduced the motifs of crossing and discipleship. The redactional *dielthōmen eis to peran* defines the purpose of Jesus' embarkation in terms of a crossing. This produces a slight shift from the original sea story toward a voyage story. Following the calming of the elements, and before the disciples are given a chance to express their admiration, Jesus rebukes them, charging them with lack of faith and, interestingly enough, cowardice. *Pistis* in conjunction with *deiloi* alters the traditional notion of belief in, or acknowledgement of, the miracle worker to an attitude of courage under stress. The rebuke singles out the disciples' weakness during the crossing, and not their lack of reverence in view of the miracle. They are admonished because, cowed by the perils of the crossing, they showed concern only for their well-being (4:38). The *oupō echete pistin* (4:40c)[13] at the beginning of the sea drama is echoed by the *oupō noeite* (8:17c) and *oupō syniete* (8:21b) at the very conclusion. This gives an indication of the pervasiveness of the theme of discipleship, or rather that of the failure of discipleship, throughout 4:35–8:21. The whole section is bracketed by the "not yet" of the disciples' courage and understanding. The motif of the disciples' fear (4:41a), "a theological, and not a psychological datum,"[14] is a functional element of Mark's discipleship theology. That he associates fear with their lack of understanding is shown by the redactional verses 9:6, 32 and also 10:32. Fear is an expression of the disciples' condition of non-perception.[15] The understanding of the fear in 4:41a is therefore not that the disciples are

---

13. The well-attested *oupō* is generally preferred over against the *pōs ouk*.
14. Aloysius M. Ambrozic, *The Hidden Kingdom*, The Catholic Biblical Quarterly—Monograph Series, No. 2 (Washington, D.C.: The Catholic Biblical Association of America, 1972), p. 161.
15. Be it noted that the whole gospel ends on this discordant note of fear.

filled with reverential fear in view of Jesus' demonstration of power, but rather that they are shocked by Jesus' rebuke of cowardice because they cannot grasp the implications of the crossing. Their final question, "Who then is this, that even wind and sea obey him?," must be viewed as a statement made in lack of faith. It is out of fear and lack of understanding that they confess the lordship of Jesus over nature.[16] Therefore the redacted story of the Stilling of the Storm will have to be considered not as a sea miracle which manifests the power of Jesus, but as a mysterious crossing which is misunderstood by the disciples as a sea miracle.[17]

Jesus himself takes the initiative for this first passage across the Lake of Galilee. It turns out to be a stormy passage, and in mid-water the disciples falter, which incurs the rebuke of Jesus. Among themselves the disciples marvel at the identity of the one who saved them by mastering the elements, but the real significance of the move across the lake escapes them. As the master pioneers the breakthrough toward new shores, they appear to be out of step with the purpose of his mission.

The exorcism story of the Gerasene Demoniac (5:1–20) owes little to Markan redaction.[18] An exception is the opening statement *kai ēlthon eis to peran tēs thalassēs*, which serves to weave the miracle into the crossing pattern. With *eis to peran* we meet Mark's technical term indicating a crossing. *Kai ēlthon* reflects Markan partiality to *erchesthai*, using it preferably in the plural.[19] Were it not for this plural, the disciples would be absent from the story. The conflict between the plural *ēlthon* in 5:1 and the singular *exelthontos* in 5:2 may mark the change from the redaction to tradition.[20] The locality of the *chōran tēs Gerasēnōn*, however, is anchored in the tradition.[21] Aside from the editorial opening line only the

16. Leander E. Keck, "Mark 3, 7–12 and Mark's Christology," *JBL*, 84 (1965), p. 356, n. 96; Jürgen Roloff, "Das Markusevangelium als Geschichtsdarstellung," *EvTh*, 27 (1969), p. 84, n. 43.

17. Against Kertelge (*Wunder*, p. 99, n. 367, p. 100) who believes discipleship is secondary to Jesus' epiphany.

18. Rudolf Bultmann, *History of the Synoptic Tradition*, trans. John Marsh, 3rd ed. (New York: Harper & Row, 1963), p. 210; Achtemeier, "Isolation," pp. 275–76.

19. Cuthbert H. Turner, "Marcan Usage: Notes, Critical and Exegetical, on the Second Gospel," *JTS*, 26 (1924–25), pp. 225–28.

20. Bultmann, *Tradition*, p. 344. But the *exelthontos autou* in 5:2 may still be redactional because of Mark's known preference for *exerchesthai* (Pesch, "Kapharnaum," p. 178) and the genitive absolute (Doudna, *Greek*, pp. 57–59).

21. Karl L. Schmidt, *Der Rahmen der Geschichte Jesu* (Berlin: Trowitzsch und Sohn, 1919; reprinted Darmstadt: Wissenschaftliche Buchgesellschaft, 1964), p. 140. The fact that Gerasa is located some forty miles southeast of the lake has precipitated a flurry of textual activity. Both the *Gadarēnōn* and the *Gergesēnōn* indicate attempts to overcome the *lectio difficilior* of the *Gerasēnōn* by moving the exorcism closer to the lake. At an earlier stage, therefore, the story must have been unrelated to the

concluding verse 5:20, Jesus' commission to proclaim the success in the Decapolis, can with a degree of certainty be identified as Markan.[22]

This exorcism is typed by the stark and dramatic notes of the *theios anēr* conception. It depicts Jesus, the venerated Son of God, exercising his supernatural powers over the unclean spirits, causing them to engineer their own destruction. Those who witness the miracle and its spectacular results are driven into flight, fear, and even the desire for the disappearance of this awesome miracle-worker. It seems curious that Mark would espouse this miracle in the first place, and stranger still that he would make little effort to trim the "excesses" of the miraculous. Leaving the miracle essentially intact, he nevertheless offers a transformed view of it by subordinating it to a "higher" purpose. 5:1 leaves no doubt that Jesus has indeed arrived at the eastern shore. Whatever the historical location of the land of the Gerasenes, Mark designated it as the eastern goal of Jesus' first crossing. A definitely Gentile coloring of the territory suggests that Jesus came to free the Gentiles from demonic uncleanliness. Mark corroborates the Gentile nature of the miracle by identifying the area as the Décapolis (5:20). Viewed in the total context of Jesus' ministry, his first exorcism in the Decapolis recalls his first public action taken in Galilee (1:21–28).[23] Just as he began his battle on behalf of the Kingdom in Galilee with an exorcism, so does he now initiate the Kingdom in the Decapolis by performing the most massive exorcism reported of him. After the miracle, Mark stresses, the cured man cannot join Jesus on his return trip to Galilee, because he has to spread the news of the Kingdom throughout the Decapolis, just as it had earlier to be proclaimed "throughout all the surrounding region of Galilee" (1:28).

Mark adopts this massive miracle because it underscores the extraordinary nature of what has happened. But for him the point of the miraculous happening does not lie in Jesus' breaking of the demonic power, but in his breaking of the Gentile barrier. He has subordinated the epiphanic miracle to his more comprehensive scheme of the expansion of the Kingdom. Similar to the conversion of Cornelius in Acts 10, the Gerasene

---

lake. Mark placed it into the voyage framework, but was not the first to connect it with the lake, as 5:13 shows. Concerning the history of tradition, see Rudolf Pesch, *Der Besessene von Gerasa*, Stuttgarter Bibelstudien, No. 56 (Stuttgart: KBW Verlag, 1972).

22. The verse is considered traditional among others by Achtemeier, "Isolation," p. 276, and Kertelge, *Wunder*, p. 101. The verse is considered redactional among others by Kuhn, *Sammlungen*, p. 192, n. 3, and Roloff, "Markusevangelium," p. 85, n. 49.

23. A correlation between 1:21–28 and 5:1–20 has frequently been observed, but never been fully evaluated within the total context of the gospel.

exorcism in Mark 5:1–20 constitutes the crucial watershed of the mission to the Gentiles.

As clearly as the Decapolis exorcism was painted in Gentile colors, so are the two miracles of the raising of Jairus' daughter and the woman with a hemorrhage placed into a recognizably Jewish milieu. Jairus, ruler of a synagogue, the woman's duration of suffering (twelve years), and the girl's age (twelve years) furnish the symbols of Jewishness. The miracles were adopted by Mark essentially in the form in which they came to him, but the interpolation of the healing miracle into the story of the raising is of his own making (5:21–24, 35–43; 5:25–34).[24] The *diaperasantos . . . palin eis to peran* (5:21) denotes a crossing from the Decapolis back to the west, and the "unnecessary phrase"[25] *para tēn thalassan* (5:21), an editorial comment exclusively used in reference to the Galilean side of the lake (1:16; 2:13; 4:1), binds the miracles to the western shore. Further Markan features include 5:24, which smoothes the rupture caused by the interpolation,[26] and 5:43, the command to silence.[27] To these commonly accepted elements of the redaction, 5:37 must be added.[28] The introduction of the three confidants, who will consistently act in the interest of the redaction, as well as the use of double negatives,[29] and the verb *synakolouthein* in a discipleship context[30] point to Mark as the author of this verse.

The intercalation of the two stories introduces an element of tension which in turn brings the focus upon the resurrection miracle. There had been hope earlier that the summons of death might be forestalled, but Jesus chose to pass up the chance. Now it is in the face of the reality of death that he gives a demonstration of his power, foreshadowing his own resurrection.[31] Knowledge of this greatest miracle of all is, however, confined to the disciples. This is the purpose of the selection of the three

---

24. Ernest v. Dobschütz, "Zur Erzählkunst des Markus," *ZNW*, 27 (1928), p. 195; Siegfried Schulz, *Die Stunde der Botschaft* (Hamburg: Furche-Verlag, 1967), p. 29; Achtemeier, "Isolation," pp. 276–79.

25. Achtemeier, "Isolation," p. 278.

26. *Ibid.*

27. Bultmann, *Tradition*, p. 214; Kertelge, *Wunder*, pp. 118–20.

28. Bultmann (*Tradition*, p. 214) acknowledges the editorial character of 5:37, but assigns the verse to a pre-Markan stage of redaction.

29. Vincent Taylor, *The Gospel According to St. Mark* (London: Macmillan and Co., 1963), p. 46.

30. Turner, "Marcan Usage," *JTS*, 26 (1924–25), pp. 238–40.

31. The *anastēnai* of 5:42 is resumed in the passion-resurrection predictions (8:31; 9:31; 10:34). But see also the important verses 9:9–10.

witnesses and the command to silence.[32] The disciples alone are granted an inside clue as to the kind of Christ they can well anticipate. They will have to keep this knowledge *in pectore* until they are called upon to use it for their own salvation (9:9!).

We must not lose sight of the all-comprehensive voyage pattern. At this point, the configuration of the sea journeys indicates neither a rejection of Israel and a turning to the Gentiles, nor even a break with Galilee and an unswerving thrust into the Decapolis. Rather, the breakthrough to the Gentiles, coupled with the return trip to the Jews—underlined by a massive miracle performed on either side—serves notice that both sides of the lake belong together. The Jewish and the Gentile parts of the lake have been sanctioned, and they both participate in the struggle of the Kingdom.

In 6:1–33 Mark compiled a block of material which was totally unrelated to the miracle tradition. By way of a major deviation from the "norm" of the tradition he inserted such diverse stories as the rejection at Nazareth, the mission of the twelve, the death of John the Baptist, and the return of the twelve. The fact that Mark decided to abandon the catenae model and take full charge of the plot provides us with an opportunity to catch the editorial viewpoint more directly than before. This section will disclose the Markan scopus, if we focus upon its placement in the gospel and the sequence of events. Why was the underlying miracle structure broken at this point, what is the plot of the insert, and how is it related to the main story?

One of the many unusual features pertaining to the story of Jesus' rejection at Nazareth (6:1–6a) is that it does not mention his home town by name. The redactional 6:1[33] introduces the scene of action with *patrida*, a term most likely derived from the *patridi* of the proverb (6:4).[34] But whereas the *patris* in 6:1 gives a non-partisan impression, it is at the height of the controversy elaborated by *en tois syggeneusin autou kai en tē oikia autou* (6:4). Since neither Matthew (13:57), nor Luke (4:24), nor John (4:44), nor Pap. Oxy. 1,5, nor Thomas log. 31 make any reference to *tois syggeneusin,* and only Matthew notes the *en tē oikia autou,* and this by adoption of the Markan text, the whole elaboration can be attributed to the redaction.[35] It stems from Mark's desire to specify and

---

32. Kertelge, *Wunder,* pp. 118–20.
33. Erich Grässer, "Jesus in Nazareth (Mark VI, 1–6a)," *NTS,* 16 (1969), p. 10.
34. *Ibid.*
35. *Ibid.,* p. 6. But most commentators will only concede the redactional nature of *en tois syggeneusin autou.*

personalize the neutral *patris* in terms of the family of Jesus. Although in the story the relatives did not cause the discord since they appear only indirectly in the testimony of the "many" (6:2b), Mark uses their citation as an opportunity to dissociate Jesus from them. It was not the town of Nazareth as much as it was Jesus' next of kin, his house and family that provoked him to make the break. The nature of this break is such that it invites immediate comparison with Jesus' earlier exclusion of the relatives (3:20–35). This second rejection finalizes the long-projected split between Jesus and his family, and we will henceforth refer to it as a schism.

Jesus responds to this schism by sending out the twelve (6:6b–13), to continue through preaching, exorcising, and healing (6:13), the very work that he had begun. As they return, the new designation of apostleship has been bestowed upon them (6:30). This registers a landmark experience in the life of the disciples, because never before or after are they called apostles.[36] Apparently, it was the missionary journey which actualized their advancement from discipleship to apostleship. An indication of this advanced stage of discipleship had already been given at the occasion of their official appointment (3:14). While the disciples live with Jesus and follow him on his way, the apostles are called to move out and continue his work away from him, and, we might add, after the master's mission is completed. The apostles are the emancipated disciples who keep the message alive after the master has gone. Apostleship in Mark's view anticipates the time of Jesus' absence and assures a measure of continuity. With the successful completion of their mission, the full identity of the twelve, as outlined in 3:14, is established. They have now been commissioned, and they ought to be ready to function in the absence of Jesus. The interpolation of the death of John the Baptist between the disciples' departure and their return effects more than the time lapse dramatically required by the duration of the mission. Theologically, it synchronizes the death of John with the apostolic mission, again foreboding events of the future. As the death of the forerunner coincided with the apostolic commission, so will the death of Jesus himself give birth to this new, apostolic community in Galilee. Then the disciples will have to act upon their assignment and assume full apostolic responsibility.

To gain a fuller understanding, we must connect this schism and mission with the earlier exclusion of the family. The earlier split had occurred on the heels of a most significant event, the above-mentioned

36. Verse 3:14 is of dubious textual quality.

appointment of the twelve (3:13–19). No sooner had the disciples been designated as the collegiate of the twelve, than were they separated from the family of Jesus (3:20–35). And no sooner had they been separated from the family, than were they initiated into the history of the Kingdom (4:1–34). The schism also comes at a crucial moment. Immediately after Jesus had broken the Gentile barrier and defined the scope of the Kingdom, he is intercepted by his family and frustrated by the unbelief of his own house. The very moment the two sides of the Kingdom have been drawn together, the line of division is sharpened to the breaking point of a schism. And as the earlier exclusion of the relatives had marked the step toward a deepening of the disciples' insight into the Kingdom, so does the schism result in the disciples' apostolic involvement in the history of the Kingdom.

The full implications of the break with the family will unfold as the story of the Kingdom proceeds, but the point Mark makes through the dramatic arrangement of events is quite clear. He is grooming the disciples in opposition to the relatives, and he is building up the Jewish-Gentile Kingdom in separation from all family influence. The disciples are the apostolic guardians of a Kingdom which is fully identified both by its Jewish-Gentile constituency and by its divorce from the family tree of Jesus. With all this the disciples are given a foretaste of, and indeed a mandate to the kind of Kingdom community which will be set free after the death of Jesus.

After this preview of the apostolic future, Mark continues to narrate the story of the Kingdom by returning to the miracle cycle once again. The redactional 6:31–33[37] produces a new variation of the voyage motif which ties the bulk of inserted material back to the catena. While the subsequent feeding of the multitude (6:34–44) is unlikely in its pre-Markan form to have been associated with a lakeside setting, it is the main purpose of the elaborate *mise en scène* 6:31–33 to locate it at a place near the *western* bank of the lake. Crowded in by the people, Jesus and his disciples fetch a boat which is to take them to a lonely place. But the crowds on this Galilean side watch the departure and anticipate Jesus' place of destination. Running "on foot" (6:33b) along the shore, they arrive ahead of Jesus at his secret landing place. There is no mention

37. Bultmann, *Tradition*, p. 244; Taylor, *St. Mark*, pp. 318–20; Julius Wellhausen, *Das Evangelium Marci* (Berlin: Georg Reimer, 1909), p. 48; Alfred Suhl, *Die Funktion der alttestamentlichen Zitate und Anspielungen im Markusevangelium* (Gütersloh: Gerd Mohn, 1965), p. 144.

of *diaperan* or *eis to peran*! This third voyage is thus not a crossing, merely a movement from one spot on the western bank to another spot on the western bank. A new, though still western place for the feeding is established and the Galilean multitude which is to be fed has arrived.

6:34 sets up the conditions for the feeding proper. Of Markan making is *exelthōn*[38] and *polyn ochlon*, which capitalizes on the fact that people had converged "from all the towns" (6:33b). The *ērxato didaskein* needs little comment, and so does the adverbial use of *polla*.[39] Mark introduces the feeding with the scene of a teaching Jesus. The distinctly traditional element of the verse is the reference to Jesus' compassion, *esplangchnisthē ep' autous*. The verb *splangchnizesthai* is not part of the Markan vocabulary (1:41; 8:2; 9:22), and 8:2 indicates that its original place was in the miracle story. We conclude that Mark, who created the teaching situation, also introduced the saying of the sheep without a shepherd as the topic of the teaching.[40] According to the traditional miracle story, Jesus takes compassion on the people because they are hungry. But Mark, breaking the logic of the miracle, has Jesus take pity on the people because they live in a leaderless situation. This is the Markan introduction to the feeding and it sets the tone for the miracle. Vice versa, the miracle must be interpreted so that it responds to the theme of the introduction. The motif of the sheep without a shepherd foreshadows the moment when the shepherd will be struck and his sheep scattered about (14:27). Then Christians will indeed be deprived of their leader. In Mark, therefore, the miracle addresses itself to the issues of the absence of Jesus and the continuity of his reign. The point does not lie in the obvious fact that Jesus assumes the role of shepherd over his people, for this would neither speak into a situation of posthumous void, nor satisfy the needs of a leaderless people. Once again, the disciples provide the clue.[41] Their involvement in the feeding goes far beyond the function of giving Jesus a helping hand. They are commissioned to feed the people (6:37b), they are instructed to make the crowds settle down in orderly camps (6:39), and they do feed the people, distributing the bread among the multitude (6:41a). Rather than their helping Jesus feed the people, this is a case of

---

38. See n. 20, above.
39. Hawkins, *Horae*, p. 35.
40. Suhl, *Funktion*, pp. 144–45; Bultmann, *Tradition*, p. 217; Erich Klostermann, *Das Markusevangelium*, 4th ed. (Tübingen: Mohr/Siebeck, 1950), p. 63.
41. P. G. Ziener, "Die Brotwunder im Markusevangelium," *BZ*, 4 (1960), pp. 282–85; B. van Iersel, "Die wunderbare Speisung und das Abendmahl in der Synoptischen Tradition," *NovTest*, 7 (1965), p. 181.

Jesus showing them how to feed the people. With this experience in mind, they ought to be able to assume their role as shepherds when the occasion arises. But their desire to dismiss the crowds (6:35–36) and to buy the bread (6:37c–e) suggests that they are unaware of what has transpired at this feeding.

With mission and mandate of the apostolic Kingdom assured, the feeding marks the act of its official designation. On the western side of the lake the Markan Jesus constitutes the Jewish part of the Kingdom, and, speaking to a time when his absence is felt, puts the disciples in charge of it.

THE GENTILE DESIGNATION

The time for the second voyage to the east side of the lake has arrived (6:45–52). *Eis to peran* (6:45a) and *diaperasantes* (6:53) leave no doubt as to the reality of the crossing. Not long ago Jesus had pioneered the Gentile breakthrough and broken fresh ground on behalf of the Kingdom. The second time around, the disciples are to be in the vanguard and truly lead the movement to the Gentiles. This is why Jesus exerts pressure (6:45a: *ēnagkasen*), forcing the disciples to spearhead the move across the lake (6:45a: *proagein eis to peran*). But they show no improvement over their first crossing, and fail again to overcome the adversities of the passage. Inextricably tied to their lack of initiative is their failure to recognize the true nature of Jesus. First they take him for a ghost,[42] and after he has revealed his full identity (6:50e: *egō eimi*) and removed the obstacle to the crossing, they are in a state of total perplexity and incomprehension. The reason for this fiasco lies in their persistent refusal to learn the lesson taught by Jesus' travels. In a general sense, this is the meaning of the strange note that "they did not understand about the matter of the loaves" (6:52a).[43] These apostles designate who had been put in charge of the Jewish constituency should have known that this

---

42. The difficult 6:48d (*kai ēthelen parelthein autous*) is widely understood to be traditional and in support of the miracle motif: Jesus does not enter the boat because he is about to reveal himself on the sea. It could, however, be a Markan insert, running counter to the miracle: Jesus does not wish to enter the boat because he intends to make the crossing.

43. Verse 6:52 by near total consensus is Markan. It serves to subordinate the epiphanic motif to the overarching discipleship-voyage drama. Quentin Quesnell (*The Mind of Mark*, Analecta Biblica, No. 38 [Rome: Pontifical Biblical Institute, 1969], pp. 257–60) sees seven different meanings simultaneously expressed by the verse, the unity motif being one of them. In our judgment, the unity motif is uppermost in the mind of Mark.

feeding was only in partial fulfillment of the Kingdom. Their experience of the first crossing was to have opened their eyes to the inclusion of the Gentiles. The fundamental truth which Jesus came to express through his voyages was that there is only "one loaf" (8:14!). In this spirit they should have recognized Jesus, as he revealed himself to them in the middle of the lake, not as the miracle worker who made an exhibition of his domination over nature, but as the unifier who calmed the storm in order to secure the passage to the Gentiles. And so this essentially abortive crossing expires with the accusation of "hardness of heart" (6:52b). It seems safe to say that the disciples, should they ever play an active role in the history of the Kingdom, would shape it in a highly exclusive fashion.

The arrival at the east coast causes a noted difficulty in the itinerary. While in 6:45 the place of destination was given as Bethsaida, one actually lands at Gennesaret (6:53). The solution to the problem lies in Mark's rearrangement of traditional material.[44] In the pre-Markan miracle catena the story of the walking on the sea, introduced by reference to departure for Bethsaida (6:45), was directly linked with the story of the blind man of Bethsaida (8:22–26), likewise introduced by reference to Bethsaida (8:22). Mark displaced the latter because he considered it the proper prelude to the eye opening mid-section of the gospel, Jesus' journey to the south.[45] But how to account for its replacement by 6:53–56, a redactional passage summarizing Jesus' healing ministry? As so often before, its place in the plot provides the clue. This exclusive report on healings among Gentiles closely parallels Jesus' Kingdom work in the west. In Galilee he had opened his active ministry with an exorcism (1:21–28) and followed up with a healing (1:29–31). Likewise among the Gentiles, he had performed an exorcism after the first crossing (5:1–20) which is now, after the second crossing, followed by healings. The Kingdom has arrived in full on the eastern shore.

The admission of the Gentiles proves to be a sensitive issue which calls for a precedential ruling (7:1–23). The arrival of the Jerusalem delegation is required by the logic of the plot, and does not transport us back to Galilee. The "Gentile issue" must be argued out on Gentile ground and prior to the Gentile ratification. Precisely what is at issue is whether the

---

44. Achtemeier, "Isolation," pp. 281–87.

45. This not only explains the geographical discrepancy between 6:45 and 6:53, but it also makes understandable why 8:22–26 in its present position is out of place in relation to the preceding voyage drama: according to 8:13 Jesus and the disciples have returned to the west, whereas in 8:22 they arrive at northeastern Bethsaida.

Gentiles have to adjust to the Jewish *paradosis*, or whether the tradition is liberalized so as to make room for the newcomers. Mark's influence is apparent in 7:14–23, a reproduction of the dramatic pattern of the mystery speech. The parabolic ruling is first pronounced to the crowd, then secretly divulged to the unenlightened disciples. The confidential piece of information concerns the fact that all ritual uncleanliness is replaced by inward impurity, and a new morality has taken the place of ceremonial cleanliness. The tradition is not merely liberalized but overruled, and the legal barrier which prevented Gentiles from full participation in the Kingdom has been removed. All this information is polemically directed against the Jerusalem authorities (7:1) and therefore tantamount to a schism with the Jewish capital. At the occasion of the mystery, we recall, the Jerusalem authorities together with the family of Jesus had been pointed out as the true opposition (3:20–22). In the meantime the point is amply confirmed. Prior to the apostolic mission the break with the relatives had deteriorated into a schism, and prior to Jesus' northern journey the relationship with Jerusalem is now completely severed. The integrity of the Kingdom is preserved so long as it stays independent from the family and the Jerusalem authorities. This the disciples can and must know.

The emancipation from the southern capital engenders new freedom of movement, and the area of the lake is left for a trip to the northernmost, Gentile point. Up to the region of Tyre (7:24) and Sidon (7:31)—this is as far as the orbit of the Kingdom is expanded. As expected, the new space is purged first by an exorcism (7:24–30), and second by a healing (7:32–37).

Embedded in the exorcism miracle is a controversy unit (7:27–28) which disrupts the story line of the miraculous recovery of the Syrophoenician woman's daughter. The removal of this unit reproduces the unbroken miracle tradition. Enclosed by near identical frame verses (7:26c: *to daimonion ekbalō ek tēs thygatros autēs*; 7:29c: *exelēlythen ek tēs thygatros sou to daimonion*), and introduced and concluded by like transitional comments (7:27a: *kai elegen autē*; 7:29a: *kai eipen autē*), the controversy section is marked as a redactional insert. The issue raised through this dialogue between Jesus and the woman is that of Jewish-Gentile priority. The resolution, first the Jews and then the Gentiles, keeps pace with the Markan story, while completely overshadowing the miracle per se. Presented between the Jewish feeding (6:34–44) and what is apparently going to be the Gentile feeding (8:1–10), this ruling confirms

Mark's dramatic sequence of events.[46] Coming in the aftermath of the unqualified approval of the Gentiles, this very Jewish principle amounts to a concession to the Jews. Even though the Gentiles were admitted at the price of the Jewish tradition, it is on Gentile ground that the Jewish prerogative of the Kingdom is affirmed. Mark, it seems, has taken every pain to give equal recognition to the Jewish and Gentile side alike.

The subsequent journey follows an awkwardly roundabout route. From northern Tyre the way leads through Sidon, which is still further north, to the southern Lake of Galilee via the southeastern Decapolis. This topological recital brings to mind an earlier review in 3:7–12, which had summarized Jesus' *total* program. It was in part designed to offer the disciples a taste of the ecumenical nature of the Kingdom, before they were officially installed into discipleship (3:13–19). With the exception of Idumea, Jesus will carry out this program by sanctioning all these places with his presence.[47] Now, at the completion of the Gentile mission, he departs from Tyre (the place of his last exorcism), moves up to Sidon (mentioned in the program, but as yet not visited), and traverses through the Decapolis (referred to in the program with *peran tou Iordanou*, and visited at the first eastern arrival) to the Lake of Galilee. In sweeping fashion 7:31 summarizes the *Gentile* mission. In the midst of it *eis tēn thalassan tēs Galilaias* appears out of place. Only at this point, at the conclusion of the Gentile mission, does Mark designate the eastern side (we have as yet not crossed over to the west) as the Lake of Galilee. In view of his skillful presentation of the unity message through the medium of travels and places, this can hardly be accidental. The whole area of Tyre, Sidon, and the Decapolis is with the aid of the prepositional connectives *ek*, *dia*, and *ana* drawn together into one Gentile domain which borders on what now is revealed to be the Lake of Galilee. The eastern side, and everything it stands for, has become Galilee. The differences between Jew and Gentile, west and east are nullified, and the Kingdom's drive to cover "all of Galilee" is consummated.[48]

A last healing, performed on a deaf mute, rounds out the work of the

46. *Chortasthēnai* (7:27b) provides the verbal link backward to the Jewish feeding (6:42) and forward to the Gentile feeding (8:4, 8).

47. T. A. Burkill, *New Light on the Earliest Gospel* (Ithaca, N.Y.: Cornell University Press, 1972), p. 88.

48. Our interpretation of the journey in 7:31 combines the insights of Burkill, *New Light*, pp. 71–95; Ferdinand Hahn, *Mission in the New Testament*, trans. Frank Clarke (Naperville, Ill.: Alec R. Allenson, Inc., 1965), pp. 111–20; Willi Marxsen, *Mark the Evangelist*, trans. Roy A. Harrisville *et al.* (Nashville, Tenn.: Abingdon Press, 1969), pp. 66–75.

Kingdom among the Gentiles (7:32–37). Throughout the course of the mission around the lake the theme of ethnic unity is accompanied by a noticeable pattern of sexual parallelism. Prior to the apostolic commission and Jewish designation Jesus showed individual concern for a man in the east (5:1–20) and two women in the west (5:21–43); prior to the Gentile designation he attended to two women (7:24–30) and now a man (7:32–37) in the east. The unity of the Kingdom embraces Jew and Gentile, as well as man and woman on either side.

After the "Gentile issue" is resolved, Jesus designates in a second feeding on the eastern side what can only be the Gentile part of the Galilean Kingdom (8:1–10). This time he explains to the disciples that the crowd has been with him for three days without food (8:2). Again we notice the anticipation of a future event. The disciples must remember, it was after three days that Jesus took pity on the Gentiles. The beginning of the Gentile mission is projected into the time after death and resurrection. As in the first feeding, the disciples are actively drawn into the event and instructed into the bread distribution (8:6). But judging from their superficial questioning (8:4), they have not penetrated any more deeply than before the implications of this feeding.

The fifth voyage (8:10) cannot be considered a trip back to the west shore, because the crossing signals (*eis to peran, diaperan*) are absent. In analogy to the third trip, it merely causes a change of place, this time along the eastern coast. At the conclusion of Jesus' great mission around the lake, Jerusalem, represented by the Pharisees, asserts its authority and throws down the gauntlet (8:11–13). A Kingdom in antithesis to Jerusalem and open to the Gentiles is totally unacceptable, unless substantiated by heavenly interposition. A sign is to verify the miracles. But Jesus' miracles had been the sign. His mission was the message. Beyond that no sign will be given.

The time of departure for the west (8:13: *eis to peran*) has finally arrived (8:14–21).[49] During this last crossing tension between Jesus and the disciples reaches an unprecedented height. Among themselves the disciples wonder about the shortage of loaves, for there is only one loaf in the boat (8:14, 16). Interpolated into this discipleship context is Jesus' warning against the leaven of the Pharisees and of Herod (8:15). This construction illustrates a correlation between the disciples' bread dis-

---

49. Verses 8:14–21 is a Markan construction, see Ambrozic, *Kingdom*, p. 69; Martin Dibelius, *From Tradition to Gospel*, trans. Bertram L. Woolf (New York: Charles Scribner's Sons, n.d.), p. 229; Taylor, *St. Mark*, p. 363.

cussion and the Pharisaic/Herodian leaven. What the Pharisees and
Herod have in common is their opposition to the Kingdom of God. The
Pharisees had objected to the Gentile inclusion (7:1–23) and challenged
Jesus' Kingdom mission (8:11–23); Herod had instigated the death of the
forerunner (6:17–29). The disciples, however, blindly wondering about
their lack of loaves, are on the verge of siding with these opposition
forces.[50] They are in possession of the one loaf, and yet their discussion
stays on the level of food supply and bread shortage. Notwithstanding
their intimate experience of Jesus' traveling pattern, they remain oblivi-
ous to the unity of the Kingdom. Frustrated over their incorrigible conduct, Jesus reinforces his charge of hardness of heart (8:17d; 6:52b) by
the accusation of the blindness of eyes and deafness of ears (8:18), the
very words which in the mystery speech had thrust the family of Jesus
and the Jerusalem authorities to the outside (4:12). In effect, the disciples
are exposed as members of the outside opposition, in league with Herod,
the relatives, and the Jerusalem authorities. One last time Jesus tries to
bring them to their senses by singling out the two epochal feeding events,
which epitomize the total purpose of the Galilean mission.[51] Do they not
recognize the abundance of blessing poured out over Jews and Gentiles
alike? On this inconclusive note of tension and blindness and with a foreboding question mark the Gentile mission comes to an end.

CONCLUSION

In 4:35–8:21 Mark comes to terms with the Gentile mission and the
ethnic identity of his community. In a plot full of complications and
dramatic surprises he narrates the elementary story of a Kingdom split in
two, but unified as one. To accomplish his purpose he utilizes the symbols of bread, boat, lake, the two seashores and the six voyages. The boat
trips are designed to dramatize, not a centrifugal course of action, spin-
ning out from the Galilean center to ever more distant lands, but a uni-
tive movement, alternating between the two sides of the sea. The lake,
losing its force as a barrier, is transposed into a symbol of unity, bridging

---

50. I owe this understanding of the puzzling interpolation 8:15 to Karl-Georg
Reploh, *Markus—Lehrer der Gemeinde*, Stuttgarter Biblische Monographien, No. 9
(Stuttgart: Katholisches Bibelwerk, 1969), pp. 81–86.

51. It may be objected to our interpretation of 4:35–8:21 that we exaggerate the
voyage pattern, discipleship and the theme of ethnic unity, while completely eliminating the christological content. But the summarizing, redactional 8:14–21 alerts us
to what is of primary importance to Mark: the two feeding events, which had taken
place on either side of the lake, and the disciples' continued incomprehension.

the gulf between Jewish and Gentile Christians. The two are the one. Galilee is no longer ethnically confined to either a Jewish or a Gentile Christian identity, rather "all of Galilee" is where Jewish Christians and Gentile Christians live together in the newness of the Kingdom.

For obvious reasons Mark found the two analogous miracle catenae highly attractive. This duplication of traditional material was ideally suited to mirror the bifocal experience of his own communal life. He mobilizes the miracle resources for his story of Jesus' mission of unity and the disciples' increasing delinquency. As a corollary of this, the epiphanic coloring of the tradition is subdued, and the miracles are transformed into signs.[52] What we fail to notice, however, is a vigorous polemic aimed pointblank at the *theios anēr* christology.[53] The miracles are not emptied of all numinous features and thrown back at their agents, but they are used to fill positive roles in the drama of a twofold, yet united Kingdom. Mark does not adopt the tradition in order to disavow it, but he modifies it with his mind set on the Kingdom program. His Jesus is still a miracle worker of massive proportions, but he performs these miracles in the service of the Kingdom and on behalf of its two-fold unity.

The polemic which does permeate the Galilean Kingdom plot is conspicuously directed at the family of Jesus and the Jerusalem authorities. But neither one of them is representative of a *theios anēr* theology. As for the family, its theological position remains obscure. Jerusalem is shown to have provoked the schism by adopting the provincial stance of southern orthodoxy and exclusiveness. More and more, however, the disciples emerge as the real powers that stand in the way of the fulfillment of the Kingdom. From the outset they are anxious to retard the movement toward "all of Galilee." Throughout, they cannot follow the logical pattern of Jesus' travels. Although they are step-by-step, and act-by-act,

---

52. In principle, Mark's handling of the miracle catenae is similar to John's appropriation of his miracle source, as clarified for us by A. Fauré, R. Bultmann, R. Fortna, E. Haenchen, J. Robinson, J. Becker and others. But this similarity was recognized before. See Ernst Lohmeyer, *Das Evangelium des Markus,* 17th ed. (Göttingen: Vandenhoeck & Ruprecht, 1967), p. 135; Raymond E. Brown, *The Gospel According to John,* The Anchor Bible, No. 29 (Garden City, N.Y.: Doubleday & Company, Inc., 1966), p. 247.

53. Recently it has become fashionable to interpret Mark's use of miracles almost entirely *via negativa.* Mark adopted the *theios anēr* miracles in order to combat a *theios anēr* christology, see for example Achtemeier, "Origin," pp. 218–21. Difficult to understand is Weeden's (*Mark,* pp. 52–69, *passim*) thesis. Prior to 8:30 Mark presents a picture of a Jesus saturated with *theios anēr* miracles. Peter's confession (8:30) to such a Jesus summarizes this christology which in turn is refuted by Jesus' suffering Son of Man (8:31). Hence, at 8:31 the whole christology of 1:1–8:30 is exposed as wrong!

guided into the purpose of his mission, the voyages find no congenial response among them. In the end they are banished to the outside, at one with the family and the Jerusalem establishment, as indeed their objections to Jesus are not unlike those of Jerusalem.

We must pause and one more time recall the facts to memory. The apostolic Kingdom is emancipated from the family of Jesus by a carefully executed schism, disestablished from the Jerusalem powers by a second schism, and finally placed in opposition to the disciples. These are extraordinary circumstances that give birth to the Galilean Kingdom, and they call for an extraordinary answer. In our discussion of the controversy stories it has become clear that Mark was engaged in an internal Christian struggle, opposing what appeared to be a Jewish-Christian identity. By now the Christianity rejected by Mark is more distinctly profiled in the form of the relatives of Jesus, the Jerusalem authorities, and above all the disciples under the leadership of Peter. At this point we postulate a Christian community which traced its origin to the relatives of Jesus, considered itself standing in unbroken tradition with the twelve under the primacy of Peter, and advocated a faith in so Jewish a fashion as to be—in the eyes of Mark, the opponent—virtually indistinguishable from, and thus guilty of cooperating with, the Jewish power structure. These features point to the mother church of Jerusalem.[54] Granted that the history of the Jerusalem community is wrapped in darkness, there can be agreement on the following points. The Jewish Christians of the city did not relinquish the law, they held the family of Jesus in high esteem, they revered Peter, at least until the rise of James, and they looked with respect upon the disciples, at times selecting a core group of three "pillars" among them. If Mark does indeed polemicize against southern Christians, his preference for Galilee may also be conditioned by his geographical experience. Perhaps Galilee came to be a positive symbol for him, because he is the spokesman of Christians who live in the largely Gentile north. More recently the thesis of a northern Christian community was advocated by Marxsen.[55] But he failed to perceive the gospel's anti-Jerusalem bias. It is our hypothesis that Mark is representative of a

---

54. In linking the Markan opposition with Jerusalem we are indebted to the insights of the following four scholars: Joseph B. Tyson, "The Blindness of the Disciples in Mark," *JBL*, 80 (1961), pp. 265–67; Etienne Trocmé, *La Formation de l'Evangile selon Marc* (Paris: Presses Universitaires de France, 1963); Kenzo Tagawa, *Miracles et Evangile* (Paris: Presses Universitaires de France, 1966); John D. Crossan, "Mark and the Relatives of Jesus," *NovTest*, 15 (1973), pp. 81–113.

55. Marxsen, *Mark*, pp. 57–95.

northern Christianity which is in opposition to a southern, Jerusalem-type Christianity.

With the conclusion of the voyages the Kingdom in Galilee has come into its own, and the disciples should likewise have come of age. But as they join Jesus on his way down south, they leave without memory of this apostolic, emancipated Kingdom in the north.

Chapter IV

THE FUTURE OF THE KINGDOM

8:22–10:52
8:27–9:13
9:2-8

The central section (8:22–10:52) more than any other part of the gospel bears the imprint of a skillfully designed composition.[1] For the interpreter this calls for a shift from redaction criticism to composition criticism. So strongly marked is the final text by the Markan purpose that we will refrain from delving into the background of the traditional sources and sayings. Whatever the history of the units of tradition, Mark has arranged them into a new context which is wholly his own. We will glean the redactional viewpoint from the structure of the composition, the organizational patterns, the arrangement of the material, and the sequence of the events.

Thematically, this mid-section is structured by the motif of the way. Quite possibly, the gospel conceives of Jesus' life from the very outset in terms of a journey. John the Baptist prepares the way which Jesus is to travel (1:2–3).[2] This way of Jesus is made up of a continuous sequence of

1. Ernst Haenchen, "Die Komposition von Mk VIII:27–IX:1," *NovTest*, 6 (1963), pp. 81–109; Norman Perrin, "Towards an Interpretation of the Gospel of Mark," *Christology and a Modern Pilgrimage* (N. Perrin Festschrift), ed. Hans D. Betz (Claremont, Calif.: New Testament Colloquium, 1971), pp. 7–30; Maria Horstmann, *Studien zur Markinischen Christologie*, Neutestamentliche Abhandlungen, No. 6 (Münster: Aschendorff, 1969), *passim*.
2. The programmatic force of the way motif in 1:2–3 was recognized by Aloysius M. Ambrozic, *The Hidden Kingdom*, The Catholic Biblical Quarterly-Monograph Series, No. 2 (Washington, D.C.: The Catholic Biblical Association of America, 1972), pp. 19–20. The possibility of a redactional compilation of this compound citation formula, 1:2–3, ought to be considered. What 1:2 and 1:3 have in common is *hodos*. Possibly Mark put together quotations on the basis of *hodos*, a concept to which he wished to draw attention from the outset.

entries and exits. Both *eiserchesthai* and *exerchesthai* appear to be part of a Markan scheme which is in evidence throughout the gospel. The entry motif is used in almost stereotyped fashion to depict Jesus' entrance into a house, a boat, a synagogue, a town, the temple, and the Kingdom. The following occurrences may be said to be redactional: 1:21, 45; 2:1; 3:1, 20; 5:39; 7:17, 24; 9:28, 43, 45, 47; 10:15, 23, 24, 25; 11:11, 15. The entry motif is complemented by an exit motif which likewise persists from beginning to end: 1:29, 35, 38, 45; 2:13; 5:2; 6:1, 12, 34, 54; 7:31; 8:27; 9:30; 10:17, 46; 11:11, 12; 14:26; 16:8.[3] This rhythmic pattern of involvement and breakup imposes a mark of urgency and restlessness upon the ministry of Jesus. He journeys from place to place as if drawn by some distant goal. Leaving behind him the formation of the Jewish-Gentile Kingdom in the north, he begins his journey southward. Outwardly, the mid-section depicts Jesus traveling from Caesarea Philippi to Jerusalem. But more is implied by the narration of Jesus' actual journey from north to south. The way, a fundamental metaphor of life, is capable of transmitting multifarious levels of truth. We shall in this chapter discuss four aspects of Jesus' way from Galilee to the south.

First, the way ties experiences into a comprehensive sequence and thereby suggests the purposefulness of Jesus' life. His journeys are not erratic wanderings, but calculated movements aimed at the full realization of the Kingdom of God. There is a purpose to his traveling ministry. If people are immobilized by the destruction of Jerusalem, and stagnating in hopelessness, the way of Jesus will take them out of despair to new hope. Second, the way has an eye opening and mind-expanding function. As Jesus journeys to Jerusalem he discloses his full identity to the disciples. Prior to entry into the city they will have been granted complete initiation into Jesus' messiahship. They are, or ought to be, fully prepared for the Jerusalem events. Third, the way has a beginning as well as an end. For the first time the goal of Jesus' way comes into view. The death bell rings loud and clear, and yet, the way is not a journey unto death alone. Prominently displayed at the center of the journey is the ultimate goal, which lies beyond death. In true Markan fashion, the sight of the goal raises the issue of the beginning. Birth and beginning are curiously interrelated to goal and ending. In this chapter we will give most of our attention to the goal which is previewed in the transfiguration account. Fourth, the way may spell tragedy and indeed turn into a pilgrimage to

---

3. The redactional use of *eiserchesthai* and *exerchesthai* is noticed by Ulrich Luz, "Das Geheimnismotiv und die Markinische Christologie," *ZNW*, 51 (1965), pp. 14–15.

death. This, of course, will be the fate of the disciples. They never grasp the teleological orientation of Jesus' travels. As a result, they lose the way, literally perish along the wayside, and never reach the goal. Theirs is the road to ruin.

ON THE WAY

The central section is placed into the framework of the "way." At the outset Jesus and his disciples are reported to be "on the way" (8:27: *en tē hodō*), and at the end Bartimaeus is said to have followed Jesus "on the way" (10:52: *en tē hodō*). Interspersed throughout this mid-section the way motif is featured four more times. The disciples are twice said to have engaged in a discussion "on the way" (9:33, 34: *en tē hodō*), Jesus continues traveling "along the way" (10:17: *eis hodon*), and toward the end of the section it is disclosed that he is "on the way" (10:32: *en tē hodō*) to Jerusalem. The way motif appears in exclusively redactional verses; both Matthew and Luke eliminate this Markan *hodos* with telling regularity.[4]

The section is skillfully subdivided by three passion-resurrection predictions (8:31; 9:31; 10:33–34), each of which is placed into a different geographical locale. The first prediction is situated in the area of Caesarea Philippi (8:27), the second one is given in Galilee (9:30), and the third one on the way to Jerusalem (10:32). Three additional place names strategically spaced through the mid-section further strengthen the effect of the journey: Capernaum (9:33), the region of Judea and beyond the Jordan (10:1), and Jericho (10:46). Of these six locations, four can be credited to the redaction (9:30; 9:33; 10:1; 10:32). The very first and last names (8:27; 10:46) are anchored in the tradition.

From a literary perspective, the formal ordering of this section, the carefully set pattern of the predictions, and the pervasiveness of the way motif reflect the understanding that there is order and purpose to Jesus' ministry. Above all, it is the underlying theme of the way which provides structure and meaning. Mark placed the Caesarea Philippi and Jericho traditions at the margins of this section, and between them inserted topological reference marks which mediate the movement from one place to the other. With the aid of the redactional device of the way and by setting up geographical signposts along this way a journey is created that

---

4. The one exception is Matthew 20:17. Outside this central section *hodos* is either located in the tradition (4:4, 15; 6:8; 11:8), or used in a figurative sense (12:14).

gives direction to the life of Jesus. The goal, Jerusalem, is for the first time announced at the occasion of the third and last passion-resurrection prediction (10:32, 33). 11:1, the transition from the journey to the Jerusalem section proper, announces Jesus' arrival in the vicinity of Jerusalem. The journey is undertaken with the definite purpose of going to Jerusalem. It remains to be seen, however, whether the city is indeed the final goal.

Thematically, the purpose of this way to the city is articulated in the three passion-resurrection predictions. Jerusalem will become the place of Jesus' death and resurrection. The *dei* in the first prediction subordinates the journey to the stern force of divine necessity. It is under the pressure of a binding obligation that Jesus travels to meet in Jerusalem his death and resurrection. An air of fatefulness and inevitability hovers over this whole journey. But despite the divinely ordained necessity of Jesus' passion and resurrection, the realm of freedom and personal decision remains untouched. Jesus himself takes the initiative and wills his fate. In full consciousness and with deliberation he embarks upon the way to the cross, and it is on this way that at three successive "stations of the cross" he reiterates his determination to go the way to the end. He *must* go to Jerusalem and there meet his personal crisis, and through crisis, his glory.

SHOWING THE WAY

The central section is enclosed by two stories, each dealing with the healing of a blind man: 8:22–26, the healing of the blind man of Bethsaida, and 10:46–52, the healing of the blind Bartimaeus. These carefully placed framing stories serve to qualify the whole intervening section, i.e., the healings cast light on the journey to Jerusalem. What Jesus does at the beginning and end of the trip, open the eyes of blind men: this he is in effect doing all along his way to the city. He opens the eyes of the disciples and initiates them into a new dimension of his messiahship.[5] The disciples, traveling the way of Jesus, pass through the "stations of the cross" and should thereby experience a broadening of their christological perception. But it is only by walking completely the road with Jesus that they would learn to see him fully, i.e., as the suffering, dying, and rising Messiah who deliberately moves to meet his fate. Aside from one notable

5. Rudolf Bultmann, *History of the Synoptic Tradition*, trans. John Marsh, 3rd ed. (New York: Harper & Row, 1963), p. 350.

event (the transfiguration), the full identity of Jesus is disclosed at the three "stations of the cross." With this christological knowledge in mind, the disciples should be almost sufficiently prepared for what is to come in Jerusalem.

Each passion-resurrection prediction is followed by a discourse on discipleship (8:34–37; 9:33–37; 10:35–45). The bulk of these conversations between Jesus and the disciples centers around the qualifications of discipleship. While walking the way with Jesus, the disciples learn that true discipleship means to deny oneself, to take up one's cross, to lose one's life, to be last and least, to drink the cup that Jesus is to drink, and to be baptized with Jesus' baptism. This radical discipleship message is both preached and dramatically executed through the medium of the way. By weaving the passion-resurrection predictions and the discipleship discourses into the narration of the way of Jesus, Mark interrelates christology with the anthropological implications, and the life of Jesus with that of the disciples. The way of Jesus is the way of the disciples, and discipleship consists in walking the way of Jesus. This is the meaning of *akolouthein*, to follow, in the gospel of Mark. Jesus leads the way (10:32b: *kai ēn proagōn autous*) and the disciples are to follow him (10:32d: *hoi de akolouthountes*). Jesus not merely preaches the way, but he literally shows the way.[6] If they follow after the Jesus *proagōn*, they will not only learn their leader's identity, but in the process find themselves and their own calling. Full knowledge of Jesus will give them insight into their own nature and destiny. But again, if they are to grasp Jesus and know themselves, they will have to go the way of Jesus, and they will have to walk it to the end. As the leader so are his followers called to walk through the strait gate of suffering to glory.

END OF THE WAY

We will focus our attention upon 8:27–9:13, the section which includes and leads up to the transfiguration event. Jesus' question concerning his identity (8:27) precipitates Peter's "confession" (8:29) which in turn undergoes correction by Jesus' first passion-resurrection prediction (8:31). This passion-resurrection credo evolves into a homily on discipleship (8:34–37) which explicates the meaning of Jesus' passion and glory to the disciples. 8:38 forms the transition from discipleship to eschatology. This

---

6. Functionally, the *hodos* motif in Mark already approaches the personalized, Johannine sense (John 14:6).

word of warning for the first time conjures up the parousia of the Son of Man. The eschatological logion 9:1, a word of consolation, constitutes the first undisguised reference to the Kingdom's future dimension. Death will be spared for some of this present generation because the Kingdom will arrive during their lifetime. It is noteworthy that the way of the disciples is outlined *after* the little credo of passion and resurrection and *prior* to the eschatological credo. This structure reflects not the logic of the ministry of Jesus (where passion, resurrection, and parousia are as yet events of the future), but rather the logic of the Markan experience of history. The Markan Christians live *between* the two salvation events of death-resurrection on one end and parousia on the other. With the death and resurrection of Jesus as their point of departure, and with the prospect of a fully realized Kingdom in the near future, they travel at present the way of Jesus. Life and conduct at present are oriented toward the eschatological advent of the Son of Man. At his parousia he will redeem their faith and efforts. Walking the way they are making their future.

Evolving from the past, moving through the present, and advancing toward the future, the way gravitates toward a peak which is marked by the high mountain of the transfiguration. In view of the Markan perspective of the present as being midway between past passion-resurrection and future parousia, it seems doubtful whether the transfiguration looks forward to the resurrection.

Despite prolific studies on the transfiguration pericope (9:2–8), not so much as a minimum of consensus has been attained.[7] The liberal Life of Christ research sought to locate the transfiguration as a personal experience in the ministry of Jesus, or in the life of Peter.[8] The unusually high density of religious motifs prompted other scholars to illuminate our understanding of 9:2–8 by exploring the Jewish background of such themes as the high mountain, the metamorphosis, the heavenly voice, Elijah and Moses, and the three booths.[9] Frequently the transfiguration was interpreted through the medium of Exodus 24, and Jesus was viewed

---

7. Heinrich Baltensweiler, *Die Verklärung Jesu*, Abhandlungen zur Theologie des Alten und Neuen Testaments, No. 33 (Zurich: Zwingli-Verlag, 1959), p. 9.

8. A good example of a liberal interpretation of the transfiguration is furnished by Eduard Meyer, *Ursprung und Anfänge des Christentums*, Vol. I (Stuttgart and Berlin: Cotta, 1921), pp. 153–57. The author considered the transfiguration to be a vision of Peter.

9. A good example of this history of religion approach is furnished by Harald Riesenfeld, *L'Arrière-Plan de Récit Évangélique de la Transfiguration de Notre-Seigneur*, Acta Seminarii Neotestamentici Upsaliensis, No. 16 (Copenhagen: Ejnar Munksgaard, 1947).

as a second Moses. The very richness of motifs has also been the source of a dilemma. Each motif lends itself to a great variety of readings, and unless an interpretative criterion is brought to bear upon the transfiguration tradition, confusion prevails. The chief weakness of most interpretations lies in their disregard of the pericope's contextual determinants. For a tradition as equivocal as the transfiguration unit, the safest method for a proper understanding lies in a study of the surrounding text.[10] 9:2–8 lies embedded in the redactionally structured mid-section. We have already noticed its locus at an eschatological culmination point, dramatically marked by the high mountain. The most immediate frame is furnished by 8:38–9:1 and 9:9–10. 9:1 is a formerly isolated logion introduced with the Markan citation formula, while 9:9–10 is a Markan composition throughout.[11] It is this intensely eschatological frame which conditions the intervening transfiguration unit. Proceeding from the external to the internal, we will commence our analysis with the frame, and then read the transfiguration motifs in relation to Mark's contextual criterion.

The Kingdom saying 9:1[12] features a number of characteristics which suggest that Mark appropriated it to his Kingdom theology. The phrase *idein tēn basileian* stands out because of its singular occurrence in the synoptic tradition.[13] In Mark, *idein* denotes the eschatological experience (13:26; 14:62), which is however anticipated by sporadic glimpses at the true nature of Jesus (5:6, 22; 9:20; 15:39). The *seeing* of the Kingdom is the appropriate designation for a crucial stage in the history of the Kingdom. Since the Kingdom exists at present in disguise, but exists thus for the purpose of being revealed, Mark in the first reference to the Kingdom's future manifestation adequately describes it as entry into the phase of visibility. Similarly, the use of *dynamis* in conjunction with *idein-opsesthai* (9:1; 13:26) implies that "the earlier coming of Jesus, and the first appearing of the Kingdom of God, were not *meta dynameōs, en*

---

10. Bultmann, *Tradition*, p. 306; Joachim Rohde, *Rediscovering the Teaching of the Evangelists*, trans. Dorothea M. Barton (Philadelphia: Westminster Press, 1968), p. 20.

11. Horstmann, *Studien*, p. 106, *passim*.

12. Among the numerous studies on 9:1 the following three are of special importance: Günther Bornkamm, "Die Verzögerung der Parusie," *In Memoriam Ernst Lohmeyer*, ed. W. Schmauch (Stuttgart: Evangelisches Verlagswerk, 1951), pp. 116–26; Anton Vögtle, "Exegetische Erwägungen über das Wissen und Selbstbewusstsein Jesu," *Gott und Welt*, Vol. I (Karl Rahner Festschrift) J. B. Metz *et al.* eds. (Freiburg: Herder, 1964), pp. 642–47; Norman Perrin, "The Composition of Mark IX, 1," *NovTest*, 11 (1969), pp. 67–70.

13. This formula occurs only one more time in the New Testament, in John 3:3.

dynamei."[14] *Dynamis* in 9:1 signifies the apocalyptic exposure of the Kingdom. The unusual perfect participle *elēlythyian* recalls the studied use of the perfect tense in 1:15. In 9:1 it denotes the continued existence of the Kingdom over a period of time and its eschatological arrival at some future point.[15] Whatever the precise formulation of this pre-Markan Kingdom logion was, it is unlikely to have referred to a seeing of the Kingdom's arrival in full power. The redaction has shaped this Kingdom saying so as to give full expression to the apocalyptic breakthrough of the hitherto hidden Kingdom.

8:38 is the first explicit announcement of the parousia and 9:1 the first undisguised forecast of the Kingdom in the future sense. On the analogy of 1:14–15, whereby Jesus' first appearance was synchronized with the present arrival of the Kingdom, Mark joined 9:1, the future arrival of the Kingdom, to 8:38, the "second" appearance of Jesus. From beginning to end Jesus is the proclaimer and bringer of the Kingdom. In the last analysis, the Kingdom can be *seen*, because its arrival entails the parousia of Jesus which is an event to be *seen* (13:26; 14:62). After the present arrival of the Kingdom was programmatically stated in Jesus' inaugural message (1:14–15), and the Kingdom's hidden dimension explained in the mystery speech (4:1–34), its future status is for the first time articulated in 9:1. With one exception (11:10), all further Kingdom sayings refer to the Kingdom solely in its future condition (9:47; 10:15, 23, 24, 25; 12:34; 14:25; 15:43). Beginning at 9:1 events precipitate toward the apocalyptic breakthrough of the Kingdom, and the transfiguration pericope stands precisely at this eschatological turning point. What the three disciples are privileged to *see* (9:8, 9) on the high mount of transfiguration is not the resurrection, but a preview of the eschatological promise of the parousia.

Passing over the transfiguration pericope we turn next to the second framing unit, 9:9–10. Both the secrecy motif (9:9) and the disciples' lack of understanding (9:10) attest to a redactional construction. The change of place (mountain scene—descent from mountain) indicates a shift in dramatic orientation. The Markan Jesus descending from the mountain delivers the commentary on the preceding mountain mystery. The *eidon* in 9:9 resumes the *eidon* of 9:8, but ultimately harks back to the *seeing* in 9:1 (*idōsin*). Exclusively accessible to the perception of *seeing*, the

---

14. Charles K. Barrett, *The Holy Spirit and the Gospel Tradition* (London: S.P.C.K., 1966), p. 73.
15. Against Charles H. Dodd's famous interpretation that the Kingdom of God has arrived in the past of Jesus, see *The Parables of the Kingdom*, rev. ed. (New York: Charles Scribner's Sons, 1961), pp. 37–38.

transfiguration is earmarked as an epiphany. What distinguishes this epiphany from others is the well-known fact that Mark has furnished it with the date of its final disclosure (9:9). The transfiguration is thus meant to be an anticipation of something the full realization of which is yet to come, or yet to be grasped. Its truth must not be divulged until the resurrection of the Son of Man has taken place.

At this point we turn against the dominant consensus of scholarly opinion which equates the guarded secret of the transfiguration with Jesus' resurrection. Precisely what is said is that the transfiguration epiphany must remain under cover until the resurrection. The resurrection opens the way to and sets the date for the full realization of the mountain experience. In itself it is not the subject matter of the epiphany, but the *terminus post quem* of its fulfillment. After the resurrection the disciples should have remembered this transfigured Son of God they had previously experienced on the high mountain in the north. According to Mark's logic, death and resurrection will release the disciples toward the road of discipleship, and the only goal ahead, the only promise unredeemed will be the parousia.

Dramatically, Mark demonstrates the coherence of 9:9–13 by staging the entire discussion between Jesus and the disciples during the descent from the mountain. Structurally, 9:9–13 forms a distinctly organized text, held together by two Son of Man sayings, one referring to the rising of the Son of Man (9:9b), the other to his suffering (9:12c, d), so as to "conform to a passion announcement with all its parts."[16] Whatever pre-Markan elements there may be in 9:11–13, in their present arrangement these verses continue Mark's commentary on the transfiguration.

The discussion carried on in 9:11–13 centers on Elijah, who had played a role in the transfiguration scene. The disciples regard him in the traditional sense as the forerunner (9:11: *dei elthein prōton*) who is to usher in not the resurrection, but the reign of God. Their concern about the dating of the eschaton echoes 9:1, the Kingdom word of consolation. Jesus' answer concentrates upon the identification of Elijah with John the Baptist. He comes first (9:12b: *prōton*) not to announce the resurrection on the third day, but the final epiphany itself. Verses 9:11–13 therefore not only tie up with the eschatological prophecy of 9:1, but the verses also single out a figure of the transfiguration scene in a highly eschatological sense.

16. Heinz Eduard Tödt, *The Son of Man in the Synoptic Tradition*, trans. Dorothea M. Barton, 2nd ed. (Philadelphia: Westminster Press, 1965), p. 197.

9:11–13 comes to life only when read against the background of a controversy revolving around the forerunner function of John the Baptist. The Markan argumentation defends the identification of the Baptist with Elijah, the eschatological forerunner, as an article of Christian faith. The apologetic nature of his argument is indicated by the double reference to Scripture (9:12c: *pōs gegraptai*; 9:13c: *kathōs gegraptai*), as well as by the polemics against the murderers of John (9:13b: *kai epoiēsan autō hosa ēthelon*). Malachi's prophecy, Mark contends, has been fulfilled. The Baptist was indeed the precursor who restores everything first,[17] and he has in fact appeared in history. The details of Mark's reasoning, however, are tied to the tragic ending of John. It is John's suffering and death which receives support from Scripture. As it was written of the Son of Man, so is it also written of Elijah! Mark argues from the death of the Son of Man backward to the Baptist's death.[18] The Son of Man's death serves to vindicate the Baptist's death. Mark's apology throws into relief the opponents' objection. In their opinion, John cannot be the promised Elijah, because his violent death contradicts his expected role as the eschatological restorer. A suffering, executed man does not fulfill the forerunner qualifications as set forth by Malachi. The controversy centered around the scandal of the death of the Baptist, and not, as H. E. Tödt[19] suggested, around the Son of Man's death. The Markan argument in 9:11–13 is designed to uphold the eschatological function of John the Baptist despite his, in the eyes of the opponents, objectionable and disqualifying suffering. It is because of his passion that John is said to be ideally qualified to prepare the way of his suffering master.

Mark has woven the transfiguration tradition (9:2–8) into an eschatological pattern (8:38–9:1, 9:9–13) of Kingdom expectation and parousia hope. 8:38–9:1 directs attention forward to the eschatological goal, and 9:9–10 comments on the post-resurrectional dating of this goal. 9:11–13 reaffirms the identity of John the Baptist as the forerunner of the eschaton. Standing at the gospel's eschatological turning point, and at the focal point of a concentrated Kingdom-parousia context, the transfiguration emerges as a parousia epiphany. Its individual features must now be interpreted in conformity to its context.

17. The future tense *apokatastēsei* of the LXX is replaced by the present tense *apokathistanei*.
18. It is one of Willi Marxsen's (*Mark the Evangelist*, trans. Roy A. Harrisville *et al.* [Nashville, Tenn.: Abingdon, 1969], p. 32) most perceptive insights into the gospel composition that "Mark composes backward."
19. Tödt, *Son of Man*, p. 196, n. 1.

A vast array of primarily Old Testament sources has been assembled to account for the transfiguration's unusual dating "after six days" (9:2). Exodus 24, as indicated above, seemed to furnish the prototypal explanation. As Moses waited on Mount Sinai for six days until Yahweh revealed Himself on the seventh day, so does God disclose Jesus' true nature on the seventh day. The similarities between the Moses on Mount Sinai and the Jesus on the mount of transfiguration are unmistakable. But there are discriminations to be made. Jesus and the chosen disciples do not ascend the mountain until after the sixth day, while Moses spends six days waiting on the mountain until Yahweh's manifestation on the seventh day. More importantly, the transfiguration scene reveals the glory of Jesus, but on Sinai it is the glory of Yahweh, and not that of Moses, which shines forth (Ex. 24:17). While some features of Exodus 24 may well have found their way into 9:2–8, the Jesus of the transfiguration is not modeled after the Moses of Sinai. Moses' own participation in the transfiguration scene together with Jesus refutes this theory.

One of the more imaginative explanations for the six days has been offered by J. Schreiber.[20] He starts with the assumption that Markan chronology structures Jesus' Jerusalem ministry into precisely seven days: first day, 11:1–11; second day, 11:12–19; third day, 11:20–13:37; fourth and fifth day, 14:1–11; sixth day, 14:12–72; seventh day, 15:1–47 (see 15:42). At one point this Jerusalem chronology forges an analogical bond with the transfiguration chronology: both the death of Jesus and the transfiguration epiphany occur on the seventh day. Since, according to Schreiber's reading of Markan theology, Jesus' death signals the moment of his resurrection and exaltation, the transfiguration is said to anticipate Jesus' death, resurrection and exaltation. While Schreiber deserves credit for trying to grasp the meaning of the six days "from within," i.e., by means of internal criticism, his thesis raises at once a methodological and a theological question. Methodologically, only a forced interpretation of chronological references arrives at the schematization of a holy week. Apparently Mark placed Jesus' pre-passion time in Jerusalem into the framework of three successive days (11:11; 11:12, 15; 11:27). But the passion chronology proper is full of ambiguities and does not continue the preceding three days into a seven day period.[21] Theologically, Schreiber's

---

20. Johannes Schreiber, *Theologie des Vertrauens* (Hamburg: Furche-Verlag, 1967), pp. 119–20.
21. Ernst Lohmeyer, *Das Evangelium des Markus*, 17th ed. (Göttingen: Vandenhoeck & Ruprecht, 1967), pp. 227–28; Ernst Haenchen, *Der Weg Jesu*, 2nd ed. rev. (Berlin: Walter de Gruyter & Co., 1968), p. 373, n. 1.

shrinking of resurrection and exaltation into the moment of death mistakes Mark's essentially apocalyptic frame of mind for John's realized eschatology.

The most ingenious suggestion in recent times comes from N. Perrin.[22] He detects a relation between the six days of the transfiguration and the three days of the passion-resurrection predictions. The *meta hēmeras hex* of the transfiguration and the *meta treis hēmeras* of all prediction units effect a discrimination between resurrection and parousia: "after three days, the resurrection; after six days, the parousia."[23] Perrin's proposal has the advantage of correlating the gospel's only time references outside the passion narrative, and correlating them in such a way as to conform to the structural pattern of 8:27–9:13: death and resurrection after three days, the way of discipleship, the parousia after six days. The separate, yet correlated time references keep the resurrection of the past apart from the parousia of the future, and confirm the intervening experience of discipleship as the way toward the parousia promise.

As mentioned a number of times, the transfiguration setting is located on a mountain. Removed from the world of humans and nearer to the heavens, the mountain peak represents the ideal place for close communication with God and the locus of revelation. After Jesus had forced the disciples into the second crucial journey to the Gentiles, he ascended a mountain and prayed (6:46). The official appointment of the disciples as the collegiate of the twelve was located on a mountain (3:13). The nature and sequence of the end time is revealed by Jesus sitting on the Mount of Olives (13:3). The mount of transfiguration, however, is an exceptional mountain, for it is the only "high mountain" (9:2: *oros hypsēlon*) in the gospel.[24] Towering above all other peaks of revelation, it designates the transfiguration as the epiphany of all epiphanies.

Both Matthew and Luke depict the transfiguration proper as an apparition immersed in a blaze of light. In the Matthean version, Jesus' countenance shines "like the sun" (17:2), and his garments appear gleaming "white like light" (17:2). According to the Lukan account, Jesus' face

---

22. Perrin, "Interpretation," pp. 27–28.

23. *Ibid.*, p. 26. The passion-resurrection predictions are widely held to be pre-Markan formulations, and the time reference in 9:2 is usually relegated to the tradition. All this Perrin rejects. He argues for a Markan composition of the predictions (with individual section parts taken from the tradition), and a redactional development of the six days out of the three days.

24. In the Revelation of John the seer is carried in the spirit to a "big and high mountain" (21:10: *oros mega kai hypsēlon*) to observe the arrival of the heavenly Jerusalem.

undergoes a transformation and his clothing gives the impression of "flashing white like lightening" (9:29). By contrast, Mark does not picture a light epiphany, nor does he even mention the face of Jesus. He focuses upon Jesus' clothes, the whiteness of which he reports twice (9:3a, 3b). The whiteness of Jesus' garments, not the brightness of the light, portrays the transfiguration in Mark. White, the apocalyptic color par excellence,[25] lends the quality of end time to the mountain epiphany. For the first and last time during his earthly ministry Jesus anticipates the nature of his post-resurrectional authentic existence. For a single moment the three witnesses are allowed to see the Jesus who is to come.

Of all the problems surrounding the transfiguration the joint appearance of Elijah with Moses is perhaps the most puzzling. Frequently overlooked is the fact that Mark himself wrote a commentary on Elijah (9:11–13). We have observed him conducting a strenuous defense on behalf of John the Baptist, alias Elijah, the eschatological precursor. Interestingly enough, he leaves the Moses appearance uninterpreted. His attention is focused upon Elijah. Already the unusual formulation *Elias syn Mōysei* in the tradition points in this direction. Both the anachronistic chronology and the preposition *syn* in place of the more neutral *kai* accords a position of priority to Elijah. On the other hand, Mark does not remove Moses from the tradition, presumably out of his known fondness for groupings of three. Now the three eschatological figures correspond to the three disciples. In keeping with the internal logic of the gospel story, the second career of Elijah, i.e., the ministry of John the Baptist, has already expired at the time of his transfiguration appearance. His role as Jesus' precursor was completed with his captivity, which marked the beginning of Jesus' public career (1:14). Strictly speaking therefore, it is not the Elijah *redivivus* who converses with Jesus on the mount of transfiguration, but the Elijah who has already accomplished his forerunner mission. If, cast into the role of forerunner, he makes still another appearance, its purpose must be to anticipate the "second" career of Jesus. As he served to usher in Jesus' first coming, so is he on completion of his own second ministry called upon to initiate Jesus into his "second" coming.

The cloud is the traditional manifestation of the nearness and presence of God (Ex. 24:16; 1 Kings 8:10–11; Ezek. 1:4), and the voice coming out

---

25. Wilhelm Michaelis, "leukos," *TDNT*, 4, pp. 241–50. White is the predominant color in the Revelation of John. The heavenly horses (6:2; 19:11, 14), the heavenly cloud upon which the Son of Man is seated (14:14), and the judgment throne (20:11) are all white. White are also the garments of those who are to become citizens of the New Jerusalem (3:4–5; 4:4; 6:11; 7:9, 13).

of the cloud is none other but the voice of God. It must be borne in mind that the suffering Jesus dies unassisted by God (15:34), and the rising Jesus conquers death without the demonstrative agency of God. He suffers a solitary passion, and he rises by his own power.[26] Once again the transfiguration emerges as the pinnacle of Jesus' ministry. It is comparable only to one other incident, baptism. At Jesus' beginning God had in a similar way and with near identical words taken the initiative (1:11). A third event, the centurion's confession (15:39) is sometimes viewed in connection with baptism and transfiguration. What these three scenes have in common is an exclusive reference to Son of God, a conspicuous placement toward beginning, middle, and ending of the gospel,[27] and an epiphanic quality (they are open to seeing, 1:10; 9:9; 15:39).

P. Vielhauer[28] sought to uncover the underlying rationale which binds these three events together. He identified them as the three stages of an oriental enthronement ritual, progressing from baptism through transfiguration to confession. Baptism constitutes the adoption or apotheosis: Jesus is presented with the divine attributes of spirit and life. Transfiguration exhibits the proclamation and presentation: the deified Jesus is introduced to the assembly of gods. The confession betokens the acclamation or enthronement: in a formal transfer of power Jesus is installed into the seat of power. This three-stage drama portrays the ministry of Jesus as a steadfast procession toward his heavenly enthronement as the eschatological king at the moment of death. Furthermore, the whole ritual is performed behind the curtain of the messianic secret. Jesus alone perceives the miraculous happening at baptism, only the three disciples witness the transfiguration, and the enthronement glory is concealed behind the outward brutality of the cross.

As a whole, Vielhauer's thesis imposes an alien schematization upon the gospel,[29] but this is not to belittle his many valuable insights. Baptism, transfiguration, and confession are indeed correlated, most directly so baptism and transfiguration. The strategic placing of Son of God highlights this title's supreme importance for Mark. In competition with Christos and Son of Man, Son of God emerges victorious. It is also true

26. This is the force of the verb *anistanai* over against the *egeirein*, see Perrin, "Interpretation," pp. 26–27.

27. If one accepts the reading of Son of God in 1:1, the strategic placement of this title is still more obvious.

28. Philipp Vielhauer, "Erwägungen zur Christologie des Markusevangeliums," *Aufsätze zum Neuen Testament*, Theologische Bücherei, No. 31 (Munich: Kaiser Verlag, 1965), pp. 119–214.

29. Heinz-Dieter Knigge, "The Meaning of Mark," *Interpr*, 22 (1968), pp. 61–62.

that at baptism and transfiguration Son of God is used in a royal, titulary sense. The royal ideology of Psalm 2:7 and Isaiah 42:1 characterizes Jesus' installation into the office of king. What Vielhauer overlooked is the fact that the transfiguration points outside and beyond the immediate gospel dramatization into the post-resurrectional life of Christ and the Christians. It thus forms not the second stage of a rationally conceived enthronement procession, but the final stage of the history of the Kingdom. To be sure, all three scenes are enmeshed in the web of the secret, but each in its own way.

Mark fails to inform his readers of Jesus' birth and descent. In lieu of a nativity, baptism assumes the role of a birth story. Baptism is Jesus' messianic birth in terms of his installation into the office of the eschatological king. But his birth is shrouded in secrecy. Nobody witnesses the eschatological irruption of the spirit, not even the Baptist himself.[30] With his installation at baptism Jesus secretly becomes the king of the end time.

At his death Jesus' sonship of God is for the first time disclosed to man. But the Gentile officer does not proclaim Jesus' enthronement in death; rather seeing (15:39a: *idōn*) the execution prompts his confession that Jesus had been the Son of God (15:39c: *houtos ho anthrōpos hyios theou ēn!*). The scales fall from his eyes as he beholds that Jesus had been the Son of God all along. But this confession at the foot of the cross constitutes merely a partial breaking of the secret, for henceforth people live in the hiddenness of the Kingdom and await the coming of the Son of God *en dynamei*. But the veil of secrecy is lifted enough to facilitate the composition of the Kingdom gospel which in turn directs the way toward the parousia.

The transfiguration, closely modeled after baptism, anticipates Jesus' parousia, his messianic birth in apocalyptic fullness. It would, however, be amiss to call this birth a *second coming*. After a covert advent and a ministry in hiddenness the parousia constitutes Jesus' overt coming and manifest birth. It is not until this ultimate point of disclosure that both the hidden Jesus and the mystery of his Kingdom will pass into the full light of revelation. The Markan condition is explained and experienced as a journey on the way to this point of apocalypse. The goal of the parousia is still ahead. Once reached, however, it will not be an end in itself, but in analogy to baptism the beginning of life in the Kingdom, undisguised and free from the pressures of partial fulfillment. The true

---

30. Matthew and Luke dismantle the secret and stress the public aspect of Jesus' baptism.

end of history is not the death of Jerusalem, but, over and beyond the ruin of this city, the birth of the Kingdom. The goal of the way marks the entry into the full possession of the Kingdom, and the gospel of the hidden Kingdom is but a prelude toward the Kingdom in full. The omega of the parousia is the alpha of the Kingdom.

LOSING THE WAY

Almost from the outset of the way of Jesus we observed the disciples filling different roles than normally expected. Inclined to hold back, they seemed to try to retard the travels of Jesus. By the end of the Galilean mission their role as unperceiving outsiders and leading opponents was firmly assured. The manner in which Mark built them up as chief opponents has given us reason to suspect that they might have been the representatives of a conservative Jerusalem Christianity which founded its existence upon the authority of Peter and the twelve.

In view of the disciples' Galilean debacle it comes as little surprise that they cut very poor figures on the way to Jerusalem. Peter, the spokesman, answers Jesus' question concerning his (Jesus') identity (8:29a, b) with the Christos "confession" (8:29c, d). It is followed by Jesus' injunction to silence (8:30), the interpretation of which is controversial. Is Peter's "confession" suppressed because it is valid,[31] or put down because it is invalid?[32] If one halts at 8:30 and reflects on Peter's Christos apart from the ensuing conflict and clash, the "confession" appears correct at least in the formal sense. Our desire to stop at 8:30, however, stems from the conviction that the "confession of Peter constitutes the decisive moment in the course of the narrative."[33] But the Markan text must not be broken asunder into 8:27–30 and 8:31–33.[34] The "confession" triggers off an acute controversy which reveals that the Christos nurtured by Peter fell disastrously short of what Jesus had in mind. Jesus' prediction of his own passion and resurrection (8:31)[35] provokes an aggressive reaction on the

31. Thus the consensus of opinion.

32. Theodore J. Weeden, *Mark—Traditions in Conflict* (Philadelphia: Fortress Press, 1971), pp. 64–66, 139.

33. Ambrozic, *Kingdom*, p. 232.

34. Ferdinand Hahn, *The Titles of Jesus in Christology*, trans. Harold Knight and George Ogg (New York: World Publishing Company, 1969), p. 223. This is different in Matthew where the *apo tote* (16:21) marks a new paragraph following the beatitude of Peter.

35. It is specified as a teaching *parrēsia* (8:32a). This is the *epilysis* (4:34) reserved for the disciples, but withheld from the public.

part of Peter (8:32b), but Jesus in turn rebukes Peter for trying to lure him off the way of suffering and cross (8:33). In the end Peter, the disciples' chief spokesman and Jesus' chief opponent, stands convicted of being Satan. Thus Jesus' suffering and rising Son of Man exposes the inadequacy of Peter's Christos, while Peter's refusal to embrace a suffering messiah earns him the incredible indictment of Satan. Clearly, Peter's "confession" was the wrong confession.

Neither the second nor the third passion-resurrection prediction meets with any success. In the wake of the second prediction (9:31–32) the disciples, not comprehending the matter and not asking for further enlightenment, in effect join ranks with Peter. The third prediction (10:33–34) is misunderstood by James and John who request positions of power and glory. It is over the issue of a suffering, rising Son of Man that Peter breaks with Jesus, James and John indulge in offensive triumphalism, and the remainder of the disciples confess their continued ignorance.

One of the principal characteristics of the Markan opponents, represented by the disciples, is their disregard for, or perhaps even rejection of a passion christology. This is the reason Peter's Christos runs into the opposition of the passion-resurrection credo. It is difficult to overlook that the three predictions uniformly affirm a suffering, rising *Son of Man*. This is a deliberate feature which calls for explanation. Resuming our earlier observation,[36] we suggest that Mark employs Son of Man at points of maximum disagreement with his opponents because it was under this title that Jesus was known to them. Whatever their notion of the Son of Man, Mark's suffering, rising Son of Man is totally unacceptable to them. And so is a humiliated John the Baptist! This we had inferred from the Markan comment 9:11–13.

We must insist, however, that the dual nature of the passion-resurrection predictions be taken seriously. If the Markan Jesus sees fit to counter Peter's christology in terms of passion *and* resurrection, the Petrine Christians are likely to have lapsed on those two points. That the disciples had difficulty in coming to terms with the resurrection is borne out by the singularly Markan verse 9:10. Only in Mark is the unperceptiveness of the disciples stretched so far as to include the resurrection of Jesus. But if they fail to grasp the resurrection of Jesus, this crucial date for the launching of the way to the parousia, how will they ever reach the goal? The answer is, they cannot, because the transfiguration epiphany itself

36. See Chap. I, p. 22.

has escaped their comprehension. The redactional 9:6[37] attributes a state of confusion to Peter and of fear to the disciples. This is Mark's way of registering discipleship failure. It follows on the heels of Peter's suggestion to build three booths. His request is motivated by the compulsion to seize upon the eschatological vision and to arrest what was only meant to be a prolepsis of the Son of God. Peter's eyes are on the present. He mistakes the future for the present and takes the now for the answer. This desire to perpetuate the transfiguration glory coupled with the inadequate awareness of the decisive resurrection date reveals the opponents' dilemma: they are guilty of a mistaken realization of eschatology.[38]

It follows that the way of the disciples is not to deliverance, but toward the edge of doom. But their route to ruin is of their own making, because they could have known the full Jesus they needed to know in order to pass through the passion and glory of Jerusalem. At an early point during his Galilean mission Jesus had chosen the three confidants and given them a demonstration of his resurrection power (5:21–24, 35–43). At Gethsemane he will for the very last time try to win the three over to his suffering messiahship.[39] At the three "stations of the cross" he had in plain, unequivocal terms disclosed what they would have to expect from following him. On the mount of transfiguration he had revealed himself to the three as the very goal of the way. "Listen to him" (9:7d), the heavenly voice had urged—to him who had spoken of his suffering, death, and rising, and who would on the way continue to speak thus. But it is impossible to dishabituate the disciples of their way of hearing and seeing. They will go their own way, miss the goal, and perish along the way.

CONCLUSION

It is virtually *opinio communis* that Peter's "confession" of the dying, rising Son of Man constitutes the crucial scene of recognition, with the transfiguration merely serving as the "heavenly ratification of Peter's confession."[40] It is argued that the Caesarea Philippi incident brings Jesus' passion in full view; henceforth, events precipitate toward passion and resurrection. This, we claim, is an *opinio errans*. All indications point

37. Bultmann, *Tradition*, p. 261; Weeden, *Mark*, p. 121, n. 11; Ambrozic, *Kingdom*, p. 80.
38. Very close to the point is Vincent Taylor, *The Gospel According to St. Mark* (London: Macmillan and Co., 1963), p. 391: "Peter wishes to prolong the blessed association perhaps in revolt against the idea of Messianic suffering."
39. Werner H. Kelber, "Mark 14, 32–42: Gethsemane," *ZNW*, 63 (1972), pp. 166–87.
40. Bultmann, *Tradition*, p. 260.

Kelber's thesis on Transfigul (handwritten annotation)

to the transfiguration as the true scene of recognition. Structurally, its place is precisely at mid-point of the gospel.[41] Topologically, its locale is the only "high mountain" in the gospel. Eschatologically, it stands at the turning of time toward the apocalyptic manifestation of the Kingdom. Christologically, it comes at the peak of a titulary progression: Peter's false Christos is corrected by Jesus' suffering, rising Son of Man, to be capped by the Son of God in his parousia glory. Theologically, it marks God's only intervention outside baptism. Dramatically, it stages God's attestation of his Son in opposition to Peter's vainglorious Christos. The fullness of Jesus lies beyond passion and resurrection, and the gospel is more than a *theologia crucis*, arguing the case of a crucified, rising Son of Man. Placed at the center of the gospel and in the midst of the eye-opening journey, the transfiguration reveals Jesus as the manifest Son of God, goal of the way.

The gospel "lacks" both a nativity story and a formal conclusion. At the beginning it furnishes no information concerning Jesus' birth and derivation, and at the end it leaves the reader with only a glimpse of what the final outcome might be. This "incomplete" beginning is closely related to the "inconclusive" ending, and the "open" ending sheds light on the "deficient" beginning. Jesus' birth in fullness remains untold at the outset, because it has as yet not occurred, but is expected shortly. Baptism, which assumes the role of a nativity story, narrates Jesus' secret installation into his kingship. The gospel is not furnished with a formal conclusion, because its main objective, the Kingdom of God, is still in progress, yet near completion. The "deficient" posture of the gospel is thus a literary means of expressing both the incompleteness and the imminent availability of redemption. This gospel of the Kingdom forms an open gate toward the realization of the Kingdom. It thrusts a way toward an ending which will in fact be the true beginning. This proclivity toward Kingdom and parousia bestows a preliminary, initiatory character upon the gospel as a whole. It functions as the introduction to the eschatological beginning, and in consequence must dispense with a formal beginning and ending. Unable to present the parousia End as the climactic ending of the gospel, but compelled to accentuate its signal importance, Mark offers it in central position. The fundamental structure of the gospel, its beginning, middle and ending, is thus dictated by the experience of an imminent parousia hope.

---

41. By sheer verse count 9:2–8 stands right at the center, with 324 verses preceding the transfiguration, and 335 following it.

Chapter V

COLLAPSE AND REORIENTATION
OF THE KINGDOM

11:1-25

Kingdom and parousia are the goal of the way. But Jerusalem is likewise the goal of the way, as spelled out in the last passion-resurrection prediction (10:33). If Mark is truly concerned about a new place and a new time, and if the Kingdom is to have a place on earth, will this place be Jerusalem? To this the Markan Jesus gives a provisional answer (10:17–31) after he has entered the south (10:1) and before he issues his third passion-resurrection prediction.

The pericope of the Rich Young Man (10:17–31), conventionally so called, has been provided with a redactional revision of considerable length. Bultmann[1] identified 10:17–22 as the traditional apophthegm, and 10:23–27, 28–31 as two blocks of redactional accretion.[2] Reploh[3] demonstrated the thoroughly redactional nature of those two secondary units, 10:23–27 and 10:28–31. Already a cursory reading of the total pericope

1. Rudolf Bultmann, *History of the Synoptic Tradition*, trans. John Marsh, 3rd ed. (New York: Harper & Row, 1963), pp. 21–22.
2. Upon closer analysis, Bultmann detects a more complex interlacing of tradition with redaction. Mark may have encountered the apophthegm already consisting of 10:17–23, 25. Verse 10:24 would be a Markan interpolation. Verses 10:23 and 10:25 properly belong together, since both verses emphasize the difficulty of entering the Kingdom for rich people. The interpolated 10:24 radicalizes the objective of the apophthegm: all men, not merely rich people, will find it hard to enter the Kingdom. Nikolaus Walter ("Zur Analyse von Mc 10:17–31," *ZNW*, 53 [1962], pp. 206–18), objecting to Bultmann's proposal, assumes a clear dividing line separating tradition from redaction between 10:24a and 10:24b. According to the stylistic pattern of an apophthegm the story reaches its peak in a Jesus logion (10:24a), and is rounded off by reference to the disciples' reaction (10:24b). Both Bultmann in his more detailed argument and Walter underrate the redactional activity in 10:23–27.
3. Karl-Georg Reploh, *Markus—Lehrer der Gemeinde*, Stuttgarter Biblische Monographien, No. 9 (Stuttgart: Katholisches Bibelwerk, 1969), pp. 191–210.

discloses a subtle shift of emphasis, but the precise Markan scopus hinges on an evaluation of tradition and redaction.

In the traditional story (10:17–22) a person asks Jesus about the conditions by which he might enter eternal life. Jesus calls his attention to the commandments, but the man has piously observed all of them since his youth. Thereupon the attainment of his goal is said to depend on one additional requirement. He is to sell his possessions and give the proceeds to the poor. But this he cannot do, and he departs in anguish. The tradition narrates the story of an abortive discipleship, which is not without a touch of tragedy. Although the man is fully qualified before the law, he stands disqualified in the eyes of Jesus. What precisely it was that prevented him from meeting the full challenge of discipleship is left unsaid, because the final gloss (10:22b) is already the redactional comment.[4] According to Mark, the moral of the story is that the man's possessions caused him to stumble. It is this point which Mark appropriates in 10:23–27 and radicalizes in 10:28–31.

In 10:23–27 the most revealing index of redactional activity is to be found in a Markan insertion.[5] A Kingdom logion warning the rich (10:23b) is almost literally repeated as a warning directed to the disciples (10:24c). The focus lies in the intervening 10:24a–b, which reports the disciples' amazed reaction[6] and Jesus' specific reply to them. The disciples are astounded because what seemed to be of concern to the rich alone, Jesus applies to them. Far from being guaranteed a free passage, their entrance into the Kingdom is a most difficult achievement. A third Kingdom saying (10:25) again names the rich, but it can now be understood that Mark has put the disciples on a par with the rich. The acute paradox of the camel and the needle's eye compounds the effect of the first two Kingdom sayings and makes the gateway to the Kingdom look virtually impassable. As expected, the disciples' response is more intense than before. They are stunned (10:26a: *perissōs exeplēssonto*) and inclined to doubt the possibility of redemption altogether. But Jesus dispels their misgivings and commends them to the power of God. The goal is attainable.

In 10:23–27 Mark thoroughly involves the disciples in the fate of an

---

4. Verse 10:22b is a Markan *gar* clause. The use of *ēn* with a participle (*echōn*) as an auxiliary is Markan, see Cuthbert H. Turner, "Marcan Usage: Notes, Critical and Exegetical, on the Second Gospel," *JTS*, 28 (1926–27), p. 350. See also Walter, "Analyse," p. 213, n. 33.

5. See Chap. I, p. 19 and Chap. II, p. 40.

6. The use of *thambeistai* in the New Testament is limited to Mark. It occurs in 1:27, a largely redactional verse, in 10:32, a redactional product throughout, and in 10:24a. The compound *ekthambeistai* is likewise Markan (9:15; 14:33; 16:5, 6).

abortive discipleship. Three times he speaks to them of entry into the Kingdom,[7] and each time he underscores the difficulty associated with reaching the goal of the way. Exactly what makes the passage into the Kingdom hard to travel is spelled out in 10:28–31.

Peter, in his role as spokesman of the disciples, alerts Jesus to the full price of discipleship already paid by them: they had abandoned everything in following after Jesus (10:28). The careful choice of words (*aphienai, akolouthein*) brings back the memory of the first calling of disciples (1:16–20). Jesus' reply is remarkable for its detail and puzzling in its meaning. What he demands is a total renunciation of all relations and possessions, and a complete dissolution of all that ties them to this present way of life (10:29). But this, one must agree with Peter, the disciples have already fulfilled. Still more perplexing, because unprecedented in the synoptic tradition, is the promise of a this-worldly compensation which would beyond all proportions offset the loss incurred on behalf of Jesus and his gospel (10:29–30). In the very end, life in the coming con of the Kingdom will turn priorities upside down. Those who have abandoned their present way of life will be given the seats of honor, while those who have failed to tear themselves away from their mode of living will be disqualified (10:31).

It is well at this point to reflect on Mark's reinterpretation of the apophthegm of the Rich Young Man. While some features of the story have remained unutilized, others have undergone a drastic revision. Ignored is the tragic aspect, i.e., the fact that the man falls short of Jesus' expectations despite his conscientious observance of the laws. Disregarded is the point that almsgiving could have assured him a heavenly deposit. Mark sees the major stumbling block on the way to the Kingdom in the "many possessions" (10:22b: *ktēmata polla*), which according to his radical interpretation take on the form of house, brothers, sisters, mother, father, children, and fields. The accent is shifted from the virtue of almsgiving and the treasure in heaven to a complete renunciation of the old, habitual way of life and a temporary redress prior to entry into the Kingdom.

The full implications of Mark's notable radicalization of the traditional apophthegm will surface when we bring the theme of complete separation in connection with similar features we observed before. From the moment the Kingdom began to involve disciples, it tended to have an

7. The three Kingdom sayings bring to mind the three passion-resurrection predictions. Both configurations of threes are deliberately designed by Mark. As Jesus spoke three times to the disciples of his dying and rising, so did he three times call their attention to the narrow gate which leads into the Kingdom.

uprooting effect upon them. Jesus' initial message of Kingdom and *meta-noia* implied a radical change of life direction, and the subsequent way of Jesus unsettled people from their own way of living. The Kingdom affirmed itself by emancipation from the family of Jesus and Jerusalem. Lastly, we had assumed that the Galilean Kingdom was established in opposition to a Jewish Christianity in Jerusalem. In 10:17–31 this theme of schism reaches an unprecedented height. As Jesus enters the south (10:1),[8] he delivers his most drastic message of separation and divorce. It had not been sufficient for the disciples to have followed Jesus' call in Galilee: they will have to sever *all* life connections. But, we resume Peter's objection, what else is there that they can dispense with? They do not possess houses or fields, and they have broken with father and mother. As so often before, Jesus' message must be understood as an anticipation of the future. He gives his disciples advance knowledge as to how to act in future times. The theme of schism is at its sharpest in the south because there is the place the disciples will be tempted to mistake for the goal of the way. In effect, Jesus gives an advance warning against settling down, striking roots, and living the life in the Kingdom. The promise of new houses and brothers and sisters and mothers and children and fields points to a new community the identity of which need not be spelled out to the disciples. Journeying through Galilee Jesus had taken meticulous care to introduce the disciples into, and put them in charge over the Kingdom of God.

On another level, the past of Jesus' message of renunciation aims directly into the Markan present. The identity of the promised community is not unlike the hidden Kingdom in Galilee. As the arrival of the Kingdom was tantamount to the fulfillment of the *kairos* (1:15), so is the replacement for the loss of the old way of life granted *nyn en tō kairō toutō* (10:30a). The fact that the new fellowship will have to coexist *meta diōgmōn* (10:30a) is in keeping with Mark's theology of the hidden Kingdom. As outlined in the Galilean mystery speech (4:17), tribulation and persecutions do not contradict the nature of the Kingdom, but they are in fact painful evidence of its secret arrival. Tribulation and persecutions strain the hidden existence of the Kingdom to the breaking point of total reversal of all values. Then darkness will be turned into light, and the last be the first, as the first will become the last. This peak event is hinted at by the golden rule of eschatological reversal in 10:31. The

---

8. The geographical note 10:1 has the character of a heading which joins together the disparate traditions of 10:2–31. See Reploh, *Lehrer*, pp. 173–74.

eschatological community will shed its disguise and emerge as the manifest Kingdom of God. Thus the description of the new order of life *meta diōgmōn* fits well the realities of the hidden Kingdom in Galilee.

As the new community, so will the total surrender of the old communal conditions likewise reflect the Markan experience. The renunciation is described as a loss "for my [Jesus'] sake and for the sake of the gospel" (10:29b). The redactional *heneken tou euangeliou*[9] lifts Jesus' message into the present of Mark,[10] and demands a reading from the evangelist's own time. As analyzed at the very outset, the gospel constitutes the new program in the aftermath of the Jerusalem catastrophe, and its message comprises the presence of the Kingdom in Galilee. If Mark, therefore, brings the end of all life relations in connection with the beginning of the gospel of the Kingdom, he may well be referring to the loss of houses and relatives and possessions Christians experienced in the destruction of Jerusalem. Their loss is explained as a loss for the sake of Jesus and his Kingdom because it opens the way into the true fellowship of the hidden Kingdom.

EXCURSUS

It is instructive to note that Jesus launches his mission in the south with a discourse on divorce for the sake of remarriage (10:1–12). If it is imperative to dissolve all earthly ties on behalf of the Kingdom, the question must force itself upon the Christian conscience whether the marriage bond is subject to this very requirement. The marriage relationship is singled out as the one exception to the eschatological experience of separation and divorce. By the same token, neither wife nor husband are included among the goods to be renounced (10:29). Membership in the Kingdom, it is implied, must not serve as a pretext for divorce and remarriage.

While the ties to the past are severed, the link to the future is strengthened. Children (*paidia*) are accepted into the Kingdom (10:13–16) and treasured as the models of new membership (10:15). The disciples, significantly, reject children, because their (the disciples') faith does not embrace the future. Their concept of the Kingdom stagnates within the narrow confines of the present, while the Kingdom of God is committed to the future. The internal breakup of families (10:29: *tekna*; 13:12) in no way contradicts the espousal of children, for the renewal of life entails the release of all former relations.

Marriage survives the eschatological divorce from all life connections, and the adoption of children, symptomatic of the new life in the Kingdom, richly recompenses for the loss of the old life.

9. See Chap. I, p. 4.
10. Well recognized by Reploh, *Lehrer*, pp. 206–07.

The redactionally built-up theme of total separation and the accompanying theme of a hundred-fold recompensation make it seem unlikely that both loss and gain would occur in the same place. If Mark intended to make the south the locus of surrender and deprivation, then the way of Jesus cannot end in the Kingdom of Jerusalem. This same idea is further reinforced by the fact that the goals of Kingdom and Jerusalem are strategically kept apart. 9:1, we noted, marks the first reference to the Kingdom as the goal of the way. Both the redactional verse 10:32 and the third passion-resurrection prediction 10:33 for the first time disclose Jerusalem as the journey's goal. But between 9:1 and 10:33 the goal of the Kingdom is placed five more times on the way of discipleship (9:47; 10:15, 23, 24, 25). Thus, having first identified the parousia with the arrival of the Kingdom (8:38–9:1), the latter is five times specified as the goal of discipleship, before Jerusalem is finally mentioned as the terminal point. This arrangement is designed to stress the Kingdom's priority over the city, and to steer clear of any possible identification of Kingdom with Jerusalem. The way of Jesus is on to the Kingdom, but first through the crisis of Jerusalem. As he approaches the outskirts of Jerusalem, a rift develops between Kingdom and city which in the city's temple will deteriorate into a complete break. At the same time the way will be rerouted to the new place of hope.

THE IMPENDING RIFT

The conventional heading, Entry into Jerusalem (11:1–10), conjures up the image of the king's triumphal procession into his royal citadel.[11] The role of the Mount of Olives and the centrality of the temple, the unused colt and the strewing of branches, the shouts of Hosanna and the acclamation of Hallel psalm 118:26—all these features appear to produce the scenario of a messianic entrance in the vein of Zech. 9:9–10.[12] It is worth noting, however, that in some quarters of the Life of Christ research a strange reserve and evasiveness, a break and new orientation even was observed just at the point of Jesus' entry into the city. This led A.

11. See for example 1 Kings 1:32–48; Psalms 24:7–10; 42:5; 43:3; 68:25–28; 89:16; 118:19–20; 132:7–10; Isaiah 9:1–2; Zechariah 9:9.
12. The messianic character has been emphasized among others by F. C. Burkitt, "W and Θ: Studies in the Western Text of St. Mark," *JTS*, 17 (1916), pp. 139–52; E. Werner, " 'Hosanna' in the Gospels," *JBL*, 65 (1946), pp. 97–122; J. S. Kennard, " 'Hosanna' and the Purpose of Jesus," *JBL*, 67 (1948), pp. 171–76; Heinz-Wolfgang Kuhn, "Das Reittier Jesu in der Einzugsgeschichte des Markusevangeliums," *ZNW*, 50 (1959), pp. 82–91; C. W. F. Smith, "No Time for Figs," *JBL*, 79 (1960), pp. 315–27; J. Blenkinsopp, "The Oracle of Judah and the Messianic Entry," *JBL*, 80 (1961), pp. 55–64.

Schweitzer[13] to postulate his well-known thesis that Jesus was hailed not as the Messiah, but as his forerunner, Elijah. R. M. Grant[14] concluded that the events portrayed in 11:1–23 designate a transition in Jesus' messianic consciousness from phase one, in which all hope was focused upon eschatological fulfillment in Jerusalem, to phase two, in which Jesus awakened to the necessity of a parousia postponement. In the wake of W. Wrede's influential thesis of the Messianic Secret the Markan entrance text was often found to be dictated by a secrecy theology.[15] But Wrede himself had not seen fit to claim 11:1–10 for the "dogma" of the secret,[16] and the technical terms of Mark's secrecy theology are in fact absent. The thesis that the acclamation words 11:9b–10 intend a muffling of the messianic aspect in the sense that the "acclamation is eschatological, but not specifically Messianic,"[17] does not touch upon the Markan purpose either because *ho erchomenos* (11:9b), He That Cometh, is an unmistakable messianic formula, and "the kingdom of our father David" (11:10a) is equally charged with messianic quality. But what these and other scholars rightly sensed was the fact that the combined features of the Markan text do not effect a royal entrance scenario.

It is first of all noteworthy that the acclamation is schemed in such a way that it does in fact not concur with the entry into the city. Mark, and Mark alone, has Jesus' companions cut leafy branches "from the fields" (11:8b), which adverts to a rural location. It is only *after* Jesus has been hailed that he enters city and temple, by himself (11:11a: *eisēlthen*), unobserved and unapplauded. Thus the acclamation incident is kept out of the reach of Jerusalem, so that strictly speaking Mark does not portray an entrance scene.[18]

13. Albert Schweitzer, *The Mystery of the Kingdom of God*, trans. Walter Lowrie (New York: Schocken Books, 1964), pp. 156–63; and *idem*, *The Quest of the Historical Jesus*, trans. W. Montgomery, 6th ed. (New York: Macmillan, 1968), p. 394.

14. Robert M. Grant, "The Coming of the Kingdom of God," *JBL*, 67 (1948), pp. 297–303.

15. William Wrede, *Das Messiasgeheimnis in den Evangelien*, 3rd ed. (Göttingen: Vandenhoeck & Ruprecht, 1963); see also T. A. Burkill, *Mysterious Revelation* (Ithaca, N.Y.: Cornell University Press, 1963), pp. 193–96; Dennis E. Nineham, *The Gospel of St. Mark* (Baltimore, Md.: Penguin Books, Inc., 1963), p. 292.

16. Wrede, *Messiasgeheimnis*, pp. 10, 44.

17. Rudolf Otto, *The Kingdom of God and the Son of Man*, trans. Floyd V. Filson and Bertram Lee-Woolf, reprint of rev. ed. of 1943 (Boston: Starr King Press, 1951), p. 224.

18. General statements to this effect were made among others by Ernst Lohmeyer, *Das Evangelium des Markus*, 17th ed. (Göttingen: Vandenhoeck & Ruprecht, 1967), p. 233; Karl L. Schmidt, *Der Rahmen der Geschichte Jesu* (Berlin: Trowitzsch und Sohn, 1919; reprinted Darmstadt: Wissenschaftliche Buchgesellschaft, 1964), pp. 297–98; Werner Georg Kümmel, *Promise and Fulfilment*, trans. Dorothea M. Barton, Studies in Biblical Theology, No. 23 (London: SCM Press, 1966), pp. 115–17.

More than anything else it is the acclamation words themselves (11:9b–10) which bring the Markan bias into focus. The verses give the impression of a studied literary construct:

> *ōsanna,*
> *eulogēmenos ho erchomenos en onomati kyriou*
> *eulogēmenē hē erchomenē basileia tou patros*
>   *hēmōn David*
> *ōsanna en tois hypsistois.*

Put into the frame of the Hosanna shouts is a central section consisting of two parts running parallel to each other ("blessed be the coming . . ." resumes "blessed be he who comes . . .").[19] Two features of this literary complex point to Markan composition. One is the Hosanna-frame which is reminiscent of the *euangelion-* frame in 1:14–15.[20] There is secondly 11:10a, the exaltation of the kingdom, which is marked as a redactional *ad hoc* formulation for the following four reasons: (1) 11:9 and 11:10a are slightly ruptured; in 11:9 a person is acclaimed, while in 11:10a it is the kingdom to which tribute is paid; (2) this rupture is reasonably explained by identifying 11:10a as a redactional extension of the preceding psalm quotation;[21] (3) what comes to expression in 11:10a is the Markan theme of the Kingdom, although it must immediately be admitted that the Kingdom's qualification as that "of our father David" seems thoroughly "un-Markan"; (4) both Matthew and Luke reject what in their view is an inadmissable Markan comment on Psalm 118:26.

Possibly, the acclamation words 11:9b–10 are a Markan construct *in toto*. But even if one is not prepared to go quite that far, our analysis points out that the most "un-Markan" statement, the reference to the Davidic kingdom (11:10a), is in all probability redactional. With this we have approached the vexing question of Jesus' Davidic sonship in Mark. Before a judgment can be made on the significance of 11:10a, we will by way of a brief digression review the gospel's other Son of David passages, because 11:10a must be read in the context of Mark's understanding of Jesus' Davidic sonship.

The first person to call Jesus Son of David is the blind Bartimaeus

---

19. See Reginald H. Fuller, *The Foundations of New Testament Christology* (New York: Charles Scribner's Sons, 1965), p. 112; Christoph Burger, *Jesus als Davidssohn,* Forschungen zur Religion und Literatur des Alten und Neuen Testaments, No. 98 (Göttingen: Vandenhoeck & Ruprecht, 1970), p. 50.

20. Chap. I, pp. 3–4; see also Chap. II, p. 31.

21. John D. Crossan, "Redaction and Citation in Mark 11:9–10, 17 and 14:27," *Proceedings,* Vol. I (1972), pp. 26–29.

(10:47c, 48c). The Bartimaeus pericope (10:46–52) forms the conclusion to the eye opening mid-section of the gospel (8:22–10:52). In view of the fact that the eyes of the disciples remain closed on their way to Jerusalem, it may not be accidental that it is *before* Bartimaeus' eyes are healed and opened that he addresses Jesus as Son of David. The repeated Son of David acclamation (10:47c, 48c) forms a Markan insertion which focuses upon a futile attempt to silence Bartimaeus' use of this title (10:48a, b). The Son of David confession is made by a man *oculis captus*! As he approaches Jesus, still *in statu erroris*, Bartimaeus greets him whom he had earlier called Son of David with *rabbi* (10:51d), a title clearly rejected by Mark.[22] On the other hand, Jesus is at this Jericho incident introduced (not by Bartimaeus!) as the *Nazarene* (10:47), a designation which carries the full blessing of Mark.[23] It is extremely doubtful whether Bartimaeus' christological awareness of Jesus as Son of David and rabbi surpasses that of the disciples. The story properly concludes the gospel's mid-section, not simply because it reports a successful healing, but because it is symptomatic of the Markan notion of discipleship. Although Bartimaeus experienced the power of Jesus and received his eyesight, he remains essentially unenlightened. His myopic perspective on Jesus is unaltered and he never improves on his former judgment. As the disciples, he follows Jesus on the way, but not to the very end. For in the end, Jesus dies forsaken and alone.

Jesus himself deliberates the issue of his Davidic sonship while teaching in the temple, the very seat of Davidic fulfillment (12:35–37a). The Jerusalem scribes advocate what appears to be their local tradition: the *Christos* must be the Son of David. With the aid of Psalm 110:1 Jesus demonstrates that the *Christos* has to be the *kyrios* of David, and thus cannot simultaneously be his son. By implication this *kyrios*, sitting at the right hand, is not the Son of David, but the Son of God. Thus Jesus rejects the Davidic sonship in favor of the sonship of God.[24] This under-

22. At the transfiguration Peter mistakes the glorified Son of God for *rabbi* (9:5); following the "cleansing of the temple" and in view of the fig tree disaster Peter again calls Jesus *rabbi* (11:21), which is totally inappropriate considering Jesus' dramatic temple activity; as he kisses Jesus, Judas calls him *rabbi* (14:45).

23. I gratefully acknowledge dependence on my former graduate assistant Kim Dewey who in his MA thesis on Peter's Denial in Mark opened my eyes to Mark's positive use of *ho Nazarēnos*. At the outset, Jesus is identified as the man from Nazareth (1:9); in his first miracle Jesus is recognized by the demons as the Nazarene (1:24); in the last miracle, the Bartimaeus healing, he is introduced as the Nazarene (10:47); he is denied by Peter in terms of the Nazarene (14:67); he will lead the way to Galilee as the Nazarene (16:6).

24. Among those who advocate this interpretation are L. Baeck, W. Bousset, R. Bultmann, C. Burger, M. Goguel, E. Haenchen, W. Heitmüller, E. Hirsch, J. Klaus-

standing of an anti-Davidic polemic is, however, contested by an interpretation in terms of a christological intensification. Fundamentally, it is argued, the Christos is the Son of David, but over and above that he is the *kyrios* of David. It is therefore assumed that by expanding the traditional concept of the Davidic Messiah, Mark construes a two-stage christology in the vein of Romans 1:3–4.[25] But in order to get an impression of a two-stage christological structure one will have to consult Matthew (22:41–46). For him, the Davidic messiahship is presupposed from the outset (22:42), and is, in and of itself, not the bone of contention. What is at issue is the compatibility between the Davidic Christos and the *kyrios*, which by implication is answered in the affirmative. Matthew, therefore, presents an argument for "the paradoxical combination of the two titles which both belong to Jesus."[26] By contrast, Mark's argumentation submits a clear alternative. The scribes' Davidic sonship has been disclaimed by the *kyriotēs* of the Son of God.

Jesus' Davidic sonship does not become an issue until he approaches Jerusalem. Not only is Mark conscious of the Jerusalem Zion tradition, but he regards it as the theology of the scribal authorities of Jerusalem (12:35). It is thus not surprising that the Bartimaeus pericope carries a negative undertone and the Son of David discussion results in the title's rejection. Our review prompts the suggestion that the Davidic acclamation 11:10a is to be understood as the wrong acclamation. Jesus' followers express the traditional hope of Jerusalem.[27] Mark dissociates the acclamation from Jerusalem and places it into an anti-Jerusalem, anti-Davidic context. One can almost detect a progressive exposure of the inadequacy of the title as Jesus approaches the seat of Davidic hopes: the confession of the blind Bartimaeus at Jericho, the wrong acclamation at the outskirts, and Jesus' personal rejection in the temple.

The "un-Markan" nature of the redactional 11:10a finds its explanation in Mark's putting the wrong confession on the lips of the acclaimers. The sheer foreignness of the Davidic acclamation is to catch the attention of the reader and to question its validity. For Mark, "Jesus is the Son of God bringing in the kingdom of God, not the Son of David introducing the

---

ner, E. Meyer, K. L. Schmidt, A. Suhl, P. Vielhauer, H. Weihnacht, J. Wellhausen, W. Wrede.

25. This case was argued *in extenso* by Ferdinand Hahn, *The Titles of Jesus in Christology,* trans. Harold Knight and George Ogg (New York: World Publishing Co., 1969), pp. 251–58.

26. Günther Bornkamm, "End-Expectation and Church in Matthew," *Tradition and Interpretation in Matthew,* trans. Percy Scott (Philadelphia: Westminster Press), p. 33.

27. Thus also Crossan, "Redaction," pp. 31, 46–47.

kingdom of David."[28] 11:1–10 does not depict Jesus' triumphal, messianic entry into Jerusalem, but the rejection of Davidic messianism outside of Jerusalem. The incident does not anticipate the realization of Jesus' messiahship in Jerusalem, rather it casts doubt upon the messianic promise native to Jerusalem. A wedge is driven between the Kingdom of God and the kingdom of David, and Jesus is on his way to the former, rejecting the latter. Thus we find in seminal form in 11:1–10 the theme which will burst into the open at Jesus' actual entry: the break with the center of Jerusalem and the reorientation toward a new goal.

THE BREAK

According to Matthew Jesus' entrance causes a commotion in the whole city (21:10). No sooner has he entered Jerusalem than he conducts the act of temple cleansing. Unlike Mark, the purification procedure is not framed by the fig tree disaster. Following the cleansing Jesus performs messianic healing miracles whereupon he is acclaimed Son of David "out of the mouth of babes" (21:15). Matthew's "dramatic Temple trilogy"[29] (cleansing–healing–acclaiming) establishes Jesus as the Son of David in the newly cleansed sanctuary. A note of opposition flares up when the traditional temple establishment objects to a Son of David who performs healing miracles and is endorsed by the children (21:15).

Luke appraises the cleansing event with his characteristic ambiguity.[30] Immediately preceding the cleansing Jesus predicts the destruction of Jerusalem and weeps over the city for having missed the chance of peace (19:39–44). Looking back upon the city's destruction Luke brings the disaster in connection with Jesus' cleansing, understanding the latter as an act of judgment which came to fatal fulfillment forty years thereafter. On the other hand, the cleansed temple not only serves as Jesus' permanent place for his daily teaching and instruction (19:47; 21:37–38), but it becomes the vital center for the emerging apostolic church.[31]

28. Aloysius M. Ambrozic, *The Hidden Kingdom*, The Catholic Biblical Quarterly-Monograph Series, No. 2 (Washington, D.C.: The Catholic Biblical Association of America, 1972), p. 43.
29. Ernst Lohmeyer, *Lord of the Temple*, trans. Stewart Todd (Richmond, Va.: John Knox, 1962), p. 54.
30. The dialectical pattern in Lukan theology has been worked out by Helmut Flender, *St. Luke Theologian of Redemptive History*, trans. Ilse and Reginald Fuller (Philadelphia: Fortress Press, 1967).
31. Günter Klein, *Die Zwölf Apostel*, Forschungen zur Religion und Literatur des Alten und Neuen Testaments, NF 59, No. 77 (Göttingen: Vandenhoeck & Ruprecht, 1961); Klaus Baltzer, "The Meaning of the Temple in the Lukan Writings," *HTR*, 58 (1965), pp. 263–77.

Far from viewing the cleansing as a wholly ruinous affair, Matthew and Luke conceive of it as a drastic reform. In each case the cleansing results in a positive reassessment of the role of the temple in the Christian history of redemption. The temple is restored to its innate purpose, and not disqualified in essence. Jesus takes possession of the purged sanctuary, thus truly becoming lord of the temple.

In the Markan plot an initial temple visit (11:11) intervenes between acclamation and "cleansing." According to the much disputed redactional verse 11:11,[32] Jesus enters the city for the purpose of visiting the temple, and he sets foot in the temple only to vacate it at nightfall and to depart from the city altogether. During his first day in the sanctuary he is said to have "looked around at everything." The Markan *periblepsesthai* intimates a critical or even judgmental look by Jesus.[33] Jesus' exodus from the temple takes place in the late evening hour (11:11c: *opse ēdē ousēs tēs hōras*). While on one level the lateness of the hour provides an explanation for his departure, on a deeper level the approaching darkness forebodes the impending hour of crisis.[34] Thus although Jesus' goal is the temple, his first visitation prior to the "cleansing" lacks any kind of messianic association. It is not a triumphal entry, but a critical examination of "everything." Jesus enters, subjects the whole place to his critical judgment, and leaves. The entry and exit motifs are tightly contracted in this one episode. As it had formerly been his habit to enter and leave a house, a boat, a synagogue, a town, so does he now go in and out of the temple.[35] In this manner the centrality of the temple is passed over and the center of life is relativized to a mere transitional stage on Jesus' way. The temple is devoid of a sense of fulfillment and finality, and there is an air of judgment about it unheard of in Matthew and Luke.[36]

Time and again 11:15-19 has been approached with the objective of

32. Vincent Taylor, *The Gospel According to St. Mark* (London: Macmillan & Co., 1963), p. 458; Joachim Jeremias, *The Eucharistic Words of Jesus*, trans. Norman Perrin, 3rd ed., rev. (New York: Charles Scribner's Sons, 1966), p. 91.

33. See Chap. I, p. 21. In the last controversy scene Jesus looks around "with anger" (3:5). Prior to the mystery speech, his look at the insiders implies judgment on his blood relatives outside (3:34). As the healing power passes from him he looks around with irritation seeking to detect the source of his depletion (5:32). Looking at the disciples he warns them of the difficulty associated with reaching the goal of the Kingdom (10:23).

34. For *opse* and *proi* as subtle indicators of judgment and salvation, see Johannes Schreiber, *Theologie des Vertrauens* (Hamburg: Furche-Verlag, 1967), pp. 94-103, *passim*.

35. See Chap. IV, pp. 67-68.

36. Vaguely to the point is Walter Grundmann, *Das Evangelium nach Markus* (Berlin: Evangelische Verlagsanstalt, 1965), p. 228: "Es wird eine eigenartige Fremdheit zwischen Jesus und Jerusalem sichtbar."

extracting a historical reconstruction of the "cleansing" event.[37] But one need only ask the vital *historical* questions to recognize that the text is not calculated to deal with them. Could Jesus have done single-handedly what he is reported to have done without being stopped by those whom he must have deeply affronted? Why did the Jewish temple guard not interfere with what to them must have appeared a blasphemy of the highest order? Did the Roman national guard stationed at the nearby *Turris Antonia* for the purpose of preserving (Roman) law and order idly stand by while peace was disturbed at the center of Jewish life? Why was this sacrilegious offense never brought up in Jesus' trial? What was the disciples' part in the incident? While the text *in its present form* is unlikely to have been recorded from the perspective of Jesus' history, it assumes a vital role in the theological program of Mark and is ultimately designed to answer Mark's historical question.

The redactional technique of composition is apparent, for it is by means of an interpolation of the "cleansing" (11:15–19) into the story of the fig tree fatality (11:12–14, 20–21) that Mark communicates a possible inter-relationship between fig tree and temple, withering and "cleansing." Any attempt, therefore, to elucidate the Markan significance of the temple "cleansing" will prove abortive, unless the whole complex, fig tree—"cleansing"—is taken into consideration.

The first half of the fig tree pericope (11:12–14)[38] appears to be a straightforward, uncomplicated story—except for the motive given for the tree's failure. It is claimed that the tree did not bear fruit "because it was not the season for figs" (11:13c). But why condemn the tree for what it could in the nature of the case not possibly have produced? At this point, scholars resort to the world of fig trees in the hope of turning up a natural explanation for the tree's failure. But Mark the theologian does not share the scholars' enthusiasm for the tree life of Israel. If 11:13c breaks the cogency of the plot, in it may well lie the clue to the whole.[39] *Ho gar*

---

37. For recent attempts at a historical reconstruction, see Victor Eppstein, "The Historicity of the Gospel Account of the Cleansing of the Temple," *ZNW*, 55 (1964), pp. 42–58; Richard H. Hiers, "Purification of the Temple: Preparation for the Kingdom of God," *JBL*, 90 (1971), pp. 82–90.

38. Summaries of various interpretations of the fig tree pericope are contained in A. de Q. Robin, "The Cursing of the Fig Tree in Mark XI. A Hypothesis," *NTS*, 8 (1962), pp. 276–81, and Gerhard Münderlein, "Die Verfluchung des Feigenbaumes," *NTS*, 10 (1963), pp. 89–104.

39. This methodological principle was recognized by Wrede, *Messiasgeheimnis*, p. 51: "Denn in der Anschauung des Markus muss die Erklärung liegen, wenn die Geschichte sie versagt." It was restated in sharpened form by Schreiber, *Theologie*, p. 125: "Die Ideen des Verfassers hat man gerade da zu suchen, wo seine Darstellung unsinnig erscheint."

kairos ouk ēn sykōn, the very clause which disrupts the logic of the story, is one of Mark's *gar* clauses which invite the reader "to understand the context in the light of something outside the data explicitly presented to us."[40] Mark's mentioning of *kairos* points outside the immediate fig tree plot to the principal affirmation of the arrival of the *kairos* in 1:15. The fig tree pericope is redacted in such a way that the impotent tree dramatizes an eschatological crisis. In a general sense, the fig tree disaster demonstrates the abortion of the *kairos* and the frustration of the arrival of the Kingdom. The *kairos* is fulfilled in Galilee, but unfulfilled in Jerusalem.[41]

The following "cleansing" proper is almost universally located in the temple's forecourt, the Court of the Gentiles. Jesus, it is argued, leaves the heart of Jewish worship intact and acts upon the threshold because his concern is "only indirectly with a Jewish Temple problem and much more directly with the problem of the 'Gentiles.' "[42] By "cleansing" the forecourt Jesus opens the temple to the Gentiles. This forecourt hypothesis has no support in the text whatsoever. Three times the setting of the "cleansing" is given as *to hieron,* and in no other terms. Jesus enters *eis to hieron,* ejects the venders and purchasers *en tō hierō,* and prohibits the carrying of a vessel *dia tou hierou.* Subsequently it is *en tō hierō* (11:27; 12:35; see 14:49), in the temple and hardly in its forecourt, where Jesus delivers his final speeches. Nor is his exodus *ek tou hierou* (13:1) and his instantaneous announcement of the destruction of the holy place merely aimed at the Gentile vestibule. Whatever the size, measurements, and architectural design of the temple, for Mark the temple is one undivided religious entity. It is the nerve center of the city, the provisional goal of Jesus' way, the seat of Davidic promises which Jesus is about to disclaim, as well as the core of hostility and opposition. The inference is that Jesus' exorcising expulsion (11:15b: *ērxato ekballein*) of the tradespeople and their sacrificial birds must be understood as an attack directed against the temple as a whole. His disruption of the business transactions wrecks the center of life. Mark is alone in reporting that Jesus bans the carrying of anything (11:16: *skeuos*) through the temple. Given the forecourt hypothesis this prohibition was assumed to imply that the Court of Gentiles was not to be used as a short cut by people who carried heavy

---

40. C. H. Bird, "Some *gar* Clauses in St. Mark's Gospel," *JTS,* 4 (1953), p. 173.
41. To our knowledge, Schreiber (*Theologie,* p. 136) is the only scholar who states unambiguously that 11:13c is "die Pointe der Geschichte," which must be understood "im Rahmen der markinischen Eschatologie."
42. Lohmeyer, *Lord,* p. 39.

burdens across the temple hill. Yet again, attention must be directed to the fact that it is *dia tou hierou* that a *skeuos* is forbidden to be carried. What other significance can *skeuos*, vessel, in conjunction with *to hieron*, temple, have but that of a sacred cult vessel?[43] Understood in a religious sense, the obstruction of the vessel's transport effects the cessation of the temple's cultic functions.[44] In the view of Mark, therefore, Jesus not only puts an end to the temple's business operation, but he also suspends the practice of cult and ritual. At this point the temple no longer operates. It is shut down in all its functions.

It is in reaction to this incident that the Jerusalem leaders, still in the temple, plot a way of eliminating Jesus (11:18). Not since the Galilean controversies (3:6) has the opponents' murderous intention been so plainly brought into the open. It is solely the view of Mark that Jesus' temple "cleansing" precipitated the plot against his life. It is in the place of Davidic promise and eschatological hope that the course of events takes a dismal turn toward destruction. The place of life becomes the breeding place of death. Appropriately, the late hour of darkness (11:19a: *kai hotan opse egeneto*) signals Jesus' abandonment of temple and city.[45]

Has the temple thus been purified and conditioned for the eschatological pilgrimage of the nations to Mount Zion?[46] Or is the incident correctly comprehended as "a sign or token that with the Lord's arrival at Jerusalem the messianic age, indeed the kingdom of God, was at the doors . . . ?"[47] Or does it under the veil of secrecy accomplish Jesus' enthronement?[48] Can this demonstration in the temple be properly classified as a "cleansing" at all? Mark himself never refers to the temple incident in terms of a purge or cleansing. For an answer to the question we turn to the second fig tree unit (11:20–21).

While prior to the temple affair the fig tree's future appeared to be

---

43. Over one-third of the references to *skeuos* in the LXX denote sacred cult objects of the tabernacle, altar, or temple, see Christian Maurer, "skeuos," *TDNT*, 7, p. 359.

44. The omission of 11:16 by Matthew and Luke is a *testimonium e silentio* to an anti-temple slant in Mark, for the two synoptics hold a considerably more positive view of Jerusalem and its temple than Mark. To our knowledge, the only scholar who comes closest to our interpretation of 11:16 is Hans-Werner Bartsch, "Early Christian Eschatology in the Synoptic Gospels," *NTS*, 11 (1965), p. 394.

45. Schreiber, *Theologie*, pp. 89, 143, emphasizes the enormity of the fact that the death plot is located in the temple.

46. Lohmeyer, *Markus*, p. 237.

47. Robert H. Lightfoot, *The Gospel Message of St. Mark* (Oxford: Oxford University Press, 1952), p. 67; similarly Erich Grässer, *Das Problem der Parusieverzögerung in den Synoptischen Evangelien und in der Apostelgeschichte*, Beihefte zur *ZNW*, No. 22, 2nd ed. (Berlin: Alfred Töpelmann, 1960), pp. 27–28.

48. Schreiber, *Theologie*, p. 193, *passim*.

doomed, it is *ex post facto* said to have been cursed and withered away. The curse has taken effect and the tree is dead. In the context of Mark's framing design the fig tree stands for the temple, and the disaster which befell the tree illustrates what occurred to the temple. Far from being "cleansed" in order to serve in a new and purified fashion, the temple is condemned and ruined beyond all hope of recovery (the tree is ravaged from the roots up, not merely from the leaves down!). The crisis, we noted earlier, demonstrates the unfulfillment of the *kairos*. The specific condemnation, we now conclude, strikes at the eschatological prestige of the temple. The *kairos* of the Kingdom is divorced from the holy city and its temple, and the latter is deprived of its eschatological credentials. We are as yet not sufficiently informed of the Markan situation, and that of his opponents, to fully appreciate this argument: chapter 13 of the gospel, the apocalypse, will give us the opportunity to observe the opponents at close range. But we will have to bear in mind that Mark's compositional arrangement, dooming of fig tree—temple incident—withering of fig tree, is meant to highlight an eschatological temple crisis. The temple is disqualified from ever serving in its Davidic, eschatological capacity, and the way of Jesus appears to have stalled in the heart of the establishment.

THE NEW PLACE

But all is not ill-fated, because the way leads out of the impasse toward a destination that takes the place of the old site. This new goal is already intimated in Jesus' temple *didache* (11:17), delivered at the site of expulsion and disqualification. The heavily redacted 11:17 is substantially made up of Isa. 56:7 (and an echo of Jer. 7:11.[49] Of the two quotations Jer. 7:11 was part of the traditional story dealing with a temple incident. Mark eliminated it with the exception of the last two words ("den of robbers") which provides the scriptural justification for Jesus' action. With the aid of an introductory formula (11:17a) Mark inserted Isaiah 56:7 (11:17b), first and foremost because he had strong feelings about opening his community "to all the nations." He "wanted the *pasin tois ethnesin* on the lips of the teaching Jesus."[50] Matthew and Luke, each for his own reason, suppress Mark's Gentile vision.[51] This ideal of Gentile

49. Crossan, "Redaction," pp. 32–36.
50. *Ibid.*, p. 36.
51. *Ibid.*, p. 34. Matthew "because the period of universalism had not yet begun." The mission to the Gentiles is the task of the church (Matt. 28:19). Luke also "found this phrase of Mark too much too soon." The breakthrough to the Gentiles marks a distinct phase in the history of the apostolic church (Acts 10).

inclusion will have commended itself to Mark out of his own communal experience, because it is a direct reflection of the expanded Jewish-Gentile community in Galilee. It might be argued that Gentile inclusion is the one feature in support of the forecourt hypothesis: the segregated temple is purged and thereby opened to all the Gentiles. But the eschatological bent of *klēthēsetai* points beyond the present time and place.[52] Mark does not dramatize the purifying transformation of the present state of corruption. Instead he pronounces an end to the temple and the beginning of a new mode of life which is approximated by his own community, but still lacks eschatological consummation.

Peter's recognition of the tree's withered condition is met by Jesus' words of hope: "Have faith in God" (11:22b). In Mark *pistis* constitutes more a state of hopefulness in the face of visible evidence than personal belief in the Christ of the cross.[53] The full profile of faith emerges in 15:32. During Jesus' agony on the cross, representatives of the establishment taunt him to save himself and come down from the cross *hina idōmen kai pisteusōmen*. In this scene, the distorted notion of faith is put on the lips of the scoffers. Their faith is grounded in *seeing*. For Mark, however, *seeing* is the eschatological experience reserved for the parousia and the Kingdom in fullness, and faith is the proper attitude in view of the present hiddenness and unfulfillment. Spoken in the face of the temple's condemnation, Jesus' injunction to have faith in God provides a hint to the effect that the situation is not totally hopeless. The impossible might yet come through and the way be found which leads to the Kingdom of God.

The saying about the removal of a mountain (11:23) illustrates the omnipotence of faith. Following on the heels of the disqualification of the temple mount, however, this aggressive anti-mountain remark may well be understood in a non-metaphorical sense. C. W. F. Smith[54] correctly observed that the demonstrative pronoun (*tō orei toutō*) points to a specific mountain, but he assumed it was the Mount of Olives which according to the prophecy of Zechariah 14 will be toppled over and flattened out. But since Mark consistently identifies by name the Mount of Olives while leaving other mountains anonymous "it seems doubtful whether the Mount of Olives can rightly be compared to cases where a

---

52. The eschatological proclivity of *klēthēsetai* in Matthew 5:9, 19; Luke 1:32; and Mark 11:17 was well brought out by Ernst Lohmeyer, "Die Reinigung des Tempels," *ThBl*, 20 (1941), p. 261.
53. See Chap. I, p. 13.
54. Charles W. F. Smith, "No Time for Figs," *JBL*, 79 (1960), p. 322.

mountain in general is mentioned."[55] Nor does Mark's eschatologically motivated topography allow for this conclusion, as will be shown below. There is in view of the antecedent disqualification of the temple every likelihood to assume that it is the temple mount against which this saying is addressed.[56] Given the power of faith, the lofty temple hill may be humiliated and toppled. If this interpretation be accepted, it provides a first indication of the actual destruction of the temple. With the fall of the temple, Jesus' eschatological annulment of the sanctuary has come true. But it is understood as living proof of the power of faith and prayer, because the end of the temple confirms the beginning of life in the Kingdom elsewhere. The disaster is turned into a symbol of hope. The precise manner in which new hope is to be realized Mark dramatizes topologically.[57]

The southern topography signals a redirection of the way of the Kingdom toward the north. It is from Bethphage and Bethany "at the Mount of Olives" (11:1) that Jesus embarks upon his temple mission. After his initial, short visit to the temple mount (11:11) he returns to his point of departure (11:11d). On the following day it is again from Bethany at the Mount of Olives (11:12) that he undertakes his second, fateful entry onto the temple mount. Mark singles out the Mount of Olives, not because Jesus could not help but cross this mountain site on his way to the temple, but rather because he intends to illustrate a singular relationship between the Mount of Olives and the temple mount. With the Mount of Olives as his temporary headquarters, Jesus sets out to divest the temple mount of its eschatological authority. As the prestige of the temple mount declines, the Mount of Olives is in the ascendant. And while the temple mount is excluded from further participation in the history of the end time, it is the Mount of Olives which in its stead constitutes the new "eschatological base of operations."[58] Hence, the Markan Jesus traveling back and forth between the two southern mountain peaks dramatizes

55. Ulrich Mauser, *Christ in the Wilderness*, Studies in Biblical Theology, No. 39 (Naperville, Ill.: Alec R. Allenson, Inc., 1963), p. 109.

56. Thus also Charles H. Dodd, *The Parables of the Kingdom*, rev. ed. (New York: Charles Scribner's Sons, 1961), p. 45, n. 2; R. J. McKelvey, *The New Temple*, Oxford Theological Monographs, No. 3 (Oxford: Oxford University Press, 1969), p. 65, n. 3; Lightfoot, *St. Mark*, p. 78.

57. With the following observations we are indebted to Werner Schmauch, "Der Ölberg. Exegese zu einer Ortsangabe besonders bei Matthäus und Markus," *TLZ*, 77 (1952), pp. 391–96; see also his *Orte der Offenbarung und der Offenbarungsort im Neuen Testament* (Göttingen: Vandenhoeck & Ruprecht, 1956), pp. 62–67, *passim*.

58. Smith, "Figs," p. 323.

both the dispossession of the natural rights from the temple mount and the temporary transference of power upon the Mount of Olives.

It is therefore in the proper sequence of an eschatologically conditioned topography when the new ordering of time is issued from the Mount of Olives (13:1–37). Seated upon the counter mountain and opposite the temple mount (13:3) Jesus unfolds the apocalyptic program of the end time. Nor is it surprising that it is upon the Mount of Olives that the new place is for the first time revealed. After the celebration of the Last Supper, Jesus and the twelve ascend the new mount of revelation (14:26), and it is from there that the disciples catch a glimpse of the new direction, the full length, and the ultimate goal of the way. The Jesus *proagōn* (14:28: *proaxō hymas*; 16:7: *proagei hymas*) will lead his followers into the Kingdom of God in Galilee. As far as Galilee the disciples will have to go in order to fully know Jesus as well as themselves. This is then the last service the Mount of Olives is to perform: to point away from itself and to reveal Galilee as the locus of the eschatological reunion. With the eschaton at a standstill upon the temple mount it has fallen upon the opposite mountain peak to revitalize and reorient the way of the Kingdom. Ultimately, the southern topography is designed in such a manner that it directs the way out of the lost center and back to the new place of Galilee.

CONCLUSION

Separation and schism, long prepared for in Galilee, take full effect in the temple of Jerusalem. Far from narrating a triumphal entry into Jerusalem, Mark argues the disqualification of the temple mount, the overthrow of the Kingdom's cause in the temple, and the refutation of the Davidic identity of Jesus. For whether he implies the priority of the Kingdom over the holy city or demonstrates the separation of the *kairos* from the temple, whether he rejects Jesus' Davidic sonship or dramatizes the eschatological temple crisis, whether he reports Jesus' judgmental look at the temple or locates the death plot in the temple—the combined impact of all these points is to break the myth of Davidic messianism and to dissociate the Kingdom from the temple. The temple is the locus of the crisis, and the central issue of this crisis is the temple's eschatological reputation.

While the temple is incapacitated from disclosing the new place in full, it is nevertheless on the site of the old system that the beginning of new life is intimated. The eschatological schism in the temple is accompanied with the promise of a turning "to all the nations." Both the schism and the ensuing broadening of the ideal of life have been in the making throughout the Galilean mission. The exclusion of the relatives (3:20–35) had led to the initiation into the mystery of the Kingdom (4:1–34). The schism with the family (6:1–6a) had ushered in the disciples' apostolic mission (6:6b–13). The break with Jerusalem (7:1–23) was followed by Jesus' northern journey (7:24, 31). Upon arrival in Jerusalem the schism in the temple entails the vision of an all-comprehensive model of life. The Galilean breaks cause a separation from Jerusalem, as much as the schism in the temple shifts the focus toward the disestablished Jewish-Gentile community in Galilee. The establishment of Galilee is contingent upon the disestablishment from Jerusalem, and the break with the old place effects a broadening of the Christian sense of reality toward the new place of ethnic universalism.

The full recovery of hope gets under way with the aid of the topological dialectic of the temple mount versus the Mount of Olives. It has been suggested that Mark's dramatization of the southern mountain rivalry is derived from the mountain symbolism of Zechariah 14.[59] Yet the prophet's vision, anticipating the splitting apart of the Mount of Olives and the elevation of Jerusalem, moves strictly within the bounds of the Davidic Zion tradition. Mark, on the contrary, reverses the traditional roles of the two mountains. And yet, his anti-Zion posture is not without precedent. It was the priestly prophet Ezekiel who had six centuries earlier argued that YHWH had ostentatiously vacated His temple to settle down "upon the mountain which is on the east side of the city" (Ezek. 11:23). It will be recalled that Ezekiel theologized in the aftermath of the Babylonian destruction of the temple. The theme of God's exodus out of the temple and his enthronement upon the rival peak is indicative of a theology of crisis which copes with the shattering experience of the destruction of the house of YHWH. Like Ezekiel, Mark elevates the Mount of Olives at the total expense of the temple mount, and enlists the former into the service of his crisis theology. Historically, it is the Roman destruction of Jerusalem and its sanctuary which forced the anti-Zion theology upon Mark. His deliberate violation of the Zion mythology serves in part as the etiological explanation of the enemy's conflagration of the temple. Mark sees the present disaster of the temple destruction originating in the past of Jesus. The disqualification of the temple has

59. William Manson, *Jesus the Messiah* (London: Hodder and Stoughton, 1943), p. 30.

become a horrible reality in the time of Mark. The details of the Markan argument, however, point to an eschatological crisis the nature of which we have as yet not fully uncovered.

The shock of the loss of the center is absorbed by the new place of Galilee. Galilee is not merely the twice-articulated (14:28; 16:7), dimly disclosed goal of the way, but it is the well-established place of Jesus' northern ministry. Long before the loss of Jerusalem was dramatized and the holy city declared a place of "No Kingdom There" (Isa. 34:12), Jesus had assured the arrival of the Kingdom in Galilee (1:14–15). Through Jesus' Kingdom message, exorcisms, and healings Galilee was cleansed and sanctioned, and by way of his voyages Galilee was enlarged to include the Gentiles. Having created the Kingdom in Galilee, the south was to be the place of loss and surrender, and the temple the center of schism. In the last analysis, Galilee was cleansed and created because it is to become the New Jerusalem for those caught in the crisis of the old Jerusalem.

Chapter VI

THE KINGDOM'S INVOLVEMENT IN THE FALL OF JERUSALEM

13:1-37

3 sections to the speech

Jesus' second speech, the apocalypse, confronts the interpreter with a number of problems which require a brief hermeneutical reflection.

The apocalyptic speech (13:5b–37) comprises the only block of material which "disrupts" the narration of the life and death of Jesus. False prophets, wars, and persecutions do not seem to have a part in Jesus' ministry. The impression is that of an erratic boulder which thwarts the gospel's story line. Furthermore, the apocalypse has been proven to be a revision of apocalyptic traditions. Both the apocalypse's seemingly isolated position in the gospel and its independent prehistory in the tradition encouraged scholars to interpret the speech in virtual isolation from the remainder of the gospel.[1] But once it is assumed that the redactor's ambition extends beyond the shaping and making of individual traditions to the creation of the total gospel unit, Mark 13 is likely to form an integral part of the gospel whole. As the apocalyptic elements have entered into the new unity of Chapter 13, so will Mark 13 have become a constituent

---

1. This holds true of the majority of major studies on Mark 13: Friedrich Busch, *Zum Verständnis der Synoptischen Eschatologie. Markus 13 Neu Untersucht* (Gütersloh: C. Bertelsmann, 1938); George R. Beasley-Murray, *A Commentary on Mark Thirteen* (London: Macmillan & Co., Ltd., 1957); Willi Marxsen, *Mark the Evangelist*, trans. Roy A. Harrisville *et al.* (Nashville, Tenn.: Abingdon, 1969), pp. 151–206; Jan Lambrecht, *Die Redaktion der Markus-Apokalypse. Literarische Analyse und Strukturuntersuchung*, Analecta Biblica, No. 28 (Rome: Pontifical Biblical Institute, 1967); Lars Hartman, *Prophecy Interpreted*, trans. Neil Tomkinson, Coniectanea Biblica, New Testament Series I (Lund, Sweden: CWK Gleerup, 1966). To this day the magisterial work on the Markan apocalypse remains Rudolf Pesch, *Naherwartungen* (Düsseldorf: Patmos-Verlag, 1968). Yet even Pesch argues that Mark 13 is not part of the gospel's structural disposition; it is something of an afterthought of the evangelist.

part of the new gospel unit. By incorporating the apocalypse into the *corpus* of the gospel, Mark has in fact divested the former of its isolation.

It might well be asked whether to assume the integrated function of Chapter 13 is not to overtax the intention or skill of the redactor. Inherent in redaction criticism, and still more so in composition criticism, is the danger of overrating the literary and theological cohesion of the gospel. Moreover, is it beyond the shadow of a doubt that it was Mark who inserted the apocalypse, or could the latter not owe its existence to a post-Markan redactor whose theological program was at variance with that of Mark? If, however, the apocalypse in its present form is traceable to Mark, why did he present it and why at this point in the gospel? For if one were to discern the motive(s) which prompted Mark to "digress" from the narrative sequence of the Jesus story, one could learn what significance he ascribed to his apocalyptic "digression." Without denying the abiding contributions made toward the reconstruction of the pre-Markan *Vorlage*, there remain questions which justify a more thoroughly contextual reading of Mark 13. Following once again the principle of composition criticism, we will almost entirely move on the level of the Markan text, focus upon the redactor's reason for his apocalyptic presentation, and relate the speech back to this motivational starting point. The structural make-up of the speech will further aid us toward recovering the Markan viewpoint.

As noted above, what gives the speech an anomalous quality is a section which abounds with historical references (13:5b–22) in a manner unparalleled in the gospel. This very part has rightly been considered rather like a window which allows a close view of Markan circumstances. While throughout the gospel the past of Jesus speaks to the present of Mark, in this one instance the Markan reality bursts through the medium of the Jesus story. The force of the present experience is such that it asserts itself in unmediated fashion. The facts speak for themselves. What comes to expression in the apocalyptic speech must be of ultimate concern to Mark. At issue, we shall see, is the very crisis which gave rise to the gospel composition, the destruction of Jerusalem and its temple.

Yet why is the fundamental crisis dealt with at this particular point in the gospel? If the gospel responds in its entirety to the traumatic experience of the Jerusalem destruction, Mark must have carefully chosen the point at which he makes explicit reference to it. He commences his gospel not with the downfall of Jerusalem, but with the creation of the new place of Galilee. With Jesus' entry into Judea and the capital Mark begins to build up toward the Jerusalem crisis. Upon arrival in Jerusalem Jesus preaches the surrender of everything for his own sake and that of the gospel of the Kingdom. Once in the temple, he forces the temple operations to a complete standstill and pronounces a fateful sentence against the holy shrine. Having disqualified the temple as the locus of eschatological fulfillment (11:12–20), and having ideologically set himself apart from the temple (12:35–37a), Jesus removes himself physically from the temple (13:1) and predicts its physical collapse (13:2). With this we have arrived at the introduction to the apocalypse (13:1–4). Jesus' second speech forms the culmination of this anti-Jerusalem, anti-temple thrust (Chaps. 11–12).[2]

When viewed from this contextual perspective, Mark 13 is not quite the erratic boulder standing apart from the total gospel story, but is wholly congruous with the antecedent development. It is not so much a "digression" from the Jesus story, as the carefully redacted climax of Jesus' anti-temple mission. The past of Jesus is designed so as to initiate the temple crisis and then lead up to the consummation of this crisis in the time of Mark.

The introduction to the speech (13:1–4), a redactional product throughout,[3] requires a careful investigation because the manner in which Mark launches the speech gives further clues to its specific purpose.

END OF THE TEMPLE, AND END OF ALL THINGS

The verses leading up to Jesus' speech proper portray two separate scenes against the background of two different locales. In 13:1–2, Jesus discourses with one of the disciples outside the temple, and in 13:3–4 the four chosen confidants question Jesus on the Mount of Olives, opposite the temple. The conventional assumption of a literary seam between 13:2 and 13:3 fails to take into account the redactional nature of 13:1–4.[4] Given the fact of Mark's composition of 13:1–4, the question arises: why did he create two distinct scenes, set apart by locality, but united in their

---

2. Pesch (*Naherwartungen*, p. 93) recognizes that the apocalypse comes at the end of the "tempelfeindlichen Jerusalemer Komplex des Evangeliums." And yet, he pleads for the "Isolierung von Mk 13 und die künstliche Anfügung des Kapitels an den Jerusalemer Komplex" (p. 95).

3. *Ibid.*, pp. 83–107; Lambrecht, *Markus-Apokalypse*, pp. 67–91.

4. The theory of a seam between 13:2 and 13:3 goes back to Karl L. Schmidt, *Der Rahmen der Geschichte Jesu* (Berlin: Trowitzsch und Sohn, 1919; reprinted Darmstadt: Wissenschaftliche Buchgesellschaft, 1964), p. 290.

relation to the temple, and in what sense do these two scenes prepare for the speech proper?

Verses 13:1–2 show how Jesus, having completed his temple activity, makes his exodus from the doomed site and instantly turns against it by issuing the prediction of its physical downfall. The subsequent speech takes its principal point of departure from this forecast. The temple saying 13:2c functions as a "peg" upon which the apocalypse hangs. Mark's ulterior motive for presenting the apocalypse is discernible from the manner in which he lays the groundwork. Placed after the temple saying, the speech as a whole constitutes a response to the forecast destruction of the temple. It is reasonable to assume that Mark introduces the apocalypse in this way because the disaster of the temple was in his experience a *fait accompli*.[5] His concern is to provide an answer to the problems triggered off by the catastrophe, and he does this by initiating Jesus' speech with a forecast of the very event upon which he and the Christians are already looking back.

According to the second scene, 13:3–4, Jesus is seated upon the Mount of Olives, opposite the temple (13:3a: *katenanti tou hierou*). Thus Jesus delivers the speech while enthroned upon the eschatological counter mountain and looking upon the temple whose downfall he has in mind.[6] Both the first and the second scene focus upon the temple, and the apocalyptic speech is firmly anchored in the temple and closely related to its predicted fall. This dramatic setting appeals directly to the Christians. They, too, have the temple in mind, because they live under the impact of its destruction and are confronted with serious questions. Jesus' subse-

5. The following scholars object to reading 13:2c as an *ex eventu* saying: H. Conzelmann, E. Grässer, G. Harder, W. Marxsen, and J. Schreiber. That the verse provides a crucial clue to the Markan redaction was recognized by Leo Baeck, *Das Evangelium als Urkunde der jüdischen Glaubensgeschichte* (Berlin: Schocken, 1938), p. 46; Pesch, *Naherwartungen*, pp. 93–96; Ferdinand Hahn, *Mission in the New Testament*, trans. Frank Clarke (Naperville, Ill.: Alec R. Allenson, Inc., 1965), p. 111, n. 4; Nikolaus Walter, "Tempelzerstörung und Synoptische Apokalypse," *ZNW*, 57 (1966), pp. 38–49. See also Neill Q. Hamilton, "Resurrection Tradition and the Composition of Mark," *JBL*, 84 (1965), p. 419: "The gospel ought to be dated, like all apocalyptically oriented literature, from the last event it knows correctly but pretends to predict. This, of course, is the destruction of the temple and Jerusalem." S. G. F. Brandon also dates the gospel shortly after A.D. 70, see "The Date of the Markan Gospel," *NTS*, 7 (1961), pp. 126–41. But he proceeds from external evidence toward documentary evidence. He commences with "the probable situation of the Christian community at Rome under the impact of the events of A.D. 70," and then turns to the Markan text to see if "the internal plan and content of the Gospel reflect the situation of the Roman Christians" (p. 130).

6. Lambrecht, *Markus-Apokalypse*, p. 80, correctly observes: "Der Ölberg steht im Dienst des Folgenden. Markus will vom Berg her eine Aussicht auf den Tempel haben. Nicht der Berg, sondern der Tempel ist ihm wichtig."

quent speech serves to respond to the dilemma caused by the ruin of the temple.

The four disciples, functioning as Jesus' opponents, ask a two-fold question (13:4) which reveals the heart of their abortive theological position and simultaneously specifies the nature of the dilemma: "When will this (*tauta*) be, and what will be the sign when these things will all be accomplished (*tauta synteleisthai panta*)." There is widespread consensus that *tauta* refers back to the forecast destruction of the temple, and *tauta synteleisthai panta* points forward to the eschaton. The conjunction of these two motifs is revealing for it shows that the end of the temple could be taken for or associated with the end of all things. From this one can draw the basic outline of the theological position represented by the disciples. In some sense the eschaton is related to the temple, or the arrival of the Kingdom to the fall of the temple.[7] With the temple lying in ruins, however, and the eschaton still unconsummated, this eschatology must be challenged, corrected even, for it proved to be "false prophecy" which misled the believers into a situation of eschatological crisis. What can under those circumstances be relied upon as *to sēmeion*? What is now the true sign which heralds the end?

We are at this point able to clarify the introductory function of the two scenes. The first scene presents the basic issue with which the Christians wrestle: the destruction of the temple. The second scene articulates in what particular sense the disaster poses a problem for the believers. The double question which forms the immediate transition to the speech reveals that the physical downfall of the temple had precipitated a crisis of eschatological quality. It is in response to this eschatological crisis and disorientation that the Markan Jesus delivers his apocalyptic address.[8]

THE PROPHETS OF PAROUSIA

It will have to be demonstrated that the apocalyptic speech addresses itself to the above-said crisis situation and proposes a corrective against an erroneous eschatology.

7. Lloyd Gaston, *No Stone On Another*, Supplements to Novum Testamentum, No. 23 (Leiden: E. J. Brill, 1970), p. 12: "It is assumed by the disciples, according to Mark, that the fall of Jerusalem and the end of the world are related, even simultaneous events."
8. Hans Conzelmann ("Geschichte und Eschaton nach Mc 13," ZNW, 50 [1959], pp. 214–15) keenly observes "dass es um Korrektur umlaufender eschatologischer Irrlehre geht, welche einen—nach der Meinung des Markus—falschen Zusammenhang zwischen Schicksal des Tempels und Weltende behauptet."

The first two verses of the speech, 13:5b–6, bear a striking resemblance to 13:21–22; both verse units deal with the issue of deception.[9] The first unit opens with *blepete* (13:5b), and the second unit concludes with *blepete* (13:23a). This *blepein* in the imperative is a redactional device which has a structural function in the apocalypse.[10] The two verse units furnished with Mark's structural imperatives signal beginning and end of a major division, the first section of the speech.[11] Once again we detect the Markan framing device. Mark interpolates the speech material of the first part of the apocalypse between two separate units each of which deals with the same subject matter, false prophecy. Since the framing units exercise a controlling influence upon the material they embrace, this first section of the apocalypse is comprehended in depth only when viewed against the background of false prophecy.[12] Thus the first part of the speech is indeed organized with the objective of opposing a particular viewpoint.

The speech proper begins, significantly enough, with a warning (13:5b: *blepete mē*) which corresponds to the warning in the second unit (13:21d: *mē pisteuete*). From the outset the apocalypse stands in relation to and takes a stand against a particular position. Advocates of this position are described as coming *epi tō onomati mou* and saying *egō eimi* (13:6a). Since the personal pronoun *mou* can only refer to the person of the speaker, i.e., Jesus, the opponents apparently come in the name of Jesus. This does not fully disclose their purpose and identity, because their coming in Jesus' name lends itself to a variety of interpretations. First, they come on the authority of Jesus, i.e., they are commissioned by him.[13] Second, they come on the authority of Jesus and invoke his name.[14]

---

9. Similarity between these two verse units is often recognized. See for example Julius Wellhausen, *Das Evangelium Marci* (Berlin: Georg Reimer, 1909), p. 101; Busch, *Verständnis*, p. 80; Beasley-Murray, *Mark Thirteen*, p. 84; Lambrecht, *Markus-Apokalypse*, pp. 100–05, 168–72; Pesch, *Naherwartungen*, pp. 107–18; Theodore J. Weeden, *Mark—Traditions in Conflict* (Philadelphia: Fortress Press, 1971), pp. 88–89; Conzelmann, "Geschichte," p. 217.

10. Theodore J. Weeden ("The Heresy that Necessitated Mark's Gospel," ZNW, 59 [1968], p. 151) calls it a "Markan key word"; Pesch (*Naherwartungen*) refers to it as a "strukturbildendes Element" (p. 77) or a "Leitwort" (p. 107), and Lambrecht (*Markus-Apokalypse*) as a "Strukturwort" (p. 94).

11. Verse 13:9 is marked as a subdivision within the first section, and 13:33 rounds out the speech by linking up with its opening phrase. Beginning, middle, and end of the first section are thus structured, as well as beginning and end of the total speech.

12. Conzelmann ("Geschichte," p. 217, n. 38) observes about the correlation of the two verse units: "Daran erkennt man, wie Markus die Akzente setzt."

13. Erich Klostermann, *Das Markusevangelium*, 4th ed. (Tübingen: Mohr/Siebeck, 1950), p. 133.

14. Wilhelm Heitmüller, "Im Namen Jesu" (Göttingen: Vandenhoeck & Ruprecht, 1903), p. 63.

Third, they invoke the name of Jesus as a demonstration of their Christian identity.[15] Fourth, they use Jesus' name because they claim his identity.[16] A choice among these options is facilitated by the *egō eimi* formula. The historical roots of the formula are traceable to the I-proclamations of the royal liturgies in ancient Near Eastern religions. It was by means of these self-revelatory proclamations that the divinity proclaimed its real presence in the temple ritual.[17] The *egō eimi* may thus be properly termed a formula of theophany. In 13:6 the *egō eimi* does not require a predicative definition, because used in this absolute sense the formula affirms the presence of Jesus. This qualifies the meaning of the ambiguous *epi tō onomati mou* in favor of the fourth option. Those who use the formula of theophany assert the identity of the very one in whose name they come. But anyone who approximately forty years after Jesus' death claimed Jesus' presence must have claimed the reappearance of the crucified Jesus of the past. This brings us to the very core of the opposition eschatology. It decreed the fulfillment of the eschaton by enacting the parousia of Jesus![18] This eschatological "heresy" is therefore not accurately designated as an outside intervention into Christian beliefs, for the parousia faith is a peculiarly Christian tenet and only Christians are likely to be interested in forcing its realization. The parousia advocates are not anti-Christian messianic pretenders who compete with or lead away from the Messiah Jesus, but they are Christian prophets who have arrogated to themselves the authority and identity of the Messiah Jesus. The Markan Jesus accuses them of "deceiving" the people. Through a serious misjudgment of time they have usurped the theophanic formula, for according to Mark's concept of time the parousia is the one promise yet to be fulfilled. The Christian opponents are guilty of a premature realization of the eschaton. What emerges as the apocalypse's main objective is the correction of an erroneously conceived realized eschatology.

15. Wellhausen, *Evangelium*, p. 101.
16. Walter Grundmann, *Das Evangelium nach Markus* (Berlin: Evangelische Verlagsanstalt, 1965), p. 263.
17. Ethelbert Stauffer, "egō," *TDNT*, 2, pp. 343–54.
18. Among the scholars who assume a parousia eschatology are: Hans-Werner Bartsch, "Zum Problem der Parusieverzögerung bei den Synoptikern," *EvTh*, 19 (1959), p. 120; Conzelmann, "Geschichte," p. 218; David Daube, *The New Testament and Rabbinic Judaism* (London: Athlone Press, 1956), pp. 325–29; Erich Grässer, *Das Problem der Parusieverzögerung in den Synoptischen Evangelien und in der Apostelgeschichte*, Beihefte zur ZNW, No. 22, 2nd ed. (Berlin: Alfred Töpelmann, 1960), p. 157; Thomas W. Manson, "EGO EIMI of the Messianic Presence in the New Testament," *JTS*, 48 (1947), pp. 137–45; Vincent Taylor, *The Gospel According to St. Mark* (London: Macmillan & Co., 1963), p. 503; Lambrecht, *Markus-Apokalypse*, p. 100; Pesch, *Naherwartungen*, pp. 108–12.

The corresponding frame unit 13:21–22 confirms and further expands our knowledge of the opponents and of Mark's reasons for denouncing them. If someone stages the parousia of Jesus by enacting his messianic epiphany, he is not to be believed (13:21). This warning contrasts sharply with the Galilean invitation to believe in the presence of the Kingdom (1:15)! The opponents are now unmasked as "false Christs" and "false prophets" who seduced the people with "signs and wonders" (13:22). Given the milieu of the parousia imposture, these signs and wonders must be considered tokens of eschatological deliverance. "False Christs" and "false prophets" do not indicate two factions among the opposition. Both labels aim at one and the same people.[19] The Christian prophets falsely endorsed and/or enacted the parousia of Jesus, and are therefore under the indictment of false prophecy. The two local adverbs *hōde* and *ekei* raise the issue of place. The parousia prophets pointing to a "here" and to a "there" seem to have associated their eschatology with a specific site. If we recall Mark's bias against Jerusalem, his deliberate effort to dissociate the Kingdom from the temple, as well as the disciples' mistaken synchronization of the end of the temple with the beginning of the Kingdom, then the holy city itself and the temple in particular emerge as the likely locale of the prophets' eschatological activity. Mark is opposed to the prophets both because they miscalculated the time and because they chose the wrong place. Their eschatological conviction had been ill-timed and out of place.

THE EPIPHANY OF THE EVIL ONE

After the denunciation of the Christian prophets the issue of wars is introduced together with the warning: *mē throeisthe* (13:7). It is doubtful whether *throeisthai* (to be frightened, agitated) expresses fear of the horrors of war. 2 Thessalonians 2:2, the only other New Testament occurrence of *throeisthai* aside from the parallel in Matthew 24:6, warns against a premature anticipation of the day of the Lord. Since it is precisely this unwarranted sense of eschatological fulfillment the apocalypse takes issue with, *mē throeisthe* is likely to be sounding a note of eschatological caution. All the more so since 13:7 explicitly rejects the assumption of the presence of the End: *all' oupō to telos* (13:7d). The experience of wars, or the rumor of wars must not tempt the Christians to plunge

---

19. What the *tis* and the *polloi*, the *pseudochristoi* and the *pseudoprophētai* have in common is the practice of eschatological deception, see Herbert Braun, "planaō," *TDNT*, 6, p. 246: "these represent, not two categories, but one and the same category of men."

into eschatological agitation. Wars come to pass in due time and in accord with a preordained necessity (13:7c), but they are not in themselves *to telos* of time. Although they are understood as a worldwide upheaval of apocalyptic dimension, they do not coincide with the End (13:8). The uprising of nations, the clash of kingdoms, earthquakes, and famines merely mark the beginning of a period which precedes the End. Is it possible to identify the historical reality of these turbulent times? In all probability it is *ex post facto* that Mark accords the war experiences a proper place in history.[20] Writing in the aftermath of the destruction of Jerusalem, he is looking back upon the Roman-Jewish War of A.D. 66–70. His repudiation of a misconstrued eschatology extends beyond the crisis of Jerusalem to the war and its identification with the eschaton. The prophets in whom we had recognized the leaders of the eschatological misconceptions must have been active already during the war years which climaxed in the fall of Jerusalem and its temple. Retrospectively Mark corrects their prophecies by setting the coefficients of a new framework of time (13:7d, 8d). The war was not meant to inaugurate the Kingdom—it merely launched the "beginning of the woes."

The structural imperative *blepete* (13:9a) marks the opening of a new paragraph which deals with the lot of the Christians. The regularly spaced *paradidonai* (13:9b, 11a, 12a) indicates that they are doomed to suffer persecutions. Both Jewish tribunals (13:9b: *synhedria—synagogai*) and Gentile authorities (13:9b: *hēgemones—basileis*) sit in judgment over the Christians. Over and above that, the Christians turn perversely against each other and betray their own blood relatives to their persecutors (13:12). These conditions are not likely to have provided the background for the persecution under Nero,[21] nor do they necessarily point to Galilee.[22] There is no compelling reason, however, for the extension of the historical horizon beyond Israel.[23] During the heat of the War years feel-

---

20. *Dei* in an eschatological context (13:7c) is frequently indicative of a retrospective contemplation of history, see Erich Fascher, "Theologische Bemerkungen zu *dei*," *Neutestamentliche Studien für Rudolf Bultmann* (R. Bultmann Festschrift), Walther Eltester, ed. (Berlin: Alfred Töpelmann, 1954), pp. 228–54. The Son of Man must suffer, die, and rise (8:31: *dei*), but from Mark's own perspective he already has suffered, died, and risen. Elijah must come first (9:11: *dei elthein*), but according to Mark's concept of history he has already appeared in the person of John the Baptist.
21. The thesis that 13:9–13 reflects the circumstances which obtained during the Neronian persecution tends to be popular with scholars who assume the Roman origin of Mark prior to A.D. 70.
22. Marxsen, *Mark*, p. 174.
23. Similarly Wellhausen, *Evangelium*, p. 102; Günther Harder, "Das eschatologische Geschichtsbild der sogenannten kleinen Apokalypse Markus 13," *ThViat*, 4 (1952), p. 78; Taylor, *St. Mark*, p. 506; Beasley-Murray, *Mark Thirteen*, p. 42.

ings are inflamed and suffering is compounded by enemies from without and denunciations from within. But the suffering of the Christians has a quality of its own. They incur the hatred of "all of them" (13:13a), Gentiles, compatriots, friends and relatives because of the name of Jesus (13:13a: *dia to onoma mou*). This brings to mind the activity of the Christian prophets who heralded eschatological liberation *epi tō onomati mou*. Their proclamation of the parousia of Jesus during the War of liberation must have been a politically explosive application of the Christian message which perforce would have involved Christians in the struggle of the Zealots who were split among themselves, the pro-Roman high priestly party, a dwindling group of moderates, and the antirevolutionary Herodian dynasty.[24] In a time when the people of Israel were divided on the issue of how to deal with the Roman threat, the exclusively apocalyptic appropriation of Jesus was suited to set Christian against Christian, Christian against Jew, and Christian against Gentile.[25]

The Christian persecutions are not to be mistaken for the eschaton either. Mark makes this point by the insertion of 13:10.[26] He placed this missionary logion into the context of persecution because he discerned a relation between the suffering and death of Christians and the movement toward the Gentiles. The persecutors force their victims into the world. Of necessity, the dispersion of the Christians effects the dispersion of the gospel of the Kingdom. This is a thoroughly Markan understanding of history. What was prophesied to be the End, causes a moving of the horizon so as to make room for a broader Christian experience. The death of Christians opens the Kingdom to the Gentiles. As the death of John the Baptist had coincided with the apostolic commission, foreshadowing the death of Jesus which was to usher in the Gentile mission, so does the death of Christians pave the road to the Gentiles.[27] Neither the war, nor

24. This approximates Marxsen's understanding of 13:9–13, see *Mark*, p. 174. But one must not infer from this a date for the gospel prior to A.D. 70. 13:5b–23 is Mark's correction of a mistaken concept of past history.

25. For a vivid description of the events of A.D. 66–70, see S. G. F. Brandon, *Jesus and the Zealots* (New York: Charles Scribner's Sons, 1967), pp. 131–45, *passim*. Brandon himself has forcefully argued for Christian involvement in the War as well as for the annihilation of the mother church of Jerusalem in A.D. 70. Although his thesis is in part a modern version of Robert Eisler's *IESOUS BASILEUS OU BASILEUSAS* and a restatement of the Tübingen thesis, redaction criticism can ill afford to overlook his many significant observations concerning the gospel of Mark and its historical milieu.

26. 13:10 is both a redactional insertion and a redactional composition. Markan linguistic features are: the paratactic *kai*, the use of *eis* for *en*, Markan key terms *euangelion* and *kēryssein*, and the use of *pas* followed by a noun.

27. See Chap. III, p. 54.

suffering and persecution, nor the Gentile mission are to be construed as *to telos.* Suffering must be endured and Gentiles pursued before (13:10: *prōton*) the End (13:13b: *eis telos*) comes.[28]

The *hotan de* in 13:14 harks back to the *hotan* of the initial question (13:4c) which postulated a correlation between the end of the temple and the end of history. Something has happened *hopou ou dei,* and the reader is directly enjoined to read with perception, *ho anaginōskōn noeitō.* Matthew correctly identifies the place Mark is alluding to as *topos hagios* (Matt. 24:15), the temple. The temple of Jerusalem has become the site of *to bdelygma tēs erēmōseōs.* This Danielic cipher conjures up the desecration of the temple under Antiochus IV Epiphanes who had ordered the installation of a Zeus altar in the sanctuary. In 167 B.C. the temple was seized, defiled, and perverted into a pagan shrine, but not in fact destroyed. But the Markan reader is for the first and last time in the gospel alerted to pay close attention to the cipher and to grasp its contemporary relevance. Reading it in the total context of Mark's depiction of Jesus' ministry and antitemple mission, and reading it in full knowledge of the temple's conflagration, the Christians in Mark's time cannot help but see in it the prediction of what came to pass during their own lifetime.

The *crux interpretum* of 13:14 consists in the puzzling fact that Mark conceives of this act of utter desecration in terms of a personal power. The masculine participle *hestēkota* endows the neuter *bdelygma* with a personal quality. Closely related is the problem as to why Mark articulates as elementary an event such as the destruction of the temple in such dark and cryptic language. There is a reluctance on the part of some scholars to interpret the "appalling sacrilege" as a manifestation in history. They point to the parallel features in 2 Thessalonians 2, 3–10, an apocalyptic passage which announces the arrival of the Anti-Christ.[29] But it is doubtful whether apocalyptic language by its very nature precludes any historical, political reference. Mark may well have the Roman power in mind in which he sees the personification of an apocalyptic figure. Or, writing after the fall of Jerusalem, he may know of the construction of a pagan altar, the erection of an image, or the placing of military standards upon the ruins of the temple, and he may regard these

28. The eschatological *prōton* in 13:10 points to the *telos* in 13:13b. Marxsen's (*Mark,* p. 177) claim that the proclamation of the gospel "helps to hasten the coming of the Parousia" exaggerates the Markan point.

29. Among them B. H. Branscomb, E. Klostermann, E. Lohmeyer, A. Loisy, B. H. Streeter. Scholars who argue in this manner as a rule date the Markan apocalypse (and the Markan gospel) prior to A.D. 70, and view 13:2c as an authentic prediction of Jesus.

idolatrous objects as the embodiment of a personal power. By whatever symbols the Roman authorities asserted their sovereignty over Jerusalem and its temple, Mark describes this transfer of power in apocalyptic imagery. He avails himself of apocalyptic symbols, not because he has no real event in mind, but because the event he is reflecting upon is of such horrendous magnitude that it is adequately conveyed only through the medium of apocalypticism. Mark indeed refers to the destruction of the temple, but for him it is far more than a political, military disaster. In his view it is *the* apocalyptic disaster. The city and its temple have been visited with evil in such unparalleled, concentrated form that it compels the definition of the personification of evil in the end time. The power which had manifested itself in the days of Antiochus had in these last days attained the rank of a person. Of such momentous significance is the disaster that it cannot be communicated within the established order of language. This singular event of violence breaks the rules of grammar. The *erēmōsis* was fulfilled in its most radical, literal sense,[30] and the *bdelygma* was impersonated by Satan himself. Satan has taken possession of the holy temple.

It is this dramatic event that the Christians are expected to be able to "see" (*hotan de idēte*). But this invitation to see, when taken literally, is nonsensical,[31] for how can they see the destruction of the temple, if they live outside Jerusalem in Judea (13:14)? How can they see Satan's take-over, if they are to flee into the mountains? We must remember that *seeing* in the gospel is used in a predominantly eschatological sense.[32] It denotes a break through the veil of secrecy, a vision of eschatological glory, and the sighting of an epiphany. Wherever Christians live, they can "see" the disaster, if they perceive its eschatological significance. What they "see" is an epiphanic event, the epiphany *ad malam partem*: the parousia of the Evil One.

The Satanic usurpation of the seat of David causes the Christians to flee. Noticeably, the order to flee is given to Christians *en tē Ioudaia*, and not to people *en tē Ierōsolymō*. The difficulties surrounding the phrase *en tē Ioudaia* are often pointed out. After the apocalyptic prediction of the destruction of the temple the reader expects the order to leave the city of Jerusalem, but not Judea. Whereas a flight from Jerusalem into

30. In the LXX *erēmōsis* refers almost exclusively to the destruction of Jerusalem, its temple, or the royal palace, see Pesch, *Naherwartungen*, p. 143.
31. Correctly pointed out by Ernst Haenchen, *Der Weg Jesu*, 2nd ed. rev. (Berlin: Walter de Gruyter & Co., 1968), p. 444.
32. See Chaps. I, n. 43; IV, p. 73; V, p. 103.

the mountains would be intelligible, the withdrawal from mountainous Judea into the mountains is obscure. Are the people to hide in the mountains of Judea, or are they to leave Judea for some mountains elsewhere? These observations prompted Lohmeyer,[33] Marxsen,[34] and Pesch[35] to affirm the redactional nature of *en tē Ioudaia*.[36] The pre-Markan apocalypse spoke of a flight into the mountains, which in the context of 13:14 could only have meant a flight from the city of Jerusalem into the hills of Judea.

A review of *Ioudaia* in the gospel casts a revealing light upon its use in 13:14. The term occurs in four instances, each time in a redactional, or partially redactional verse, and each time indicating a movement away from Judea. John the Baptist's baptism effected an exodus of "all the country of Judea and all the people of Jerusalem" (1:5).[37] The ecumenical gathering at the Lake of Galilee[38] is also attended by people "from Judea and Jerusalem" (3:7). Upon arrival in Judea (10:1) Jesus preaches the total surrender of the old mode of living on behalf of the gospel of the Kingdom (10:29–31).[39] In the apocalypse he predicts a flight for those who are living in Judea in the aftermath of the destruction of the temple. Judea, like Galilee, is a place of immediate relevance to Markan times. As the reassessment of past history arrives at the point of disaster which is at the root of the gospel composition, and reaches beyond it into Mark's own time, the evangelist updates the text so as to make it respond to Christians who live disoriented in Judea. If they read the gospel with care they must know that Judea was never meant to be a place to stay. Rather it is the land of destruction, dislocation, and exodus after the fall of the temple. It is true, the apocalypse itself provides no clue for reading *ta orē* in the sense of Galilee. But within the broader system of Mark's geographical coordinates the *orē* ultimately point to Galilee, the new place of redemption. The flight of the Judean Christians is an eschatological exodus out of the land of Satan into the promised land of the Kingdom.

The flight ushers in the period of "those days" (13:17), namely the

---

33. Ernst Lohmeyer, *Das Evangelium des Markus*, 17th ed. (Göttingen: Vandenhoeck & Ruprecht, 1967), p. 276.

34. Marxsen, *Mark*, p. 182.

35. Pesch, *Naherwartungen*, p. 147.

36. Hartman (*Prophecy*, p. 208) finds no evidence of *Ioudaia* in the midrashic substrate underlying the Markan apocalypse.

37. See Chap. I, p. 13.

38. See Chap. III, p. 46.

39. See Chap. V, pp. 87–92.

eschatological time of *thlipsis* (13:19a) which extends "until the now" (13:19b) of Mark's own time. Following the loss of the center, a time of unparalleled crisis begins which precedes the End. "Those days" lie between the parousia of Satan on the one hand and the parousia of the Son of Man on the other. They are not the End yet, but the beginning of the woes, the time of the great tribulation.

In the first section of the apocalypse (13:5b–23) Mark rewrites a period of history in repudiation of Christian parousia prophets. He de-eschatologizes the time of the Roman-Jewish War, calls for flight in view of the desolation of the temple, and interprets the present as *the* eschatological crisis. With the apocalyptic prediction of 13:14 he reaches the religious depth of his anti-Jerusalem theology. His objection to Jerusalem as the place of eschatological fulfillment stems from the conviction that the Roman destruction of the temple has constituted the personal victory of Satan. The Kingdom cannot manifest itself in the city and its temple, because what used to be the seat of David has become the seat of Satan. This more than anything else refutes the prophets who had upheld the eschatological vocation of the city and temple. With the concluding words *proeirēka hymin panta* (13:23b) the Markan Jesus departs from his speech and reflects upon what he has spoken up to this point. The whole first section is thus expressly qualified as having issued from Jesus' foreknowledge. Because Mark is correcting a view of history which had proven disastrous, he is anxious to place his version of history under the auspices of Jesus' providence. According to Mark, up until his time nothing has digressed from Jesus' eschatological masterplan. Long before the prophets deceived their Christian followers, Jesus had already "outprophesied" them, and he had "outprophesied" them in terms of an anti-parousia prophecy.

THE PAROUSIA OF THE SON OF MAN

The second and central section of the apocalypse (13:24–27) deals exclusively with the parousia of the Son of Man. *En ekeinais tais hēmerais meta tēn thlipsin ekeinēn* (13:24a) sets an intriguing date for the parousia. According to the previously outlined chronology (13:19a) "those days" ought to coincide with the period of "tribulation." The slight deviation from the eschatological schedule and the resultant cumbersome dating in 13:24a is indicative of Mark's[40] effort to keep the parousia as near as

40. *Meta tēn thlipsin ekeinēn* is an editorial insertion, see Pesch, *Naherwartungen*, p. 157.

possible to his own present, while at the same time preserving a necessary distance. The parousia is so close as to virtually fall into "those days," but it will be an event distinct from the "tribulation." It arrives in connection with, but is not itself part of the present crisis. It is thus a tenuous borderline which separates the Markan present from the parousia.

The Son of Man who manifested his authority on earth (2:10, 28), who suffered, died, and was resurrected (8:31; 9:31; 10:33–34; 9:9, 12; 14:21, 41), and who through his passion redeemed the many (10:45), is the same who will be revealed at his parousia (8:38; 13:26; 14:62). Despite the sameness of the title which spans the ministry, death, and life of Jesus, his parousia will manifest him in a fashion hitherto unperceived. While his power and glory, sensed only by the demons and at last by the centurion, were largely obscured from the public and thoroughly misunderstood by the disciples, they will on the day of his coming be *seen* in the open (13:26: *opsontai*). The eschatological *opsontai* denotes a seeing in fullness of what was up to this point only dimly perceived. The parousia signals the apocalyptic break through hiddenness and misconception. Only at the parousia will Jesus present himself in the *doxa* of his father (13:26).[41] This apocalyptic function of the parousia is of a piece with Mark's theology of the Kingdom. For as the Kingdom arrived with Jesus, is hidden at present, but will be seen shortly *en dynamei* (9:1), so also did the Son of Man walk on earth with authority, is absent at present (2:20; 13:34; 14:25), but will be seen *meta dynameōs pollēs* (13:26).

The darkening of the sun, the absence of moonlight, the tumbling of the stars, and the convulsion of the heavens are apocalyptic metaphors traditionally associated with judgment on "the great and terrible day."[42] What is absent, however, are the more expressly stated features of judgment, such as the trembling of the earth and the fear of the people, the wrath of the Lord and the doom of the sinners, the slaughter of the wicked and the overthrow of evil.[43] In Mark the Son of Man does not

41. *Doxa* is a thoroughgoing eschatological term in Mark. The transference of the glory of God upon Jesus is fully visible in the eschaton (8:38; 10:37; 13:26).
42. See for example Isaiah 13:10; 34:4; Joel 2:10; 3:15–16; Zephaniah 1:15.
43. Among the scholars who noticed the absence of judgment features are: Bennett H. Branscomb, *The Gospel of Mark* (New York: Harper and Brothers Publishers, 1937), p. 239; Wilhelm Bousset, *Kyrios Christos*, trans. John E. Steely, 6th ed. (Nashville, Tenn.: Abingdon, 1970), p. 41; Grundmann, *Markus*, p. 269; Harder, "Geschichtsbild," p. 97; Robert H. Lightfoot, *The Gospel Message of St. Mark* (Oxford: Oxford University Press, 1952), p. 54; Lohmeyer, *Markus*, p. 279; Rudolf Schnackenburg, "Kirche und Parusie," *Gott und Welt*, I (Karl Rahner Festschrift), J. B. Metz *et al.*, eds. (Freiburg: Herder, 1964), p. 565; Taylor, *St. Mark*, p. 517; Johannes Schreiber, *Theologie des Vertrauens* (Hamburg: Furche-Verlag, 1967), p. 132; Heinz Eduard Tödt, *The Son of Man in the Synoptic Tradition*, trans. Dorothea

arrive to execute judgment. 8:38 is a word of warning, not a true judgment saying. The word asserts that Jesus will refuse to come to the rescue of those who refused to follow his way through suffering and death. 14:62 depicts the Son of Man's session at the right hand and his coming at the parousia. The purpose of his coming is to gather in the dispersed Christians, and to this end even the angels have to leave their heavenly abode; the Son of Man is solely concerned with "his elect ones" (13:27). In 13:24–27 the apocalyptic metaphors do not operate in a judgmental context. The conspicuous absence of the theme of judgment is explicable as a reflection of and adaptation to the Markan experience. For the judgment which Jesus executed over the temple has come to pass in Mark's time. The Christians have already *seen* the epiphany of the Evil One. They are called to go the way to the parousia, away from the site of judgment, and they look forward to the consolidation of the eschatological people of God. Hence, the day of the parousia is a day of salvation which belongs entirely to the elect ones. The tribulation of the present does not usher in judgment, but being itself a corollary to judgment, it inaugurates life in the Kingdom.

THE NEARNESS OF THE PAROUSIA

The first section of the apocalypse disavowed the prophets' parousia claims, while the second section reaffirmed the parousia once again. Christians who were caught in this crisis of time, and suffered the destruction of Jerusalem and the collapse of their parousia hopes, will not rest content with a simple restatement of this same hope. The timing of this both new and old hope is the overriding issue. Provided the parousia is coming, how soon is it coming, and what is its connection with the experienced destruction of the temple? This is the question answered by the third section of the apocalypse (13:28–37).

The initial parable (13:28–29) resumes the eschatological fig tree symbolism. In 11:12–14, 20–21 the fig tree had served to illustrate how the Kingdom had come to grief in the temple (11:15–19). At that time all Kingdom hope was crushed, although hints had been given to the effect that all was not lost (11:17b, 22). Speaking now from the Mount of Olives and looking upon the place of the Evil One, the Markan Jesus once again

M. Barton, 2nd ed. (Philadelphia: Westminster Press, 1965), pp. 32–47. Neither John the Baptist nor Jesus in his inaugural message (1:15) preaches judgment, see Franz Mussner, "Gottesherrschaft und Sendung Jesu nach Mk 1, 14 f.," *Praesentia Salutis* (Düsseldorf: Patmos, 1967), p. 85.

avails himself of the fig tree, this time offering hope for the possible realization of the Kingdom.

The *hotan* in both the picture part (13:28b) and the reality part (13:29a) raises the issue of time which is of fundamental concern to the apocalypse, and ultimately goes back to the initial question (13:14: *hotan,* 13:11: *kai hotan,* 13:7: *hotan,* 13:4: *pote . . . hotan*). Nearness is the *tertium comparationis* (13:28c, 29c: *ginōskete hoti engys*), and the object of nearness can only be the Son of Man whose coming had been assured. The condition of nearness is fulfilled *hotan idēte tauta ginomena* (13:29b). The *hotan idēte* harks back to the *hotan de idēte* of 13:14, which spoke of the temple abomination, and the *tauta* responds to the *tauta* of 13:4b which likewise implied the fall of the temple. As the fresh foliage of the fig tree harbingers the nearness of the summer, so does the destruction of the temple indicate the nearness of the parousia. If a *sēmeion* is given at all, the Satanic usurpation of the temple is the negative sign presaging the beginning of the End.

In 13:30–32 three formerly isolated sayings are joined into a new unit. 13:30 gives an emphatic assurance of fulfillment to "this generation." At times *hē genea hautē* connotes a pejorative meaning (8:38; 9:19), but in the present context it is the temporal not the moral aspect which is accentuated. This generation is the eschatological generation of the end time. The assurance is directed to the present generation of Christians who will not (entirely) pass away before *tauta panta,* the eschaton,[44] arrives. This is fully consistent with 9:1. Verse 13:30 sharpens the motif of nearness which was already implied in 13:24 and specified in 13:28–29. The parousia is timed to materialize in the present generation which lives in the wake of the destruction of the temple. 13:31 extols the authority of the words of Jesus. Taken by itself, the fallen temple must not serve as the authoritative basis for hope. The only reliable ground for certainty is Jesus' words of the apocalyptic speech and ultimately the totality of the gospel of the Kingdom which interprets the meaning of the Jerusalem disaster.[45] The words of the gospel will remain in force until they come to fruition. 13:32 sets a limit to more detailed specifications. After the destruction and during this generation—that much is certain. As for day and hour, not even the protagonists of the parousia, Jesus and the angels,

---

44. While 13:29 responds to the first half of the initial double question 13:4 (13:29b: *tauta ginomena;* 13:4b: *pote tauta estai*) concerning the destruction of the temple, 13:30 resumes the second half of the question 13:4 (13:30: *tauta panta genētai;* 13:4c: *tauta synteleisthai panta*) concerning the eschaton.

45. *Hoi emoi logoi* is synonymous with *to euangelion,* compare 8:35 with 8:38.

are informed. Day and hour remain the ultimate secret which rests with the Father. Hence, the people cannot know and they must not know, for Jesus himself does not know. 13:30–32 set the time of the parousia as succinctly as possible. This generation is the last generation; Jesus' words warrant the truth of the promise; God reserves the right to determine day and hour.

The structural *blepete* introduces the last unit of the apocalypse, the parable of the doorkeeper (13:33–37), which forms the *parenetic* conclusion to the speech. Subsequently identical verbs mark beginning and ending of both picture and reality part (13:33b: *agrypneite*, 13:34c: *grēgorē*, 13:35a: *grēgoreite*, 13:37c: *grēgoreite*). Watchfulness is the principal theme of the parable. The situation of the disciples is likened to that of the servants who during the temporary absence of the master are vested with his *exousia* (13:34; see 6:7). The reality part, however, assigns the *exousia* motif to a subsidiary position and develops solely the vigilance of the doorkeeper. The Christians are enjoined to wake and watch, as did the doorkeeper. The parable presupposes the nearness of the parousia (13:30), but argues in view of the uncertainty of the date (13:32; 13:33c, 35b: *ouk oidate gar pote*). The Christians have to be on the alert at all times, because Jesus may well come suddenly and without further advance sign. Watchfulness is thus imperative because the parousia is near at hand and yet incalculable.

CONCLUSION

The apocalyptic speech is divided into three parts: a revision of past history (13:5b–23), the parousia (13:24–27), and the nearness of the parousia (13:28–37). Each of the three parts is further subdivided into three sections. 13:5b–23 deals with the War years (13:5b–8), persecution and Gentile mission (13:9–13; 13:9: *blepete*), and the abominable destruction of Jerusalem (13:14–23; 13:14: *hotan de idēte*). 13:24–27 is composed of the cosmic drama (13:24–25), the coming of the Son of Man (13:26: *kai tote*), and the ingathering of the elect ones (13:27: *kai tote*). 13:28–37 consists of the parable of the fig tree (13:28–29), three sayings concerning the nearness of the parousia, the authority of Jesus' words, and the uncertainty of the end (13:30–32), and the parable of the doorkeeper (13:33–37; 13:33: *blepete*). Since a predilection for triads is a well-known Markan feature, the overall structuring of the apocalypse can be attributed to Mark.

As structure of the apocalypse, so is also its place in the gospel the work of the redaction. At precisely the spot at which the plot of Jesus' ministry touches upon the neuralgic point in the Markan life situation, the biographical medium is ruptured and the destruction of Jerusalem comes to the fore. In the gospel's plot, this Jerusalem crisis constitutes the dramatic peak of a carefully built up anti-Jerusalem, anti-temple momentum (Chaps. 11–12), the main purpose of which had been to discredit the eschatological prestige of the city and its holy place. In Mark's view, the disaster of Jerusalem is of eschatological proportions. The conflagration of the temple consummates the parousia of the anti-Messiah, an apocalyptic spectacle which utterly refutes the propagation of the parousia of Jesus by Christian prophets. Their parousia faith has come to an end with the destruction of the place of messianic hope, and all parousia believers are left without future time, i.e., without hope. In depth this is the crisis situation to which the Markan apocalypse addresses itself at the height of the Jesus story prior to the passion narrative.

In the first part (13:5b–23) Mark rewrites the past history of immediate Christian concern, and he rewrites it in repudiation of the parousia prophets. He defuses a history pregnant with parousia expectations. This he does not because he objects to a parousia theology, but because he intends to preserve the parousia hope for his own generation. And this is the crucial point of the Markan apocalypse. Having purged the parousia hope of its unfortunate involvement in history, he can once again offer it as the unbroken promise of a true future. In the second and central part of the apocalypse (13:24–27) Mark offers the very hope which had come to grief with the prophets. The precious promise is by no means discredited, merely rescued from its prophetic misemployment. Mark acts both as the opponent of the prophets, and as the custodian of their parousia apocalypticism. Placed in central position of the speech, the parousia comprises the true novelty of the future. Extricated from past history and projected into the future, the parousia is then in the third part (13:28–37) firmly anchored in the present of the Markan generation.

There is a long-standing tradition in New Testament scholarship which holds that the Jesus of the gospels either takes a deliberate anti-apocalyptic stand, or at least smooths the rough edges of apocalypticism and moderates the embarrassing voice of imminent hope.[46] Not so the Markan

---

46. Marxsen (*Mark*, p. 189) expresses the view of many: "Mark transforms apocalyptic into eschatology." Busch (*Verständnis*, p. 53) maintains that Mark 13 is "keine Apokalypse im Sinne des Spätjudentums," but an esoteric instruction of the Gentile

Jesus! Far from abandoning or moderating the parousia, he tenaciously holds on to it. The Markan apocalypse is exclusively concerned with the parousia despite its recent bankruptcy. All its energies are devoted to the preservation and reinstatement of the parousia as imminent hope. Mark does not transpose an apocalyptic theme into a different key, rather he revises the score in order to retain this apocalyptic theme in precisely the same key. Out of the ruins of misconstrued time he reconstructs new time. The Markan Jesus, true maker of time, outprophesies the parousia prophets, the fakers of time. What they took to be the end of time was but the beginning of the present critical period which precedes the End.

Christian Mark, directed against an apocalyptic Jewish Christianity. Schreiber (*Theologie*, p. 127) sees in Mark 13 "die totale 'Christianisierung' der jüdischen Apokalyptik im Sinne des Heidenchristentums," in short "die 'Hellenisierung' der Apokalyptik" (p. 131). Weeden (*Mark*, p. 93) assumes that the redactional arrangement of Mark 13 "at times neutralizes the entire apocalyptic emphasis of this special apocalyptic material," thus amounting to a "rupturing of the apocalyptic process." Just a little more balanced now Charles B. Cousar ("Eschatology and Mark's Theologia Crucis," *Interpr*, 24 [1970], p. 328) who admits that "in one sense the Evangelist follows an apocalyptic perspective." Yet despite his recognition of "the highlighting of the parousia" in Mark 13, he still concludes that Mark "takes an antiapocalyptic attitude toward speculation and unwarranted enthusiasm." This must not be our last judgment of Mark 13. Mark's so-called antiapocalypticism is an integral part of his fundamental apocalypticism.

Chapter VII

CONCLUSION:
THE GENESIS OF THE
GOSPEL OF THE KINGDOM

The basic data pertaining to the Markan gospel's time and place of composition had seemed well-established. Most scholars have claimed that the gospel came into existence prior to A.D. 70 outside of Israel, preferably Rome,[1] and was addressed to a Gentile audience. By and large this thesis is derived from such *external* sources as Papias, the anti-Marcionite Prologue, Justin Martyr, Irenaeus, the Muratorian Canon, Clement of Alexandria, Origen, Jerome, and Eusebius. The gospel's *internal* rationale, however, does not support these basic data. Mark designed a spatial configuration of north–south–north, or more specifically of Galilee–temple mount–Mount of Olives–Galilee, which provides the topological framework of the gospel. The most conspicuous dynamic operating within this frame of spatial references is the Galilee-Jerusalem polarity. In broad strokes, this is the topological universe of the Markan gospel in which the drama is performed and religious meaning produced. Mark's conceptual world must find its natural explanation arising out of this circumspectly controlled space world and in full conformity with the inherent Galilee-Jerusalem antithesis.

---

1. Latin loan-words are frequently cited in support of the gospel's Roman origin. *Modios* (modius): grain measure (4:21); *legiōn* (legio): legion (5:9, 15); *spekoulator* (speculator): executioner (6:27); *dēnarion* (denarius): silver coin (6:37); *xestēs* (sextarius): liquid measure (7:4); *kēnsos* (census): tax (12:14); *kodrantēs* (quadrans): Roman coin (12:42); *phragelloun* (flagellare): to flog (15:15); *praitōrion* (praetorium): governor's residence (15:16); *kentyriōn* (centurion): Roman officer (15:39, 44–45). Upon analysis, the Latin loan-words in Mark fall exclusively into the category of military and economic terms. This reflects the situation not of Rome, but of an occupied country, because it is there that the imperial power imposes its military might and economic structure most tangibly upon the people. Roman origin of the gospel would have resulted in a penetration of Latinisms into the domestic, social, and religious language of the gospel.

S. G. F. Brandon[2] rightly sensed a conflict between his advocacy of the Roman origin of Mark and the gospel's own set of geographical priorities when he asked "why Mark, writing for a Gentile public who lived far from Palestine, concerned himself in his narrative of the life of Jesus with enhancing the reputation of Galilee at the expense of Jerusalem." Indeed, why should the Galilee-Jerusalem configuration point to Roman composition, or appeal to Roman Christians? Of course, it is entirely defensible to argue that the religious dramatization of the temple of Jerusalem is conceivable anywhere, be it Israel or the Diaspora. Perhaps one might want to go as far as to maintain that the whole Markan space world is purely symbolic, owing little or nothing to the live situation of the evangelist who shaped this tradition. But if one opts for an autonomous mythological universe, unconnected with the real Galilee and Jerusalem, the historical search for the gospel's setting in life has come to an end, and Rome is as unprovable a place of origin as any other location.

Our own study has shown that the gospel is in close touch with a historical event of weighty proportions. The gospel's apocalypse is dramatically and thematically pegged to the forecast destruction of the temple which for Mark is past history. The evangelist makes an issue of the disaster because Christians were profoundly affected by it. The conflagration of the temple precipitated an eschatological crisis which undermined the foundation of a Christian faith. Since the apocalyptic speech registers the historical pulse beat more conspicuously than any other part of the gospel, and since it is furthermore integrated into, i.e., dramatically anticipated by, the gospel composition, the historical situation underlying Chapter 13 must apply to the gospel as a whole. If Mark's negative assessment of Judea, Jerusalem, and the temple is thus historically conditioned, the correspondingly positive role assigned to Galilee may likewise be historical reality in Mark's time. Galilee is the locus of the Kingdom of God. It is where the history of the Kingdom began and where in Mark's own generation it will be consummated. So much in sympathy with Galilee is the author, and so tangibly does he argue from the perspective of its Jewish-Christian community that it seems plausible to see in him the spokesman of Galilean Christians. Galilee in its broadest sense, including the Decapolis and the area of Tyre and Sidon as outlined by Mark, furnishes the setting in life for Mark the evangelist. To draw any further inferences as to the precise localization of this Galilean Christian-

---

2. S. G. F. Brandon, *The Fall of Jerusalem and the Christian Church* (London: S.P.C.K., 1951), p. 197.

ity of Mark (is he representative of a single community, or of a loosely bound body of Christians spread over a wide area?) would at this stage in Markan research be imprudent. But the destruction of Jerusalem and the accompanying involvement of Christians on one hand and Mark's own Galilean background on the other provides us with a tentative explanation for the gospel's dramatically executed conflict between north and south. The gospel sponsors a Christianity of the north which in the aftermath of A.D. 70 militates against a southern tradition.

But is the gospel nothing but a retrospective legitimization of a new Christian situation in the wake of the Roman victory? Does Mark merely sanction the facts after the fall? Throughout we have tried to show that the gospel is not an exercise in confirming the obvious, but a creative reconsideration of the past of Jesus so as to be of immediate service to the present of Mark. Whom does the Markan gospel serve? We have arrived at the vexed question of the Markan audience. Is the gospel's kerygmatic purpose exclusively oriented toward Gentiles? In the case of the oldest known Christian gospel we must not immediately embrace the form-critical and redaction-critical assumption of a sociologically constricted situation of preacher versus community. The fundamental bipolarity of the gospel points to more intricate circumstances.

The destruction of Jerusalem and the concurrent crisis of southern Christianity makes the Galilean Christianity appear in a new light. Thus Mark redefines his own identity in opposition to a ruined tradition of the south, and discovers the Galilean centrality in view of the broken center in Jerusalem. The considerable emphasis on the Gentile inclusion must not deceive us into assuming the gospel's appeal is limited to Gentiles. Seeing that a type of Christianity which had withheld the Kingdom from the Gentiles became implicated in God's judgment upon Jerusalem, Mark reaffirms the Galilean openness toward the Gentiles as a hallmark of the Kingdom and a sign of the end time. The Kingdom consists of Jews *and* Gentiles, and the mission to the Gentiles precedes the End. Despite the understandable enthusiasm over the Gentiles, the Christian constituency in Galilee is comprised of a dual membership, and Mark goes to great pains not to elevate the Gentile Christians at the expense of the Jewish Christians.

While on the one hand the gospel refashions the identity of the Jewish and Gentile Christians of Galilee, it may on the other hand also have a southern point of reference. Mark deposes Jerusalem and promotes Galilee in a significant order of succession. The Markan Jesus cleanses and creates Galilee, then judges and disqualifies Jerusalem, and lastly leads the way to Galilee. Why this last movement away from the ruins of the old place to the Kingdom in Galilee? This north—south—north schematization could simply explain the Galilean existence of Christians after A.D. 70, but it could also have a direct bearing upon Christians in the south. The redirection of the way of Jesus toward the north might well appeal to Christians who survived the destruction of Jerusalem and live in the dispersion of Judea (13:14). To them the Markan Jesus' opposition to southern Christianity might serve as an explanation of the crisis which jeopardized their faith, and Jesus' return to Galilee might constitute an invitation to join the people of the Kingdom in Galilee. In the last analysis, we shall see, this understanding will disclose the mythological dimension of the gospel. In principle, however, the Markan gospel is capable of functioning in different ways, for different people, and in different places.

FALSE DAWN IN JERUSALEM

The Roman-Jewish War of A.D. 66–70 and in particular the destruction of Jerusalem and its temple form the historical background and motivational starting point for the gospel of Mark. Josephus'[3] antiapocalyptic reporting of the war years barely conceals the fact that the revolt against Rome was deeply stirred by eschatological convictions. What had begun as a Zealotic uprising broadened into a full-scale war, but what gave the whole resistance movement ideological continuity was the apocalyptic anticipation of the imminent irruption of the Kingdom of God. Eschatological prophets aroused hopes for liberation by dating the time of messianic deliverance. They spread end-time rumors through the city of Jerusalem, engaged in miracles of apocalyptic quality, and interpreted the calamities of the war as the incontestable signs of the impending rescue. Ominous signs and portents, many associated with the temple, were the order of the day, and Josephus refers to them as either *sēmeia* or *terata*. Immediately preceding the conflagration of the temple a prophet called upon the people of Jerusalem "to go up to the temple court, to receive there the tokens of their deliverance." This prophet evidently interpreted the peak of the battle over Jerusalem as the apocalyptic turning of the eons. An "ambiguous oracle" (*chrēsmos amphibolos*) which according to Josephus was "found in their sacred scriptures" pro-

---

3. Josephus, *Bellum Judaicum*, VI.

vided the proof text for many apocalyptic prophecies.[4] This messianic oracle, based upon Jewish tradition, vouched that "one from their [the Jewish] country would become ruler of the world."[5]

The Jewish historian portrays the apocalyptically aroused milieu of the besieged Jerusalem with the cynical logic of one who had managed to survive on less than honorable terms. Apart from his personal entanglements, however, his view on the apocalyptic dimension of the war, not unlike Mark's, reflects the wisdom of hindsight: the prophets had been false prophets (*pseudoprophētēs tis*) and deceptive representatives of the deity (*katapseudomenoi tou theou*), deluding the people and unwilling to believe that the miracles had been the plain warning of God, foreboding disaster rather than deliverance.

There is every appearance that the Jewish war strategy was not solely based upon military considerations, but was to a considerable degree swayed by religious, apocalyptic determination. Apocalyptic calendar speculations centering around Daniel's seventy weeks of years (Dan. 9:24–27) appear to have been of signal importance.[6] The author of Daniel reinterpreted Jeremiah's seventy years of exile (Jer. 25:11–12; 29:10) in terms of seventy weeks of years, or 490 years. Following the disconfirmation of Daniel's prophecy, these seventy weeks of years became the subject of still more intricate calculations. It was during the final war years that speculations on Daniel's reckoning of the end time entered into a crucial phase. Prophetic interpretations of Daniel concluded that the 490 years would come to fulfillment sometime between A.D. 68 and 70. Since oracles derived from the apocalypse of Daniel appear to have played an influential role in the Roman-Jewish War, it has been conjectured that the *chrēsmos amphibolos* mentioned by Josephus had its scriptural basis in the writing of Daniel.[7] While there is no direct evidence to support this thesis, there is every reason to assume that the War was on the Jewish side fought under the guiding influence of prophetic leaders who relied heavily upon the scriptures of Daniel from which they extrapolated their

4. *Ibid.*, VI, 312–13.

5. *Ibid.*

6. An extensive discussion of the apocalyptic speculations concerning Daniel's seventy weeks of years during the years preceding A.D. 70 is presented by Hermann L. Strack and Paul Billerbeck, *Kommentar zum Neuen Testament aus Talmud und Midrasch*, 4 Vols. (Munich: C. H. Beck'sche Verlagsbuchhandlung, 1922–28), IV, pp. 996–1015; see also August Strobel, *Kerygma und Apokalyptik* (Göttingen: Vandenhoeck & Ruprecht, 1967), pp. 104–05; Lloyd Gaston, *No Stone On Another*, Supplements to Novum Testamentum, No. 23 (Leiden: E. J. Brill, 1970), pp. 433–68.

7. Istaván Hahn, "Josephus und die Eschatologie von Qumran," *Qumran-Probleme*, H. Bardtke, ed. (Berlin: Akademie-Verlag, 1963), pp. 167–91.

end time prophecies. In their interpretation, the final battle over the holy city assumed the proportions of the apocalyptic Armaggedon.

It is widely held that the Jerusalem Christians migrated in a body to the Trans-jordanian city of Pella immediately preceding the outbreak of the war. It would be well beyond the scope of our study of the gospel of Mark to enter into a discussion of the controversial Pella thesis.[8] Whatever the historical reality underlying the Pella exodus, our investigation of the Markan gospel disputes a total Christian departure from Jerusalem prior to A.D. 70. The manner in which the gospel wrestles with and responds to the destruction of the city and its temple testifies to Christian involvement in the abortive Armaggedon. Mark's singling out of Christian prophets associated with the fall of Jerusalem makes Christian involvement in the Jewish catastrophe virtually certain.

If the gospel's apocalypse addresses itself to a crisis situation which, in Mark's judgment, evolved out of the activity of the parousia prophets, then their influence among the southern Christians can hardly be overestimated. Mark's negative characterization of the prophets must not induce us to minimize their impact. What in retrospect is condemned as false prophecy and imposture, must in point of fact have constituted a movement of considerable weight and number. Mark's elaborately staged repudiation of the prophets bears indirect witness to their prominence and authority. The evangelist had to go to such lengths in revising a history totally misconstrued by the prophets, because it was in fact a substantial group of Christians who had pledged their allegiance to the parousia prophets.

It can hardly be accidental that an upsurge of parousia expectations occurred approximately forty years after the death of Jesus. The prophets' followers could conceive of themselves as still belonging to the first generation of Christians. They were *the* eschatological generation which after forty years of wandering in the wilderness would be led into the promised land of the Kingdom by Jesus at his parousia.[9] The prophets' focal point becomes intelligible if one deduces from Mark's anti-Jerusalem theology that they had been located in Jerusalem, had propagated the city's eschatological, messianic vocation, and had in a particular sense

8. More recently the Pella theory has been disputed by Brandon, *Fall*, pp. 168–73, and *idem Jesus and the Zealots* (New York: Charles Scribner's Sons, 1967), pp. 208–16. The author considers it a piece of Christian apologetic designed to certify early Christian uninvolvement in their nation's abortive struggle for freedom.
9. There is fragmentary evidence in Qumran that forty years were expected to elapse between the death of the Teacher of Righteousness and the Last Judgment, see CD XX. 13–15; 4QpPs 37:7–8.

focused their parousia hope upon the temple. It remains hazardous to speculate in what specific sense Christian hopes were centered in the temple, but Mark's involved argument concerning the incompatibility between Kingdom and temple could well have been designed to disprove the prophets' claim that Jesus would manifest himself in the temple. Suffice it to say that in the last analysis their faith was intimately bound up with the temple.

In view of the predominant role played by the apocalypse of Daniel in the turbulent years of the war, it is highly significant that the Markan apocalypse is permeated with quotations from and allusions to Daniel.[10] Ever since the days of T. Colani[11] an increasing number of scholars have studied Mark 13 with the assumption that it was built around the nucleus of an apocalypse of independent origin. In our time L. Hartman has come closest to identifying "a distinguishable eschatological discourse."[12] He extracts from Chapter 13 "an exposition or meditation on Daniel texts,"[13] in short a "midrash" on Daniel, which dealt with the great distress of the last days and the arrival of the Son of Man. The setting in life of this pre-Markan midrash is "early Christian teaching."[14] Hartman stops just short of saying, but in fact strongly implies,[15] that the recovered Danielic apocalypse might in fact be the "Little Apocalypse" predicated over a century ago by Colani.[16] Since Chapter 13 exposes the theological crisis which lies at the very root of the gospel, could not the identifiable theology underlying the Markan apocalypse be that of his opponents? At this climactic point in the gospel story Mark redacts, i.e., corrects, the theology of none other but his opponents! The Danielic midrash in effect was a parousia apocalypse. Mark opposes a Christianity which had been under the guidance of parousia prophets. The existence of an apocalyptic nucleus in Mark 13 accounts for the fact that the evangelist reinstates the very theology which had gone bankrupt earlier. What was valid before the siege of the city, Mark has to revise after the fall of the temple and

---

10. Lars Hartman, *Prophecy Interpreted*, trans. Neil Tomkinson, Coniectanea Biblica, New Testament Series I (Lund, Sweden: CWK Gleerup, 1966), pp. 172–74.
11. Timothée Colani, *Jésus-Christ et les Croyances Messianiques de son Temps*, 2nd ed. (Strasbourg: Treuttel et Wurtz, 1864).
12. Hartman, *Prophecy*, p. 175.
13. *Ibid.*, p. 172.
14. *Ibid.*, p. 236.
15. *Ibid.*, pp. 174–75.
16. The spectacular nature of Hartman's discovery is somewhat buried under his massive scholarship. His bias against form criticism must not prevent one from giving careful consideration to his analysis of Jewish and Christian apocalyptic texts.

the ruin of parousia faith. If the prophets' parousia hope was indeed based on the little apocalypse of Daniel, then Jesus must have been known to them as the Son of Man. This is a thesis which we had stated at an early point in our study.[17] Interestingly enough, their Jesus was not the Son of Man who has earthly authority, nor the one who suffers and rises, but the apocalyptic Son of Man who comes on the clouds of heaven. At this point the Markan scope of vision comes into view.

Prior to A.D. 70 the Jerusalem Christians appear to have derived apocalyptic prophecies from Daniel and shared the messianic expectations of their fellow Jews. But they will have differed with them in their ability to name and identify their expected Son of Man. The defenders of the besieged city were principally united in their craving for messianic intervention, "some hoping that he [the Messiah] might come, others hoping that he might return."[18] At times this must have provoked bitter feelings and led to the persecution of Christians, because their Son of Man was known to have been executed as a Zealotic rebel in Jerusalem. But at the peak of the battle and during the last months of the city exclusive Christian claims are not likely to have caused a serious conflict between Jews and Jewish Christians, for their apocalyptic interests concurred in the defense and defiance of a common enemy.

Throughout the gospel we observed Mark affirming his Galilean position over against a Christianity which we suspected of being the mother church of Jerusalem.[19] At the gospel's historical pulse point this observation is confirmed. A Jerusalem-based Christian community emerges which came to grief in A.D. 70. One reason Mark composes his whole gospel in response to these Christians is because he is dealing with the disaster of a hitherto highly respected and "established" Christianity. It was a church conscious of its impeccable tradition and background. These Christians considered themselves as successors to the twelve disciples, originally headed by a triumvirate, with Peter as the *dux et princeps*.[20] They also held the family of Jesus in high esteem.[21] This could possibly be due to the fact that the principle of dynastic leadership was in effect in the Jerusalem church. At some point during the short history of the mother

---

17. See Chap. I, p. 22; see also Chap. IV, p. 83.
18. Leo Baeck, *Judaism and Christianity*, trans. Walter Kaufmann (Cleveland, Ohio: World Publishing Company, 1961), p. 199. Baeck does not use this phrase in reference to Jerusalem prior to A.D. 70.
19. Chap. III, p. 64.
20. *Ibid.*
21. Chaps. II, pp. 35–36; III, pp. 53–54, 64.

church members of the family of Jesus appear to have achieved positions of supremacy (James; Symeon?). Obviously the members of the church were Jewish Christians who remained fundamentally loyal to their Jewish way of life. They observed the Jewish days of fasting,[22] celebrated the Sabbath day,[23] and had a strongly developed sense of clean and unclean.[24]

At least during the last years of the war the parousia of Jesus as the Son of Man became their life-sustaining force. In the increasingly apocalyptically aroused atmosphere of Jerusalem it was the apocalyptic Son of Man within reach or realized at present who could deliver liberation from oppression and servitude. Ecstatically aroused prophets, adept at performing signs and miracles, propagated and perhaps impersonated the parousia of Jesus, considering themselves the incarnate representations of the Messiah. Taking the present for the eschaton, they made no provisions for the future of their church, as their rejection of children demonstrates.[25] Their unadulterated *theologia gloriae* did not attach any soteriological significance to the death and resurrection of Jesus.[26] Not the crucified and resurrected Jesus of the past, but the Son of Man in his eschatological power and glory was to fulfill the messianic promise of deliverance.

From what we could infer from the disciples' conduct during Jesus' Galilean mission,[27] it seems that the Peter-Christians who followed in the footsteps of the disciples were less than enthusiastic about Gentiles who sought to join their church. There was no place for the evangelization of the Gentiles in this essentially closed, exclusively Jewish Christian church of Jerusalem. But if the Jerusalem Christians saw the mission of Jesus as limited to Israel, they will hardly have left the holy city as the hour of eschatological crisis and epoch-making decision approached. These apocalyptically incited Jewish Christians are likely to have joined their compatriots in the final battle against the armies of Satan. Expecting the restoration of the "Kingdom of our father David,"[28] they will have fought to the bitter end, the great majority of them dying together with their fellow Jews.

22. Chap. I, p. 20.
23. Chap. I, pp. 20–21.
24. Chap. I, p. 19.
25. Chap. V, p. 91.
26. Chap. IV, pp. 82–83.
27. Chap. III, pp. 48–65.
28. Chap. V, pp. 96–97.

A NEW PLACE AND A NEW TIME

The destruction of Jerusalem and the conflagration of the temple constituted a crisis for Jewish and, we now have reason to assume, Christian faith which cannot be exaggerated. Approximately forty years after the crucifixion of Jesus, Christian hopes were once again thwarted in the southern citadel. Not the Kingdom of David, but the Kingdom of Satan had arrived, and instead of messianic deliverance the dark age of annihilation was born. Loyalty to prophetic words and faithfulness to Jesus was answered by death. Christian history had not been redeemed by the crucial breakthrough, but was instead doomed to a total breakdown. Those Christians who survived the fall of the city were now a dispersed people whose Kingdom hopes had gone up in the flames of the temple conflagration. They were at once displaced and without hope. There seemed to be no way out of this cruel impasse. Indeed, it was the end of the temple and the end of all things, but not as foretold by the prophets.

In a situation of anomaly only extreme measures promise a solution. Old words and famililar forms of expression can no longer cope with an experience out of the ordinary. What is needed is a new voice. For this reason, religion and the arts respond to the experience of social breakdown and political crisis by a renewal of language and the creation of new paradigms of death and life. The dissolution of the existing symbols may effect a reshuffling of the data of human experience and thus give impetus to the discovery of new symbols. In this sense, crisis can serve as a catalyst of new styles of locution and create the precondition for the emergence of a new perspective on life. These considerations cast some light upon the genesis of the gospel of Mark as a style-setting document in Christian literary history. This all the more so since the gospel is not the logical end-product of the prehistory of its individual building blocks. The traditional material made up of logia, parables, miracles, and catenae does not, as if driven by an immanent force, merge into the unity of the gospel whole. On the contrary, so disparate is the material that it "scatters in every direction."[29] This earliest known Christian gospel is thus not the natural and expected stage in Christian literary history, but the unexpected, yet willed product in a time of crisis. The new gospel form, this utter novelty of the Markan voice, presupposes, negatively speaking, discontinuity with and possibly distrust of the proven literary models of

29. Willi Marxsen, *Mark the Evangelist*, trans. Roy A. Harrisville *et al.* (Nashville, Tenn.: Abingdon, 1969), p. 17.

the past. Some dislocation has occurred which required a new perspective on life. It is our contention that it was the iconoclastic moment of the destruction of Jerusalem and its temple which gave rise to this new Christian synthesis, called gospel.

At the heart of the dilemma lies a mistaken sense of time and place. A realized eschatology tied to the center of life had, expired with the demise of this place. Undeniably, eschatology is closely interwoven with christology, both carrying anthropological consequences. An erroneous eschatology discloses an inaccurate conception of Christ and a miscarriage of discipleship. In any event, Mark will have to rebuild the image of Christ and the way of Christian discipleship. But at the bottom of the crisis remains a false concept of time and the wrong choice of place: the Kingdom did not come at its appointed time and promised place.[30]

It is against the background of this spatio-temporal exigency that we recall the gospel's fundamental program: the realization of the Kingdom in Galilee (1:14–15). This manifesto is truly gospel message for a people who had suffered the loss of the Kingdom, and were bereft of orientation in space and time. It reaffirms the Kingdom in a new spatio-temporal configuration.

According to Mark, more than forty years ago Galilee had been designated by Jesus to be the center of life. Then the new place had been exorcized, cleansed, and sanctioned in its Jewish-Gentile constituency, and the new order of life had crystallized into the Kingdom of God. The Kingdom which appeared to have perished in the temple conflagration is thus firmly anchored in Jesus' past ministry. Because it became reality in Galilee long before the Jerusalem disaster had ever occurred, it is immunized against any involvement in the fall of the historical cult place. But the past speaks to the present. Galilee is the New Jerusalem because this is where in the time of Mark the authentic future lies. At the place of its arrival the Kingdom will enter into the phase of its manifestation. As it was in the beginning, but then in fullness. Conversely, Mark rejects the traditional localization of the parousia in Jerusalem, holding the firm conviction that the traditional site of eschatological manifestation had become a broken center, void and empty. Thus when the evangelist gives

---

30. The controversial issue of the priority of either christology or eschatology in Mark may ultimately be a moot question. One is not without the other, and the extraction of a pure christology unrelated to eschatology, or a pure eschatology detached from christology is incommensurate with the religious world of Mark. Noticeably, the gospel's overriding concern for place is neither covered by christology, nor by eschatology! And yet, Christ cannot be without a place, and time is always space-bound in Mark.

his last directions in the so-called story of the Empty Tomb (16:1–8), he is disinclined to display the resurrected Christ in Jerusalem, for to him the city is the place of absence. *Ouk estin hōde* (16:6e), the young man in the tomb explains to the women, refuting the prophets' *ide hōde ho christos* (13:21b). *Ekei* points to the new place of Galilee (16:7b: *ekei auton opsesthe*), not to the prophets' choice of Jerusalem (13:21c: *ide ekei*).[31] The gospel ends by urging the Christians to go back to the origin, the Galilean starting point. Where the Kingdom came in the beginning, there it will achieve its breakthrough in the end. And this end will be the true beginning.

The Christians are therefore informed both of their past history and of their future possibility, while they are also assigned a new place of orientation. There is in this system a distinct meaning reserved for the present of Christians who live in the aftermath of the collapse of the center. Time did not come to an end at A.D. 70. They are neither without time, nor out of time, but in the midst of time. They live in the crucial period between the epiphany of Satan and the advent of the Son of Man, between Jesus' death and resurrection on one side and his parousia on the other, or, in the broadest perspective, between Kingdom and Kingdom. In the twilight of its past fulfillment and at the dawn of its future apocalypse they migrate at present in the shadow of its hiddenness. Theirs is the Middle Time.[32] It is the very nature of this Middle Time that it concurs with the eclipse of the Kingdom. It is *the* time of crisis. Persecutions do not denote a dead end, but open the door to the world, and dislocation is not the sign of Christian bankruptcy, but a chance to reach the new place of life. Tension and conflict are the very symptoms of an existence in the shadow of a Kingdom which was itself born out of conflict. Nor must on the other hand suffering and death be denied. The prophetic opponents had exalted the moment of instant fulfillment and disregarded the suffering of John, the passion of Christ and the reality of death amidst their own. In the wake of A.D. 70 Mark recognizes suffering as an integral part of Christ and the Christian experience. As John the Baptist suffered,

---

31. Elias Bickermann, "Das leere Grab," *ZNW*, 23 (1924), pp. 281–92; Neill Q. Hamilton, "Resurrection Tradition and the Composition of Mark," *JBL*, 84 (1965), pp. 415–21. Mark 16:1–8 offers no ground for resurrection belief, but extends a last invitation to submit to total eschatological reorientation.

32. This model of the Middle Time is used by man to account for and sanctify the experience of a precarious present. The term Middle Ages, for example, has its medieval origin in the understanding of the present as the *medium aevum* between Jesus' first and his second coming, see Marc Bloch, *The Historian's Craft*, trans. Peter Putnam (New York: Alfred A. Knopf, Inc., 1953), pp. 178–80.

so did Christ, and so must the Christians.[33] Suffering is integrated into the Middle Time—and thus made sufferable.

Mark breaks a Christian perspective confined to the present by creating the vision of a temporal continuum, consisting of past, a present interval, and a future. It is not, of course, the discovery of the infinity of time, but merely that of a limited stretch which binds together the ministry of Jesus and the first and last generation of Christians. Jesus' past becomes the model for Mark's present. True to Jesus' Galilean mission the Christians, endowed with his *exousia* (6:7), are to preach *metanoia* (6:12), and to exorcize and heal (6:13). They are not, for example, to baptize, for their Jesus never baptized. Their present time of tribulation is analogous to Jesus' tribulation, because they are being "delivered" (13:9, 11) just as Jesus was "delivered" (9:31; 10:33; 14:41). Participating in the past of Jesus, they are assured a part in his future. In Markan terms, they walk the way of Jesus which will facilitate the exodus out of the present crisis. Similarly, Mark ties the future closely to the present. Ever since the fall of Jerusalem future redemption is within sight. If they walk the way to the end and complete the exodus out of the dispersion to the place of reunion, *thlipsis* will be replaced by *doxa*, and faith by *seeing*. While it remains true that Mark creates the process of time, his vision of time is subject to rapid erosion by time itself.[34] He can build the bridge which spans past and future, because Jesus' past and the Christians' future are still conceivable as the beginning and end of one generation. But as the gulf between Jesus and the eschaton widens, this bridge will be too short and the Markan basis for Christian existence too narrow. However with these observations we are already looking back upon Mark from the later perspective of Matthew, Luke, or the gospel's longer ending.[35]

Affected by the passage of time, Mark shows concern for continuity. What is the constant amid the flux of time? It is the Kingdom that furnishes a sense of stability and not Jesus who is absent during the time of

---

33. This commonness of the passion experience is expressed by Mark's deliberate distribution of the term *paradidonai*, see Norman Perrin, "The Use of *(Para)didonai* in Connection with the Passion of Jesus," *A Modern Pilgrimage in New Testament Christology* (Philadelphia: Fortress Press, 1974).

34. See Marxsen, *Mark*, p. 210. The author correctly observes that the Markan gospel could not have stood the test of time for long. On the other hand, Marxsen believes that the "unity in Mark results from an orientation to place," whereas time lay beyond the gospel's horizon (pp. 105–06). This view requires correction. The gospel addresses itself to a spatio-temporal dislocation, reorienting the Christian world toward a new place and a new time.

35. The so-called longer ending (16:9–20) forms not simply an extension of the gospel, but causes a shift of the gospel's total perspective.

tribulation (2:20; 13:34; 14:25) and whose resurrection engenders no assurance of the Lord's presence. The Kingdom holds together past, present, and future. We recall that Kingdom and parousia had lain at the heart of Christian faith in Jerusalem. Our analysis of the Markan apocalypse disclosed Mark's efforts to reaffirm the parousia, the very faith which had been wrecked in A.D. 70. What holds true of the apocalypse, holds true of the gospel's total purpose. Far from relaxing, let alone abandoning, hope for the Kingdom, Mark offers it anew as the live option for his own Galilean community.

This reinstatement of the Kingdom forms the one link with an otherwise broken Christian past. The same hope which had guided life prior to the catastrophe is made operative for Christian life after the catastrophe. Despite disruption and dislocation Mark affirms substantive continuity with the Christian past. He meets the disconfirmation of Kingdom apocalypticism by restating the old prophecy in the new configuration of time and space. In the process of reconfirming the prophetic truth of Kingdom and parousia Mark lapses into the past of Jesus and uncovers a more comprehensive view of the Kingdom. The Kingdom is no longer the static entity it was in Jerusalem, but an agent of temporal continuity. It is both Jesus' legacy of the past, representing him in the present (motif of *repraesentatio!*), and his promise for the future. In a word, the Kingdom has a living history. It could therefore not have been crushed in a single moment, because its history is still in progress. The gospel breaks the eschatological impasse of A.D. 70 by encouraging participation in this ongoing movement of the Kingdom. The one Markan symbol most expressive of this dynamic concept of the Kingdom is the motif of the way. As long as Christians are on the way, they cannot be in the fullness of the Kingdom. Jerusalem discounted the wisdom of the way and settled for fulfillment in the present—which was to turn into agony. For Mark, not the permanent holiness of the temple, but the impermanency of the way is the catalyst of transcendence.[36] The gospel is the unfinished gospel and its Christ not fully revealed because the Kingdom is a Kingdom-in-the-making.

The fundamental incompleteness of salvation finally illuminates the gospel's dimension of secrecy.[37] Secret, mystery, and hiddenness are es-

---

36. That the motif of the way is an ideal means of combating the opponents' realized eschatology was first suggested to me by Marty Kastelic, graduate student at the University of Dayton.

37. This is not, of course, meant to be an exhaustive discussion of the so-called Messianic Secret. More recently we have learned to differentiate at least between the

sentially apocalyptic categories. When viewed from the perspective of its impending apocalyptic breakthrough, history appears not fully revealed, but wrapped in secrecy. It is the belief in a forthcoming disclosure which veils present history, endowing it with mystery. Apocalyptic thinking, therefore, tends to deprive history of autonomous significance, reducing it to a succession of corrupt earthly kingdoms which precede the Kingdom of God. History is merely a period of transition pointing beyond itself toward consummation. The secret surrounding Jesus and the hiddenness of the Kingdom are likewise imposed upon the gospel from the imminent point of eschatological revelation.

The past of Jesus cannot have been the time of *seeing*, because the full revelation is yet to come, and the present of Mark is not what it ought to be, because one is still en route to the goal. It is not until (in Matthew and Luke) the eschatological horizon widens, that the shadow of the secret vanishes and the gospel receives a formal ending, thus becoming a type of *Vita Jesu* in its own right. In Mark, however, the eschatological vantage point is so close as to cast a shadow upon the present of Mark and the past of Jesus. Past and present stand under the shadow of an overhanging future. Salvation under these circumstances constitutes the personal manifestation and final disclosure of the secret, and the parousia marks the entry into full time, the time of unimpeded *seeing*. Under the apocalyptic dynamic of revealing and concealing the gospel shrinks into a prologue to the parousia.

Out of the cataclysmic experience of a present destroyed and a future void Mark reaches into the past. With Jesus' parousia foiled at A.D. 70, he returns to Jesus' messianic advent some forty years earlier. The ministry of Jesus makes a usable past, because it alone contains a solution to the present and the key to the future. The future lies in the past, and the End is foretold in the beginning.[38] Out of the sacred past of Jesus Mark carves a new perspective for the present, and charts a way into the future. The result is neither escape into timelessness, nor a journey into the

---

secrecy motif and discipleship failure. On the latter, see below. It is merely suggested here to view the notion of secrecy as an integral part of the gospel's apocalyptic thrust. On this, see Dietrich Rössler, *Gesetz und Geschichte. Untersuchungen zur Theologie der Jüdischen Apokalyptik und der Pharisäischen Orthodoxie*, Wissenschaftliche Monographien zum Alten und Neuen Testament, No. 3, 2nd ed. (Neukirchen: Neukirchener Verlag, 1962), pp. 60–70.

38. *En ekeinais tais hēmerais* in 13:24a, indicating the time of the parousia, resumes the *en ekeinais tais hēmerais* of 1:9, which describes Jesus' first appearance in Galilee. His advent in Galilee foreshadows his Galilean future, and his parousia is the consummation of his Galilean coming.

heavenly sanctuary, but an extension of the boundaries of time and space, as well as a broadening of the Christians' sense of Christ and man. While the Jerusalem prophets had canonized the present, Mark views it as a product of the past and in tension toward the future. By recapturing the prophetic vision of the Kingdom, he discovers the full dimensions of the Kingdom which arrived in the past and is in the process of fruition in the future. The evangelist designs a movement from the old place to the new place, but the new place is not merely a replica of the old place. Galilee is not bound to city and temple, but essentially is open space. Its boundaries are flexible, and it makes a place for Jews *and* Gentiles. Galilee thus reveals a broader consciousness of man than Jerusalem. The walled city and its locative, compact standpoint is replaced by a more dynamic, differentiated experience of the world. Jesus himself is not fully grasped as the apocalyptic Son of Man of the present. He is the apocalyptic Son of Man who had *exousia* in the past, was subjected to suffering, and rose on the third day. Only the Son of Man who had a history of power and passion is to have a future in glory. His own future is grounded in his past. In sum, Jerusalem immortalized the present and in consequence immobilized its future. Mark overcomes its restricted perception of reality, and can thus speak for man in a more total sense. His gospel furnishes the new spatiotemporal universe in which one can breathe again, relate and orient oneself, find identity, and undertake new action.

THE HERMENEUTICS OF CRISIS

In response to a world out of joint, the gospel narrates an elaborate explanation. This is the function of the theme of discipleship failure, a feature overshadowing the total ministry of Jesus. All along the way from Galilee to Jerusalem the disciples, representatives of what came to be the Jerusalem church, aid and abet the tragedy by continuously misunderstanding the message and mission of Jesus.

In Galilee Jesus had called the disciples into the service of a Kingdom which he formed and formulated in defiance of an exclusive Jewish-Christian way of life.[39] In his Galilean speech he had initiated them into the mystery of this Kingdom, its conflict-laden, hidden present and its imminent revelation.[40] If the Jerusalem Christians, however, pro-

39. Chap. I, pp. 18–22.
40. Chap. II.

ceeded to find eternity in the present, this message of the hidden Kingdom must have fallen on deaf ears. Furthermore, Jesus had taken great pains to separate the Kingdom from the influence of his family and the authority of Jerusalem.[41] How could they have missed this hint against building the Kingdom in Jerusalem? The formation of the Jewish-Gentile community, thoroughly explicated by Jesus' voyages, had made little sense to them, even though they were in two separate incidents put in charge over the Jewish and the Gentile parts of the Kingdom.[42] In anticipation of his absence Jesus had elevated them to apostleship, entrusting them with responsibility over this Galilean mission field.[43] Despite Jesus' meticulous efforts at explaining the nature and implications of the Galilean Kingdom, the disciples journey down southward without a lasting recollection of it. How are they ever to heed Jesus' call to go back to Galilee (14:28), if his sanctification of the New Jerusalem had left them with nothing but a hardened heart?

Once embarked upon the way to Jerusalem Jesus had three times pronounced passion and resurrection as the hallmark of his messiahship, but his disciples remained obstinate in the face of his repeated expositions.[44] Upon arrival in Jerusalem they will promptly perpetuate a Christian faith which makes no allowance for a dying, rising Messiah. The transfiguration epiphany they had taken for an instant solution to their problems, without paying attention to the crucial relationship between the resurrection and the parousia fulfillment.[45] After the resurrection they should embark upon the road of discipleship toward Kingdom and parousia (9:9; 14:28). But what if they never learn of the resurrection? In Judea Jesus had reminded them of the impending loss and dispersion, and in Jerusalem he had in an act of high drama disqualified the temple.[46] After all this, how could they still wish to settle in Jerusalem and build the Kingdom in this city of death and destruction?

To further prepare the disciples for what was to come, their chosen representatives had received special initiation into the very aspects of Jesus' mission which they should never and under no circumstances have dismissed from their minds. They had been privileged to witness Jesus'

41. Chaps. II, pp. 25–27; III, pp. 53–54, 59.
42. Chap. III.
43. Chap. III, p. 54.
44. Chap. IV, pp. 82–84.
45. Chap. IV, pp. 83–84.
46. Chap. V.

most spectacular miracle, the raising of a dead woman[47]—which should have conditioned their hearts and minds for the kind of Messiah Jesus was going to be. On the mount of transfiguration they had been granted a glimpse of Jesus' eschatological glory[48]—which should have encouraged them to keep their future open. On the Mount of Olives Jesus had forecast the temple disaster and the ensuing eschatological crisis[49]—which should have alerted them, *not* to invest life and hope in the city of David. At Gethsemane, on the threshold of the passion, they had been given a last chance to come to terms with a suffering Messiah[50]—which should have enabled them to follow Jesus through passion and resurrection toward the goal of the parousia.

All the clues had been given to the disciples! If they had remembered what they could have known, they would be in possession of the key to the mystery of the Kingdom of God. From the depths of their memory they could have known the way to the Kingdom. They should have waited for the signal of resurrection and then proceeded to Galilee.

But Jesus' efforts were to no avail, and the bitter harvest which had been growing all along was going to be reaped in Jerusalem. While the disciples deteriorate from misconception to betrayal and denial and flight, Jesus accepts death and moves through suffering and resurrection toward the parousia.

But his resurrection, this crucial date which was to initiate the disciples' departure from Jerusalem (16:6–7), is never reported to them, due to the failure of the women (6:8). This is the missing link which fully discloses the disciples' failure to ever leave Jerusalem. It is because they had been in flight from the facts of Jesus' ministry throughout, unable and unwilling to grasp the logic of his Kingdom gospel, that they did not receive the signal to depart for Galilee, and mistook Jerusalem for the goal of the way. Thus they forfeited entrance into the Kingdom of God. They made Jerusalem their permanent home and never learned their lesson from the past of Jesus. The signal toward the new goal had long been missed when they engineered a false dawn of the Kingdom, living in the euphoria of the here and now—until they got caught in the fall of the city.

This Markan drama of discipleship explains why Jerusalem had to

---

47. Chap. III, pp. 52–53.
48. Chap. IV, pp. 77–82.
49. Chap. VI.
50. Werner H. Kelber, "Mark 14, 32–42: Gethsemane," *ZNW*, 63 (1972), pp. 166–87.

become a place of no return, and it provides the rationale for the calamity of Jerusalem Christianity.

The gospel of Mark does not so much have the significance of a foundation, but that of an explanation. It refreshes the Christian memory and brings back to mind how it all had happened. This is the mythological function of the gospel. It relates "how it began," because the events at the beginning explain the present condition. Specifically, the gospel narrates the genesis of a crisis, and by doing so produces its resolution. The gospel is not an historical account of the life of Jesus, but the mythological reconstruction of a critical moment in Christian history. The Christians, especially those who survived the disaster in the south, must relearn their past, understand the cause of the crisis, if they still are to have a future. For this reason they are put at the very origin. They will not reach the New Jerusalem unless they make the journey over again from the beginning to its tragic ending in the old city of Jerusalem. Then, but only then, if they begin at the beginning, will it dawn on them that the end of Jerusalem was but the beginning of the period preceding the End.

BIBLIOGRAPHY

Selective Bibliography

Achtemeier, Paul J., "Person and Deed. Jesus and the Storm-Tossed Sea," *Interpr*, 16 (1962), 169–76.

———— "Toward the Isolation of Pre-Markan Miracle Catenae," *JBL*, 89 (1970), 265–91.

———— "The Origin and Function of the Pre-Marcan Miracle Catenae," *JBL*, 91 (1972), 198–221.

Ambrozic, Aloysius M., *The Hidden Kingdom*, The Catholic Biblical Quarterly —Monograph Series, No. 2. Washington, D.C.: The Catholic Biblical Association of America, 1972.

Bacon, Benjamin Wisner, "The Markan Theory of Demonic Recognition of the Christ," *ZNW*, 6 (1905), 153–58.

———— "The Prologue of Mark: A Study of Sources and Structure," *JBL*, 26 (1907), 84–106.

———— *The Gospel of Mark: Its Composition and Date*, New Haven: Yale University Press, 1925.

Baeck, Leo, *Das Evangelium als Urkunde der jüdischen Glaubensgeschichte*, Berlin: Schocken, 1938.

———— *Judaism and Christianity*. Translated by Walter Kaufmann, Cleveland, Ohio: World Publishing Company, 1961.

Baltensweiler, Heinrich, *Die Verklärung Jesu, Historisches Ereignis und Synoptische Berichte*. Abhandlungen zur Theologie des Alten und Neuen Testaments, No. 33, Zurich: Zwingli Verlag, 1959.

Baltzer, Klaus, "The Meaning of the Temple in the Lukan Writings," *HTR*, 58 (1965), 263–77.

Barbour, R. S., "Gethsemane in the Tradition of the Passion," *NTS*, 16 (1970), 231–51.

Bartsch, Hans-Werner, "Parusieerwartung und Osterbotschaft," *EvTh*, 7 (1947), 115–26.

———— "Zum Problem der Parusieverzögerung bei den Synoptikern," *EvTh*, 19 (1959), 116–31.

———— "Die 'Verfluchung' des Feigenbaumes," *ZNW*, 53 (1962), 256–60.

———— "Early Christian Eschatology in the Synoptic Gospels," *NTS*, 11 (1965), 387–97.

Beasley-Murray, George Raymond, *Jesus and the Future*, London: Macmillan & Co., Ltd., 1954.

———— *A Commentary on Mark Thirteen*, London: Macmillan & Co., Ltd., 1957.

Berkey, Robert F., "ENGIZEIN, PHTHANEIN, and Realized Eschatology," *JBL*, 82 (1963), 177–87.

Best, Ernest, *The Temptation and the Passion. The Markan Soteriology*, Society for New Testament Studies, Monograph Series, No. 2, Cambridge: Cambridge University Press, 1965.

Bickermann, Elias, "Das Messiasgeheimnis und die Komposition des Markusevangeliums," *ZNW*, 22 (1923), 122–40.

———— "Das leere Grab," *ZNW*, 23 (1924), 281–92.

Bird, C. H., "Some *gar* Clauses in St. Mark's Gospel," *JTS*, 4 (1953), 171–87.

Black, Matthew, "The Kingdom of God has Come," *ExpT*, 63 (1952), 289–90.

Blatherwick, David, "The Markan Silhouette?" *NTS*, 17 (1971), 184–92.

Blenkinsopp, Joseph, "The Oracle of Judah and the Messianic Entry," *JBL*, 80 (1961), 55–64.

Bonner, Campbell, "Traces of Thaumaturgic Technique in the Miracles," *HTR*, 20 (1927), 171–81.

Boobyer, G. H., *St. Mark and the Transfiguration Story*, Edinburgh: T. & T. Clark, 1942.

———— "The Eucharistic Interpretation of the Miracles of the Loaves in St. Mark's Gospel," *JTS*, 3 (1952), 161–71.

———— "Galilee and Galileans in St. Mark's Gospel," *BJRL*, 35 (1953), 334–48.

———— "The Miracles of the Loaves and the Gentiles in St. Mark's Gospel," *ScJTh*, 6 (1953), 77–87.

———— "The Secrecy Motif in St. Mark's Gospel," *NTS*, 6 (1960), 225–35.

———— "The Redaction of Mark IV, 1–34," *NTS*, 8 (1961), 59–70.

Bousset, Wilhelm, *Kyrios Christos*, 6th ed. Translated by John E. Steely, Nashville, Tenn.: Abingdon, 1970.

Brandon, S. G. F., "The Apologetic Factor in the Markan Gospel," *SE*, II, *TU*, LXXXVII, Berlin: Akademie-Verlag, 1964.

———— "Tübingen Vindicated?" *HibJ*, 49 (1950), 41–47.

———— *The Fall of Jerusalem and the Christian Church*, London: S.P.C.K., 1951.

———— "The Date of the Markan Gospel," *NTS*, 7 (1961), 126–41.

———— *Jesus and the Zealots*, New York: Charles Scribner's Sons, 1967.

———— *The Trial of Jesus of Nazareth*, New York: Stein and Day Publishers, 1968.

Branscomb, Bennett Harvie, *The Gospel of Mark*, New York: Harper and Brothers Publishers, 1937.

Braun, F. M., "L'Expulsion des Vendeurs du Temple," *RB*, 38 (1929), 178–200.

Braun, Herbert, "'Umkehr' in Spätjüdisch-Häretischer und Frühchristlicher Sicht," *ZThK*, 50 (1953), 243–58.

———— "*planaō*," *TDNT*, 6, 236–51.

Brown, John Pairman, "An Early Revision of the Gospel of Mark," *JBL*, 78 (1959), 215–27.

Brown, Raymond E., "The Pre-Christian Semitic Concept of Mystery," *CBQ*, 20 (1958), 417–43.

Brückner, M., "Die Petruserzählungen im Markusevangelium," *ZNW*, 8 (1907), 48–65.

Bultmann, Rudolf, *History of the Synoptic Tradition*, 3rd ed. Translated by John Marsh, New York: Harper & Row, 1963.

Burger, Christoph, *Jesus als Davidssohn*, Forschungen zur Religion und Literatur des Alten und Neuen Testaments, No. 98, Göttingen: Vandenhoeck & Ruprecht, 1970.

Burkill, T. Alec, "The Cryptology of Parables in St. Mark's Gospel," *NovTest*, 1 (1956), 246–62.

———— "Anti-Semitism in St. Mark's Gospel," *NovTest*, 3 (1959), 34–53.

———— "Strain on the Secret: An Examination of Mark 11, 1–13, 37," *ZNW*, 51 (1960), 31–46.

———— "The Hidden Son of Man in St. Mark's Gospel," *ZNW*, 52 (1961), 189–213.

———— *Mysterious Revelation. An Examination of the Philosophy of St. Mark's Gospel*, Ithaca, N.Y.: Cornell University Press, 1963.

———— *New Light on the Oldest Gospel*, Ithaca, N.Y.: Cornell University Press, 1972.

Burkitt, Francis Crawford, "W and Θ: Studies in the Western Text of St. Mark," *JTS*, 17 (1916), 139–52.

Busch, Friedrich, *Zum Verständnis der Synoptischen Eschatologie. Markus 13 Neu Untersucht*, Gütersloh: C. Bertelsmann, 1938.

Campbell, J. Y., "The Kingdom of God has Come," *ExpT*, 48 (1936), 91–94.

Carrington, Philip, *The Primitive Christian Calendar. A Study in the Making of the Marcan Gospel*, Cambridge: Cambridge University Press, 1952.

Clark, Kenneth W., "Worship in the Jerusalem Temple after A.D. 70," *NTS*, 6 (1960), 269–80.

Colani, Timothée, *Jésus-Christ et les Croyances Messianiques de son Temps*, Strasbourg: Treuttel et Wurtz, 1864.

Conzelmann, Hans, "Gegenwart und Zukunft in der Synoptischen Tradition," *ZThK*, 54 (1957), 277–96.

———— "Geschichte und Eschaton nach Mc 13," *ZNW*, 50 (1959), 210–21.

Cousar, Charles B., "Eschatology and Mark's Theologia Crucis," *Interpr*, 24 (1970), 321–35.

Coutts, J., " 'Those Outside' (Mark 4, 10–12)," *SE*, II, *TU*, LXXXVII, Berlin: Akademie-Verlag, 1964.

Crossan, John Dominic, "Redaction and Citation in Mark 11:9–10, 17 and 14: 27," *Proceedings*. Edited by Lane C. McGaughy, Vol. I, Society of Biblical Literature, 1972.

✓ –––––––– "Mark and the Relatives of Jesus," *NovTest*, 15 (1973), 81–113.

Crum, John Macleod Campbell, *St. Mark's Gospel*, Cambridge: Heffer & Sons Ltd., 1936.

Daube, David, "Public Pronouncements and Private Explanation in the Gospels," *ExpT*, 57 (1946), 175–77.

–––––––– *The New Testament and Rabbinic Judaism*, London: Athlone Press, 1956.

Dewar, Francis, "Chapter 13 and the Passion Narrative in St. Mark," *Theology*, 64 (1961), 99–107.

Dibelius, Martin, *From Tradition to Gospel*. Translated by Bertram Lee Woolf, New York: Charles Scribner's Sons, 1935.

Dobschütz, Ernst, "Zur Erzählkunst des Markus," *ZNW*, 27 (1928), 193–98.

Doeve, J. W., "Purification du Temple et Desséchement du Figuier," *NTS*, 1 (1955), 297–308.

Dodd, Charles Harold, "The Kingdom of God has Come," *ExpT*, 48 (1936), 138–42.

–––––––– *The Parables of the Kingdom*, rev. ed., New York: Charles Scribner's Sons, 1961.

Doudna, John Charles, *The Greek of the Gospel of Mark*, Journal of Biblical Literature, Monograph Series, No. 12, Philadelphia: Society of Biblical Literature and Exegesis, 1961.

Drews, Arthur, *Das Markusevangelium als Zeugnis gegen die Geschichtlichkeit Jesu*, Jena: E. Diederichs, 1928.

Ebeling, Hans Jürgen, *Das Messiasgeheimnis und die Botschaft des Marcus-Evangelisten*, Berlin: Alfred Töpelmann, 1939.

Elliott-Binns, L. B. *Galilean Christianity*, Studies in Biblical Theology, No. 16, London: SCM Press, 1956.

Eppstein, Victor, "The Historicity of the Gospel Account of the Cleansing of the Temple," *ZNW*, 55 (1964), 42–58.

Evans, C. F., "I Will Go Before You into Galilee," *JTS*, 5 (1954), 3–18.

Farrer, Austin M., *A Study in St. Mark*, Westminster: Dacre Press, 1951.

Fascher, Erich, "Theologische Bemerkungen zu *dei*." Edited by Walther Eltester, *Neutestamentliche Studien für Rudolf Bultmann*, Berlin: Alfred Töpelmann, 1954.

Feuillet, André, "Les Perspectives Propres à Chaque Évangéliste dans les Récits de la Transfiguration," *Bib*, 39 (1958), 281–301.

Flückiger, Felix, "Die Redaktion der Zukunftsrede in Mark 13," *TZ*, 26 (1970), 395–409.

Freese, N. F., "Der Anfang des Markusevangeliums," *ThStKr*, 104 (1932), 429–38.

Friedrich, Gerhard, *"euangelion,"* TDNT, 2, 721–37.

Fuller, Reginald H., *The Mission and Achievement of Jesus*, Studies in Biblical Theology, No. 12, Chicago: Alec R. Allenson, Inc., 1954.

———— *The Foundations of New Testament Christology*, New York: Charles Scribner's Sons, 1965.

Gaertner, Bertil, *The Temple and the Community in Qumran and the New Testament*, Cambridge: Cambridge University Press, 1965.

Gaston, Lloyd, *No Stone On Another*, Supplements to Novum Testamentum, No. 23, Leiden: Brill, 1970.

Gealy, Fred D., "The Composition of Mark IV," *ExpT*, 48 (1936), 40–43.

Gnilka, Joachim, *Die Verstockung Israels*, Studien zum Alten und Neuen Testament, No. 3, Munich: Kösel-Verlag, 1961.

Goguel, Maurice, *L'Evangile de Marc et ses Rapports avec Ceux de Mathieu et de Luc*, Paris: E. Leroux, 1909.

———— "'Avec des Persécutions' Etude Exégétique sur Marc 10:29–30," *RHPhR*, 8 (1928), 264–77.

Grässer, Erich, *Das Problem der Parusieverzögerung in den Synoptischen Evangelien und in der Apostelgeschichte*, 2nd ed., Berlin: Alfred Töpelmann, 1960.

———— "Jesus in Nazareth (Mark VI. 1–6a)," *NTS*, 16 (1969), 1–23.

Grant, Frederick C., *The Earliest Gospel*, Nashville, Tenn.: Abingdon, n.d.

Grant, Robert M., "The Coming of the Kingdom of God," *JBL*, 67 (1948), 297–303.

Grob, Rudolf, *Einführung in das Markus-Evangelium*, Zurich: Zwingli Verlag, 1965.

Grundmann, Walter, *Das Evangelium nach Markus*, 3rd ed., Berlin: Evangelische Verlagsanstalt, 1965.

Haenchen, Ernst, "Die Komposition von Mk VIII:27-IX:1," *NovTest*, 6 (1963).

———— *Der Weg Jesu*, 2nd ed., rev., Berlin: Walter de Gruyter & Co., 1968.

Hahn, Ferdinand, *Mission in the New Testament*. Translated by Frank Clarke, Studies in Biblical Theology, No. 47, Naperville, Ill.: Alec R. Allenson, Inc., 1965.

———— *The Titles of Jesus in Christology*. Translated by Harold Knight and George Ogg, New York: World Publishing Company, 1969.

Hahn, Istaván, "Josephus und die Eschatologie von Qumran," *Qumran-Probleme*. Edited by Hans Bardtke, Berlin: Akademie-Verlag, 1963.

Hamilton, Neill Q., "Resurrection Tradition and the Composition of Mark," *JBL*, 84 (1965), 415–21.

————— *Jesus for a No-God World*, Philadelphia: Westminster Press, 1969.

Harder, Günther, "Das Gleichnis von der Selbstwachsenden Saat. Mark. 4, 26–29," *ThViat*, 1 (1948/49), 51–70.

————— "Das Eschatologische Geschichtsbild der sogenannten kleinen Apokalypse Markus 13," *ThViat*, 4 (1952), 71–107.

Hartman, Lars, *Prophecy Interpreted*. Translated by Neil Tomkinson, Coniectanea Biblica, New Testament Series I, Lund, Sweden: C. W. Gleerup, 1966.

Hawkins, John C., *Horae Synopticae*, 2nd ed., rev. and supplemented, Oxford: Clarendon Press, 1909.

Heitmüller, Wilhelm, *"Im Namen Jesu,"* Göttingen: Vandenhoeck & Ruprecht, 1903.

Hiers, Richard H., "Purification of the Temple: Preparation for the Kingdom of God," *JBL*, 90 (1971), 82–90.

Honey, T. E. Floyd, "Did Mark use Q?" *JBL*, 62 (1943), 319–31.

Horstmann, Maria, *Studien zur Markinischen Christologie*, Neutestamentliche Abhandlungen, No. 6, Münster: Aschendorff, 1969.

Hutton, W. R., "The Kingdom of God has Come," *ExpT*, 64 (1952), 89–91.

Iersel, B. van, "Die Wunderbare Speisung und das Abendmahl in der Synoptischen Tradition," *NovTest*, 7 (1965), 167–94.

Jeremias, Joachim, *The Parables of Jesus*, 6th ed. Translated by S. H. Hooke, New York: Charles Scribner's Sons, 1963.

————— *The Eucharistic Words of Jesus*, 3rd ed., rev. Translated by Norman Perrin, New York: Charles Scribner's Sons, 1966.

Joüon, P., "Notes Philologiques sur les Évangiles," *RSR*, 17 (1927), 537–40.

Karnetzki, Manfred, "Die Galiläische Redaktion im Markusevangelium," *ZNW*, 52 (1961), 238–72.

Keck, Leander E., "Mark 3, 7–12 and Mark's Christology," *JBL*, 84 (1965), 341–58.

————— "The Introduction to Mark's Gospel," *NTS*, 12 (1966), 352–70.

Kee, Howard Clark, "The Terminology of Mark's Exorcism Stories," *NTS*, 14 (1968), 232–46.

Kelber, Werner H., "Mark 14, 32–42: Gethsemane," *ZNW*, 63 (1972), 166–87.

Kertelge, Karl, *Die Wunder Jesu im Markusevangelium*, Studien zum Alten und Neuen Testament, No. 23, Munich: Kösel-Verlag, 1970.

Kilpatrick, George Dunbar, "The Gentile Mission in Mark and Mark 13, 9–11," *Essays in Memory of R. H. Lightfoot*. Edited by Dennis Eric Nineham, Oxford: Blackwell, 1957.

Klostermann, Erich, *Das Markusevangelium*, 4th ed., Tübingen: J. C. B. Mohr/ Paul Siebeck, 1950.

Knigge, Heinz-Dieter, "The Meaning of Mark," *Interpr*, 22 (1968), 53–70.

Kuby, Alfred, "Zur Konzeption des Markus-Evangeliums," *ZNW*, 49 (1958), 52–64.

Kümmel, Werner Georg, *Promise and Fulfilment*. Translated by Dorothea M. Barton, Studies in Biblical Theology, No. 23, London: SCM Press, 1966.

Kuhn, Heinz-Wolfgang, "Das Reittier Jesu in der Einzugsgeschichte des Markusevangeliums," *ZNW*, 50 (1959), 82–91.

———— *Ältere Sammlungen im Markusevangelium*, Studien zur Umwelt des Neuen Testaments, No. 8, Göttingen: Vandenhoeck & Ruprecht, 1971.

Kuschke, Arnulf, "Die Menschenwege und der Weg Gottes im Alten Testament," *StTh*, 5 (1951), 106–18.

Lambrecht, Jan, *Die Redaktion der Markus-Apokalypse*, Analecta Biblica, No. 28, Rome: Pontifical Biblical Institute, 1967.

———— "Die fünf Parabeln in Mk 4," *Bijdr*, 29 (1968), 25–53.

Lightfoot, Robert Henry, *History and Interpretation in the Gospels*, New York: Harper and Brothers Publishers, 1934.

———— *Locality and Doctrine in the Gospels*, New York: Harper and Brothers Publishers, 1938.

———— *The Gospel Message of St. Mark*, Oxford: Oxford University Press, 1952.

Lindars, Barnabas, *New Testament Apologetic*, Philadelphia: Westminster Press, 1961.

Linton, Olaf, "The Demand for a Sign from Heaven," *ST*, 19 (1965), 112–29.

Lohmeyer, Ernst, *Galiläa und Jerusalem*, Göttingen: Vandenhoeck & Ruprecht, 1936.

———— *Lord of the Temple*. Translated by Stewart Todd, Richmond, Va.: John Knox Press, 1962.

———— *Gottesknecht und Davidssohn*, 2nd ed., Göttingen: Vandenhoeck & Ruprecht, 1953.

———— *Das Evangelium des Markus*, 17th ed., Göttingen: Vandenhoeck & Ruprecht, 1967.

Luz, Ulrich, "Das Geheimnismotiv und die Markinische Christologie," *ZNW*, 51 (1965), 9–30.

Manson, Thomas Walter, "The EGO EIMI of the Messianic Presence in the New Testament," *JTS*, 48 (1947), 137–45.

Maurer, Christian, "*skeuos*," *TDNT*, 7, 358–67.

Marxsen, Willi, "Redaktionsgeschichtliche Erklärung der sogenannten Parabeltheorie des Markus," *ZThK*, 52 (1955), 255–71.

———— *Mark the Evangelist*. Translated by Roy A. Harrisville *et al.*, Nashville, Tenn.: Abingdon Press, 1969.

Masson, Charles, *L'Evangile de Marc et l'Eglise de Rome*, Neuchatel: Delachaux et Niestlé, 1968.

Mauser, Ulrich, *Christ in the Wilderness*, Studies in Biblical Theology, No. 39, Naperville, Ill.: Alec R. Allenson, Inc., 1963.

McKelvey, R. J., *The New Temple. The Church in the New Testament*, Oxford: Oxford University Press, 1969.

Meye, Robert P., "Mark 4, 10: 'Those about Him with the Twelve'," *SE*, II, *TU*, LXXXVII, Berlin: Akademie-Verlag, 1964.

———— *Jesus and the Twelve*, Grand Rapids, Mich.: Eerdmans Publishing Company, 1968.

———— "Mark 16:8—The Ending of Mark's Gospel," *BiR*, 14 (1969), 33–43.

Minette de Tillesse, G., *Le Secret Messianique dans L'Evangile de Marc*, Lectio Divina, No. 47, Paris: Cerf, 1968.

Mussner, Franz, "Die Bedeutung von Mk 1, 14f für die Reichsgottesverkündigung Jesu," *TTZ*, 66 (1957), 257–75.

———— "Gottesherrschaft und Sendung Jesu nach Mk 1, 14f. Zugleich ein Beitrag über die innere Struktur des Markusevangeliums," *Praesentia Salutis*, Düsseldorf: Patmos Verlag, 1967.

Nineham, Dennis Eric, "The Order of Events in St. Mark's Gospel," *Studies in the Gospels. Essays in Memory of R. H. Lightfoot*. Edited by D. E. Nineham, Oxford: Blackwell, 1955.

———— *The Gospel of St. Mark*, Baltimore, Md.: Penguin Books, Inc., 1963.

Perrin, Norman, *The Kingdom of God in the Teaching of Jesus*, Philadelphia: Westminster Press, 1963.

———— "Mark 14:62: End Product of a Christian Pesher Tradition?" *NTS*, 12 (1965), 150–55.

———— "The Son of Man in Ancient Judaism and Primitive Christianity," *BiR*, 11 (1966), 17–28.

———— *Rediscovering the Teaching of Jesus*, New York: Harper & Row, 1967.

———— "The Son of Man in the Synoptic Tradition," *BiR*, 13 (1968), 1–25.

———— "The Creative Use of the Son of Man Traditions by Mark," *USQR*, 23 (1968), 357–65.

———— *What is Redaction Criticism?* Philadelphia: Fortress Press, 1969.

———— "The Composition of Mark IX, 1," *NovTest*, 11 (1969), 67–70.

———— "Towards an Interpretation of the Gospel of Mark," *Christology and a Modern Pilgrimage*. Edited by Hans D. Betz, Claremont, Calif.: New Testament Colloquium, 1971.

———— *A Modern Pilgrimage in New Testament Christology*, Philadelphia: Fortress Press, 1974.

Pesch, Rudolf, *Naherwartungen*, Düsseldorf: Patmos Verlag, 1968.

———— "Ein Tag vollmächtigen Wirkens Jesu in Kapharnaum (Mk 1, 21–34. 35–39)," *BibLeb*, 9 (1968), 114–28, 177–95, 261–77.

———— "Anfang des Evangeliums Jesu Christi," *Die Zeit Jesu*. Edited by Günther Bornkamm and Karl Rahner, H. Schlier Festschrift, Freiburg: Herder, 1970.

———— *Der Besessene von Gerasa*, Stuttgarter Bibelstudien, No. 56, Stuttgart: KBW Verlag, 1972.

Potterie, I. de la, "De Compositione Evangelii Marci," *VD*, 44 (1966), 135–141.

Preisker, Carl Heinz, "Konsekutives *hina* in Markus 4, 12," *ZNW*, 59 (1968), 126–27.

Pryke, E. J., "IDE and IDOU," *NTS*, 14 (1968), 418–24.

Reploh, Karl-Georg, *Markus—Lehrer der Gemeinde*, Stuttgarter Biblische Monographien, No. 9, Stuttgart: KBW Verlag, 1969.

Reedy, Charles J., "Mk 8:31—11:10 and the Gospel Ending. A Redaction Study," *CBQ*, 34 (1972), 188–97.

Riddle, Donald W., "The Martyr Motif in the Gospel according to Mark," *JRel*, 4 (1924), 397–410.

———— "Die Verfolgungslogien in formgeschichtlicher und soziologischer Betrachtung," *ZNW*, 33 (1934), 271–89.

———— "Mark 4: 1–34. The Evolution of a Gospel Source," *JBL*, 56 (1937), 77–90.

Riesenfeld, Harald, *Jésus Transfiguré. L'Arrière-Plan du Récit Évangelique de la Transfiguration de Notre-Seigneur*, Acta Seminarii Neotestamentici Upsaliensis, No. 16, Copenhagen: Ejnar Munksgaard, 1947.

Robin, A. de Q., "The Cursing of the Fig Tree in Mark XI. A Hypothesis," *NTS*, 8 (1962), 276–81.

Robinson, James M., *The Problem of History in Mark*, Studies in Biblical Theology, No. 21, London: SCM Press, 1957.

———— "The Problem of History in Mark, Reconsidered," *USQR*, 20 (1965), 131–47.

Robinson, William C., "The Quest for Wrede's Secret Messiah," *Interpr*, 27 (1973), 10–30.

Rohde, Joachim, *Rediscovering the Teaching of the Evangelists*. Translated by Dorothea M. Barton, Philadelphia: Westminster Press, 1968.

Roloff, Jürgen, "Das Markusevangelium als Geschichtsdarstellung," *EvTh*, 27 (1969), 73–93.

Roth, Cecil, "The Cleansing of the Temple and Zechariah," *NovTest*, 4 (1960), 174–81.

Schenke, Ludger, *Auferstehungsverkündigung und leeres Grab*, Stuttgarter Biblische Studien, No. 33, Stuttgart: KBW Verlag, 1969.

Schille, Gottfried, "Bemerkungen zur Formgeschichte des Evangeliums. Rahmen und Aufbau des Markus-Evangeliums," *NTS*, 4 (1957), 1–24.

Schmauch, Werner, "Der Ölberg. Exegese zu einer Ortsangabe besonders bei Matthäus und Markus," *TLZ*, 77 (1952), 391–96.

————— *Orte der Offenbarung und der Offenbarungsort im Neuen Testament*, Göttingen: Vandenhoeck & Ruprecht, 1956.

Schmidt, Karl Ludwig, *Der Rahmen der Geschichte Jesu*. Reprint, Darmstadt: Wissenschaftliche Buchgesellschaft, 1964.

Schmithals, Walter, *Wunder und Glaube. Eine Auslegung von Markus 4,35–6,6a*, Biblische Studien, No. 59, Neukirchen-Vluyn: Neukirchener Verlag, 1970.

Schnackenburg, Rudolf, *God's Rule and Kingdom*. Translated by John Murray, New York: Herder and Herder, 1963.

————— "Kirche und Parusie," *Gott in Welt*, Vol. I. Edited by Johannes Baptist Metz *et al.*, Karl Rahner Festschrift, Freiburg: Herder, 1964.

Schniewind, Julius Daniel, "Messiasgeheimnis und Eschatologie," *Julius Schniewind. Nachgelassene Reden und Aufsätze*. Edited by Ernst Kähler, Berlin: Alfred Töpelmann, 1952.

————— *Das Evangelium nach Markus*, 10th ed., Göttingen: Vandenhoeck & Ruprecht, 1963.

Schreiber, Johannes, "Die Christologie des Markusevangeliums," *ZThK*, 58 (1961), 154–83.

————— *Theologie des Vertrauens*, Hamburg: Furche-Verlag, 1967.

Schulz, Siegfried, "Markus und das Alte Testament," *ZThK*, 58 (1961), 184–97.

————— "Die Bedeutung des Markus für die Theologiegeschichte des Urchristentums," *SE*, II, *TU*, LXXXVII, Berlin: Akademie-Verlag, 1964.

————— *Die Stunde der Botschaft*, Hamburg: Furche-Verlag, 1967.

Schweizer, Eduard, "Anmerkungen zur Theologie des Markus," *Neotestamentica*, Zurich: Zwingli Verlag, 1963.

————— "Mark's Contribution to the Quest of the Historical Jesus," *NTS*, 10 (1964), 421–32.

————— "Die Theologische Leistung des Markus," *EvTh*, 24 (1964), 337–55.

————— "Zur Frage des Messiasgeheimnisses bei Markus," *ZNW*, 56 (1965), 1–8.

————— *The Good News According to Mark*. Translated by D. H. Madvig, Richmond, Va.: John Knox Press, 1970.

Seitz, Oscar J. F., "Praeparatio Evangelica in the Markan Prologue," *JBL*, 82 (1963), 201–06.

Slusser, Dorothy M., "The Healing Narratives in Mark," *The Christian Century*, No. 87 (1970), 597–99.

Smith, Charles W. F., "No Time for Figs," *JBL*, 79 (1960), 315–27.

Smith, Morton, "Comments on Taylor's Commentary on Mark," *HTR*, 48 (1955), 21–64.

Stauffer, Ethelbert, "*egō*," *TDNT*, 2, 343–62.

Stein, Robert H., "The Proper Methodology for Ascertaining a Markan Redaction History," *NovTest*, 31 (1971), 181–98.

Strobel, August, *Kerygma und Apokalyptik*, Göttingen: Vandenhoeck & Ruprecht, 1967.

Suhl, Alfred, *Die Funktion der alttestamentlichen Zitate und Anspielungen im Markusevangelium*, Gütersloh: Gerd Mohn, 1965.

Synge, F. C., "The Transfiguration Story," *ExpT*, 82 (1970), 82–83.

Tagawa, Kenzo, *Miracles et Evangile*, Paris: Presses Universitaires de France, 1966.

Taylor, Vincent, *The Gospel According to St. Mark*, London: Macmillan and Co., 1963.

Tödt, Heinz Eduard, *The Son of Man in the Synoptic Tradition*. Translated by Dorothea M. Barton, 2nd ed., Philadelphia: Westminster Press, 1965.

Trocmé, Étienne, *La Formation de l'Evangile selon Marc*, Paris: Presses Universitaires de France, 1963.

———— "Marc 9,1: Prédiction ou Réprimande?" *SE*, II, *TU*, LXXXVII, Berlin: Akademie-Verlag, 1964.

———— "L'Expulsion des Marchands du Temple," *NTS*, 15 (1968), 1–22.

Turner, Cuthbert H., "Marcan Usage: Notes, Critical and Exegetical, on the Second Gospel," *JTS*, 25 (1923–24), 377–80; 26 (1924–25), 12–20, 145–56, 225–40; 27 (1925–26), 58–62; 28 (1926–27), 9–30, 349–62; 29 (1927–28), 275–89, 346–61.

Tyson, Joseph B., "The Blindness of the Disciples in Mark," *JBL*, 80 (1961), 261–68.

Vielhauer, Philipp, "Erwägungen zur Christologie des Markusevangeliums," *Aufsätze zum Neuen Testament*, Munich: Kaiser Verlag, 1965.

Vogt, Ernst, " 'Mysteria' in Textibus Qumran," *Bib*, 37 (1956), 247–57.

Walter, Nikolaus, "Zur Analyse von Mc 10:17–31," *ZNW*, 53 (1962), 206–18.

———— "Tempelzerstörung und Synoptische Apokalypse," *ZNW*, 57 (1966), 38–49.

Weeden, Theodore J., "The Heresy that Necessitated Mark's Gospel," *ZNW*, 59 (1968), 145–58.

———— *Mark—Traditions in Conflict*, Philadelphia: Fortress Press, 1971.

Weihnacht, Harald, *Die Menschwerdung des Sohnes Gottes im Markusevangelium*, Tübingen: J. C. B. Mohr (Paul Siebeck), 1972.

Weiss, Johannes, *Das Älteste Evangelium*, Göttingen: Vandenhoeck & Ruprecht, 1903.

———— *Jesus' Proclamation of the Kingdom of God.* Translated, edited and with an Introduction by Richard Hiers and D. Larrimore Holland, Philadelphia: Fortress Press, 1971.

Wellhausen, Julius, *Das Evangelium Marci,* Berlin: Georg Reimer, 1909.

Werner, Eric, " 'Hosanna' in the Gospels," *JBL,* 65 (1946), 97–122.

Werner, Martin, *Der Einfluss Paulinischer Theologie im Markusevangelium,* Giessen: Alfred Töpelmann, 1923.

Wikgren, Allen, "ARCHE TOU EYANGELIOU," *JBL,* 61 (1942), 11–20.

Windisch, Hans, "Die Sprüche vom Eingehen in das Reich Gottes," *ZNW,* 27 (1928), 163–92.

Wingren, Gustaf, " 'Weg,' 'Wanderung' und Verwandte Begriffe," *StTh,* 3 (1949), 111–23.

Wrede, William, *The Messianic Secret.* Translated by J. C. G. Grieg, Cambridge: James Clarke & Co. Ltd., 1971.

Zerwick, Maximilian, *Untersuchungen zum Markus-Stil: Ein Beitrag zur stilistischen Durcharbeitung des Neuen Testaments,* Rome: Pontifical Biblical Institute, 1937.

Ziener, P. Georg, "Die Brotwunder im Markusevangelium," *BZ,* N.F. 4 (1960), 282–85.

Ziesler, J. A., "The Transfiguration Story and the Markan Soteriology," *ExpT,* 81 (1970), 263–68.

INDEXES

Index of Authors

Index of Scripture References

OLD TESTAMENT

Exodus
24 — 72, 77
24:16 — 79
24:17 — 77

1 Kings
1:32-48 — 92n
8:10-11 — 79

Psalms
2:7 — 81
24:7-10 — 92n
29:10 — 27n
42:5 — 92n
43:3 — 92n
68:25-28 — 92n
78:2 — 32n

89:16 — 92n
110:1 — 95
118:19-20 — 92n
118:26 — 94
132:7-10 — 92n

Isaiah
6:9-10 — 35
9:1-2 — 46, 92n
13:10 — 123n
34:4 — 123n
34:12 — 107
42:1 — 81
56:7 — 102

Jeremiah
7:11 — 102

25:11-12 — 133
29:10 — 133

Ezekiel
1:4 — 79
11:23 — 106
28:2 — 27n

Daniel
9:24-27 — 133

Joel
2:10 — 123n
3:15-16 — 123n

Zechariah
9:9-10 — 92
14 — 103, 106

INTERTESTAMENTAL LITERATURE

Damascus Document
(CD)
XX, 13-15 — 134n

Psalm Commentary
(4QpPs)
37:7-8 — 134n

NEW TESTAMENT

Matthew
3:2 — 10
3:17 — 10
4:4 — 10
4:7 — 10
4:10 — 10
4:17 — 10
4:23 — 10

5:9 — 103n
5:15 — 38
5:19 — 103n
7:2 — 38n
12:28 — 7, 16n
13:14 — 35
13:15 — 35
13:16 — 35

13:25 — 37n
13:35 — 32n
13:57 — 53
17:2 — 78
20:17 — 79n
21:10 — 97
21:15 — 97
22:41-46 — 96

169

NON-CANONICAL CHRISTIAN LITERATURE

Gospel of Thomas